MASOUD BARZANI

BARZANI AND THE KURDISH LIBERATION MOVEMENT

The Gulan Revolution
1975-1990
Fourth Edition

TRANSLATED BY: DAVAN YAHYA KHALIL

Part Two

Barzani and the Kurdish Liberation Movement
Fourth Edition
Part Two

Copyright © 2023 By Davan Yahya Khalil

ISBN 978-1-3999-6191-2

Manufactured in the UK

Interior and cover design by Kimberly Martin of Jera Publishing

Contents

CHAPTER SIX

Peshmarga Military Activity

The importance of organising and working with peshmerga.

AFTER THE FALL of the revolution in 1975, the regime did every-thing in its power to prevent the resurgence of that revolution. It limited the activities of the peshmerga, the party work of friends and public, and for this purpose, tried to attack us in many ways.

- Establishing and forming a special detachment of so-called Kurds who belonged to themselves and were against their people and their legitimate cause. Most of them were fully affiliated with the Ba'athists and were against anyone with Kurdish thoughts. With all their might, they helped and supported the Ba'athists and their institutions in beating and torturing our activists and looking for the peshmerga.

- After the start of the War between Iraq and Iran in September 1980, the regime launched a campaign to register Kurdish citizens and youths to establish and organise them within the framework of squadrons that led to the regiment known as a basic squadron.

Most of them were questioned about political parties before, during, and after their registration. Each was asked the party they had sympathy for, or ties to, the PDK, PUK and other parties. Because we were financially unable to contain the large number of young people and we did not wish them to become refugees in Iran, in response, we thought it would be better for Kurdish youth to be protected in some way in Kurdistan, not the middle and south or on the frontlines of the war between the two countries. They had become fuel for Ba'athists' belligerence, although not all who worked with the regime had to be our enemies, provided they were not against the masses and peshmerga, so avoiding harming and hurting civilians in Kurdistan. A large number of them were good and did not have bad intentions, and they even had contact with us. During the spring uprising of 1991 of our nation, most of the advisers played a significant role in opposing and facing the force and the Ba'athist institutions in Kurdistan were recounted.

Throughout, Kurdistan was surrounded by huge forces and armed forces and the regime stationed several brigades in Kurdistan, as well as creating several Jash regiments, trying to reach their goals. Ba'athists established the objective of these forces in Kurdistan:

1. Division 50 in Kalar.
2. Division 56 in Qaradagh and Sulaymaniyah.

3. Division 47 in Shler and Penjwen areas.
4. Division 39 of four areas.
5. Division 44 in Qaladze.
6. Division 32 in Rwandese.
7. Division 33 in the Sidakan and Mergasor areas
8. Division 1 in Kirkuk.
9. Division 11 in Zakho.

In Erbil province, the regime forces were deployed as follows:

Erbil: the headquarters of the 8th Division were divided into the centre of Erbil, brigades and regiments as follows:

The regiments of Masif Salahaddin, Shaqlawa, Spilk, Rwandese and Diana (Regiment of Hamia), Korek, Khalifan and Zozk, a brigade headquarters in Diana and a regiment were set up in Delzian.

The Mergasor Brigade, whose brigade headquarters was in Mergasor consisted of its regiments, was located in the Shakawtan, Sherwan, and two military units were established in Goyazha.

The Sari Barde Brigade, consisting of brigade headquarters, regiments, two commando units, and several regiments, such as the Hassanbag regiments and the Sari Barde.

According to official statistics, the number of Jash (Kurdish traitors) in Erbil reached 20,000, and the number of Shaabi's militia was about 20,000.

The regime forces in Zakho were deployed as follows:

The headquarters of the brigade were in the centre of Zakho and were armed with the same weapons:

Six helicopters, three tanks, two 130mm cannons, two 122mm cannons, four 120mm mortars, several light mortars.

The contingent consisted of brigades, regiments and military unit to control the area's roads and monitor residents on the border, these were armed with all kinds of weapons. A brigade and a regiment were stationed in the centre of Duhok, a brigade, and a regiment in Bagira; their duty was to monitor roads, activities citizen and peshmerga.

These brigades and regiments were stationed in these places:

1. The brigade headquarters of regiments was based in Sarsng, consisting of Amedi, Deraluk, Sheladze, Bamarne Airport.
2. The Begova Brigade consisted of several regiments: the Sotke Regiment, the Garmke Regiment, the Batifa Regiment, the Ravina Regiment, and the Kani Masi Regiment.
3. The Shekhan district was surrounded by these forces: the Ain Safne Brigade, the Atrosh regiments and Ban Givrke.
4. The headquarters of the regime's armed men was established in Akre: Akre Brigade, Dinarta Regiment, Akre Seri Regiment, Shosh, Sharman and Bakorman Regiment, Bijil district, Goran district, Grdasen area.
5. The Jash also helped the government protect the area and prevent peshmerga activities whilst monitoring the citizens and residents of the border.

Despite all the harsh Ba'athist military plans and procedures, the brave peshmerga of Kurdistan and the fearless cadres of our Party faced the enemy's attempts and plans. They proved that will is stronger and more effective than force, especially the brave peshmerga of the September revolution who played a great role in managing the activities and instructions, and in the development of new generations to protect, continue and keep the revolution and struggle of our nation alive.

The holy name of the peshmerga had become the basis of the continuation of the struggle.

That's why, after the start and resumption of the Gulan revolution on 26th May 1976 with the blood of Said Abdullah, they gave hope to our people, through the activities of our Party's brave and fearless peshmerga, in launching strikes on regime bases and strongholds, which increased dramatically. Peshmerga were active daily in different parts of Kurdistan.

One of the important and effective decisions of the ninth congress was the drafting, enactment, and exercise of the law of the Revolutionary Army of Kurdistan, as this led to the organisation and determination of the rights and duties of the peshmerga, and the lives of the people of Kurdistan. This law was amended properly in the second meeting of the central committee and with the unanimous votes of the participants of the meeting, and it was decided that the Revolutionary Army of Kurdistan should be organised according to its articles and the leadership.

The rule consisted of four sections and ten chapters.

The law defined the peshmerga, the conditions for receiving the duties and orders of the peshmerga, those who are not accepted, the rights of the peshmerga, the forms of punishment, the transfer and holidays of the peshmerga, their organisational structure, and the way they, and their leadership relations, were discussed. In article 10 and the end of the law, the form and type of relationship between the peshmerga and the masses, and the behaviour of the peshmerga, were revealed to the public. The law of the Revolutionary Army of Kurdistan had a great impact on the strengthening of the peshmerga forces of Kurdistan, in conjunction with raising the spirit of sacrifice and revolution among the peshmerga and the people of Kurdistan.

After the congress, the reorganisation and establishment of a new structure for the peshmerga was approached in in a more modern way, to adapt to the new situation, the needs of the era and the stages of the struggle. Although after the failure, some peshmerga remained in different parts of Kurdistan, preparations were made to send more peshmerga into the country to defend the rights and territory of the country. For this purpose, several meetings were held with the platoons and forces for a while, but this took a long time.

On 16th July 1979, a temporary military leadership consisting of friends Jawhar Namiq Salim, Lieutenant Muhammad, Lieutenant Ali and Lieutenant Younis Rozhbayani was established. The establishment of temporary military leadership had a significant impact on the organisation and advancing military and peshmerga affairs.

On 10th August 1979, we established the peshmerga headquarters in the Kawpar and Badinawa areas.

On 18th November 1979, in Zewa, a group of peshmerga from branch one were prepared to send them to the borders of branch one. Between the 20th and 21st November 1979, I saw some of the brave peshmerga preparing to return to the border of branch one of Badinan. Their loyalty in this unpleasant and sensitive situation toward their nation and homeland is respected.

Considering the situation in the region, Iraq, and Kurdistan, and in order to gather more forces of friends and peshmerga, it was decided that a joint organization should be formed, so, between the 8th and 12th of December 1979, we were busy organising, preparing, and meeting with friends and peshmerga of branch one, the heads of the detachments and of the areas. In the meetings I reminded Barzani about continuing our party's path, programme and struggle until our nation reached its national goals, advice and instructions.

On 24th December 1979, friends Khurshid Shera and Lieutenant Ali visited us. In this meeting, we discussed the situation in the area in general and branch two in particular. We gave them a considerable amount of heavy weapons and military equipment. After a lot of effort, on 30th December 1979, the supply of equipment and needs of branch three were complete, so, as well as Sergeant Darwesh's force, to support our forces in the area, they agreed to travel to the border of branch four.

After the start of the Iraq-Iran war, we made a full effort to take advantage of the war, so we began to reorganise and strengthen the peshmerga forces in Kurdistan, including:

- The Barzan peshmerga forces in the Hayat area, under the command of Dr Saeed Barzani.
- The Bradost forces in the Sidakan border, led by Hamid Afandi

After reorganising and strengthening the peshmerga, they were able to take advantage of the war-ravaged situation, and after the start of the war, more areas were liberated and fell into the hands of the peshmerga.

After reviewing and reorganising the peshmerga forces into a good, suitable and developed institution within the stages and conditions of the era, the activities of the brave peshmerga on

Ba'athist strongholds and bases increased. They attacked regime forces daily.

On 2nd January 1980, we moved our headquarters from Nove to Rajan, because there were more houses in Rajan, and larger places were found. The truth is that our place in Nove was narrow and constricting.

On 10th January 1980, friends Dr Jarjis Hassan, Abu Antar, Khalid Sheli, Slobandi and Sergeant Yassin returned to the same branch. Ismail Zayer (Abu Zafar) also returned to Beirut, and it was decided that Dr Jarjis Hassan should cross the Zakho border to visit the Alwatan area.

Visiting the Alwatan area

On 12th January 1980, we agreed to visit our forces in the area from the Razhan to Kawpar. We stopped for a short time in Zewa and tried to supply and prepare the necessary equipment. Then we went to Daze and Shno. Before our battle, two cars carrying weapons and equipment were stopped, and it seemed that they would not able to succeed because of the lack of good equipment. Then the cars attempted to return because roads were bad. M. Abdullah was in charge of organising the convoy. Before we arrived in Shno, because of ice on the road, what was left for our cars other than to turn around? We were near the village of Naliwani in Shno and sent Haval Fazil Mirani to Shno to tell the Kurdistan Democratic Party (KDP) about our arrival and passage. Shortly after, Mr Fazil Mirani returned and said, "The Democratic Party will send guards with us, and guard us until we arrive at the Piranshar house." We rejected Colonel Maham and greeted him with a greeting from the commander of the house brigade. It was about five o'clock in the evening that we arrived at the headquarters of branch two, in Kawpar. We spent about seven hours trying to visit the forces. The roads were very unpleasant, especially the heights of the Kani Spai before Shno.

We and our weapons arrived at branch two headquarters, and the Democratic Party later complained that we had not warned them that we would be coming, although they did not prevent us, and we argued that they had taken an inappropriate stance by seizing branch two weapons a while ago.

We had taken a significant number of heavy weapons with us, including mortars (81mm, 70mm and 57mm) anti-tank weapons and about 150 rifles, which were distributed to the peshmerga who had been unarmed for a long time and were waiting to receive rifles. Mustafa Amedi tried to contact Abdullah Darwesh station in Rajan at 9 pm. After the failure of 1975, this attempt became the first relationship between our forces through wireless, but this was not successful due to technical reasons.

On 13th January 1980, we held a multi-party seminar for branch two forces in Kawpar village, detailing the general situation, the area, and the revolution. It was a successful meeting. Then we visited the headquarters of the political office and had a meeting with these detachments.

Those present included Abdullah Amedi, Hamo Kamaki, Abdullah Qado, Siso Dolamari, Rashid Isomeri, Muhammad Ali Kurani, While Sheroki, Hassan Shekho, Jamil Akrayi, head of the district guards, Zikri Bargarai, Wakil Ramazan Koyi and other friends. After a detailed discussion on their issues and problems, and the importance of organising within the peshmerga ranks was defended but we agreed to abide by local procedures. The following points were agreed:

- Abiding by the local rules
- One-third of the forces must have permission to rest and two-thirds of the forces must be on duty.
- The increase in peshmerga's budget and Nasria would be 5.7 dinars each.
- Opening of general training and weapons training courses.
- Eliminate the shortcomings of peshmerga weapons.

The meetings continued and the peshmerga organisation was organised in general. The questioning and the implementation of the process was well-placed. Revolutionary zeal among our forces was at a high level.

On the 14th and 15th January 1980, our meetings with the detachments and our forces continued on the Kawpar border. In the afternoon, we visited Abdullah Amedi' headquarters, numbering 21 peshmerga, and the detachment consisting of a group of warm and educated young men. Their names, weapons and numbers were recorded, and they did whatever was necessary. Because of their arrangements, it was decided to send them a pleasant letter. We saw high and strong feelings in the platoon, and then we visited Abdullah Qado's headquarters and recorded the names of the peshmerga, their weapons, numbers, and details.

On 15th January 1980, we visited all the peshmerga bases and headquarters in Kawpar to be aware of the situation in the peshmerga and to review and reorganise their affairs. In the meetings, the general situation of the region, Kurdistan, PDK, and the sacred duties of the peshmerga were discussed, and the importance of organising and adhering the peshmerga to the law, advice and instructions was reaffirmed.

On 17th January 1980, in the village of Kani Ashkawt, we visited the Headquarters of Mala Rasul and felt that the Mahla Rasul detachment had more Kalashnikov weapons than any other detachment. There, at the suggestion of a resident of the Cave, we visited the village mosque where a significant number of villagers were present.

We discussed the situation in the area and the relations between the parties. It was at that time that a member of Kurdistan Democratic Party talked and, in his speech, he strongly criticised Jalal Talabani.

In Konalajan, we visited the Balak force headquarters of branch two. Their forces appeared regular, although not completely ready and slow. We returned to the political office headquarters in Kawpar, until 4 am with friends, who were busy recording their weapons and numbers. We identified the shortcomings there.

After evaluating, reading and discussing the situation in the area, it was decided to visit the Alwatan area, a strategically important location close to Sulaymaniyah province, particularly in Galadze, and a suitable area for traffic during the winter season. We needed to visit there because the bases and headquarters of most political forces and parties where in the region.

For a long time, we were busy preparing and sending forces. In this context, on 30th and 31st August 1980, we met with the officials of all the positions and forces, and we intended to prepare, advise and send them to the Kawpar area and the military department to make it easier for them and we took the necessary measures for them.

On 1st September 1980, in a special meeting with the political bureau, we discussed the time and form of our agreement and decided to try to contact the political bureau from the top, and to do so to escape without conflict, but if prevented, we felt obliged to defend ourselves.

On 2nd September 1980, we went to the political office and conducted the affairs related to our departure. We agreed that during the days of the 4th, 5th and 6th September 1980, this would be with groups of about 300 people.

On 10th September 1980, we reached the valley behind the Tarkan along with friends of the political bureau in Rajan, on the Wrme-Naghada road to Kawpar. At night, the officials of all the forces were called for the purpose of discussing our departure to the area.

On 11th September 1980, commemorating the start of the Great September National Revolution, we were busy visiting our peshmerga headquarters on the Kawpar border, as well as Mr Mala Hassan Rastgar and M. Azizman in Hadka, who had come with Haso Jajoki. At a meeting with them, the general situation in the region and Kurdistan were discussed and their views were good. They promised to help us escape.

On 13th September 1980, we were informed that on 9th September 1980, in the village of Jara Qaraman, Dr Abdul-Rahman Suleiman Zrari, along with five other peshmerga, had been martyred by the enemy, and that Jash had helped the government, such as Saeed Shatnaei and Muhammad Tahir, the leaders. Dr Abdul-Rahman was wounded in the hands of the government and was thrown alive and wounded from a helicopter. I was very worried and upset with this news.

On 17th September 1980, we were busy meeting with force officials to set up necessary measures to move. At the meeting, necessary measures were taken to distribute tasks and to determine the number and size of the forces.

Fortunately, all the forces agreed to the distribution method and demanded that we move as soon as possible, meaning that Haji Omaran should be attacked and that he should be captured with the support of the Balak artillery. All of them supported the proposal.

On 21st September 1980, we visited the peshmerga of the Fourth Branch to be aware of their situation. In a meeting, the latest developments and struggles of the Party to defend the rights of our people, were discussed. Indeed, the peshmerga were fearless, courageous, and thoughtful.

On 2nd October 1980, we met with the forces to prepare for an agreement. In the evening, we arrived at the headquarters of branch two in Badinawa and necessary measures were taken, and affairs were completed by agreement. On the same day, Khidir Daoud visited us from Haji Omaran and received important information about the bombing of Haji Omaran.

We were informed of the arrival of an Iraqi army brigade in the area. They seemed to be planning to attack the military base of our peshmerga homes and headquarters. About 450 Jash also came to Haji Omaran. For the sake of stronger programme management, we decided to consolidate the Qaladze border with all our forces, be together and then separate.

On the 3rd and 4th October 1980, Haso Zhazhoki visited his forces to prepare for our plan.

On the evening of 4th October 1980, our first peshmerga group agreed to attend the Qaladze border. The group consisted of the forces of branch four and Rashid Isomeri, Ghazali Zhazoki, and without problems on Sadr and mountain, Jasusan and Dolakok settled.

On 2nd and 5th October 1980, another force, most being peshmerga from branches 2, 3 and 4, arrived at their positions. On 3rd and 6th October 1980, the branch four forces left, followed by the battalions of Saeed Bosali and Abdullah Amedi, under the supervision of Lieutenant Muhammad, and on 7th October Ali Khalil's forces went.

On 20th October 1980, we were in the plains of Wazne, and woke early in the morning. The weather in this area is colder than elsewhere, it has a border line, high lands and no trees. After noon, it was decided that we would visit one side at the border of branch three. We took two and a half hours to get there. At 5:20, we reached the final point, which meant we entered Iraqi Kurdistan. When I got to my beloved land, I thanked Allah with the depths of my heart.

My biggest wish was for me to come back to my beloved land. We thanked the patience and strong will of our nation and the defence of our brave peshmerga. From there we looked away at the area. Sangasar, Rania, Zharawa, Mount Kewarash and Asos appeared, and we felt great joy. On the other hand, I felt sad, because we lived with the Barzani for days. These were the bright days of the Kurdish people. We stayed at night at Faizo headquarters and a simple cottage, and we made Sakar, but it was very pleasant.

On the morning of 21st October 1980, we were on the border. We looked at the enemy's barricades far away. Then we went to the villages of Shene, Zale, and Tuzha. It seemed to be the case everywhere that the headquarters of the political parties were mixed.

In the Valley of Shenem, I was very surprised at how all these parties had been treated. However, in their view, not everyone had visited Shenem, and it was as if they had not visited Kurdistan. In the evening, Mr Rasul Mamand and Qadir Jabari came to welcome us.

We were scheduled to meet with representatives of the Communist Party, the Baathists of Syria and Pasuk in the morning, to discuss the issue between the PUK and PDK. Rasul Mamand invited us to visit in the morning to meet them and we agreed to their request.

Hearing far-reaching information about the situation of the parties in the region is different from seeing the situation directly; of course, the information we received earlier from Hask, Pasok and other people talked about the instability, the PUK's situation and weakness were not the same.

On the evening of 22nd October 1980, we reached the greenery, the trees, and the Nawaz, and we were together. It looked more like Konagurk, and it was very pleasant. In the evening, we received the news of the arbitration committee. The meeting suggested four points for both sides:

1. To stop media attacks.
2. Both sides warn their peshmerga not to fight each other.
3. A direct meeting would be held between the two sides.

4. Anyone who did not abide by these points would be held accountable.

Mahmoud Faqe Khidir Qaladzaie, a member of the Communist Party, told us his points, and we met with the political bureau and agreed, to the PUK's embarrassment.

Later, the parties demanded that we withdraw our forces in order to prevent tensions from developing, and we showed our readiness at their request, and announced that because Jud forces are in the area, we would withdraw from some of our forces. So, on 29th October 1980, we met with the political bureau at the headquarters of branch one and decided to establish a force in the area. In order to participate in the Haji Omaran attack on Piranshar, other forces would be withdrawn, as well as the branch two forces who would march towards Balak. Although rumours were initially circulated that the purpose of our visit to the Alwatan area was to beat, or attack the PUK, in reality this rumour was untrue and baseless.

On 23rd January, 1980, we attended the graduation ceremony for participants in an 81mm, 60mm and 57mm cannon training course. The artillery was tested at the ceremony, but Seoniu's Bazooka failed and did not shoot. This day was historic, because after the 1975 setback, this was the first heavy weapons course.

All thanks to Allah, it was successful. The ceremony was attended by friends Ali Abdullah, Fazil Mirani, Falakadin Kakayi, and the course's teachers, Ahmed Badakh, Ali Bajluri and Lieutenant Younis. The 60mm ball was more accurate and better than all the cannons, and the 79M rifle was tested that day, which was a good rifle.

We visited Zewa on 11th March 1980, to lead a group of Hamid Afandi's peshmerga. I told the peshmerga that they should be very careful, we should do everything in our power to satisfy our people and that people should not be hurt. More attention should be paid to party organisation and work. There are some principles which we told the peshmerga in a brief statement.

On 24th April 1980, Haval Ali Obaidullah, a member of branch one, was martyred by a road mine explosion.

On 25th August 1980, we went to the village of Nove to participate in an artillery training course opened for peshmerga from branch three, branch four and the political bureau forces. After the end of the course with the 81mm cannon and 60mm mortar, a real and direct shot was fired, the Bazooka and 57mm anti-tank hit its target very well and we were happy.

On 3rd August 1980, we visited the Margawar to see the area. It was the first time I had seen or visited the area. In this context, we visited Tahir Khanum. We didn't stop and went to the border of Russia and Turkey, a pleasant area with compatible weather.

Unfortunately, on 5th March 1981, five Barzan peshmerga were martyred in Dalanpar Mountain after being trapped in the snow. The five peshmerga were Salih Hajijuma Akrai, Adil Rajab Akrayi, Azad Muhammad Amin Akrayi, Ghazi Ramazan Akrayi and Sheikh Jaafar.

Establishing a leadership headquarters in Berkme and Lolan

In June 1982, we went to the Sidakan, Berkme and Lolan areas, and established leadership headquarters in the area, making it an important place for leadership and the peshmerga. The opening of the headquarters in the area, and the readiness of the leadership friends at the headquarters, was an important turning point in our people's revolution and struggle, as it brought the leadership and bases of the Party, the masses, and our peshmerga closer together. There was an increase in peshmerga attacks and activities against the Ba'athist dictators. There, twice a month, fighter planes and helicopters were coming at us.

Shortly afterwards, we established a permanent headquarters in the Lolan area. I sent the news to Haji Muhammad Sheikh Rashid. With permission, we would cut some white trees as necessary and use them to build our headquarters houses. He replied that 'all the property in the area belongs to you'. In this way, I warned all peshmerga that they should not build any headquarters in the village of Lolan, out of respect for Khanaqa and the Sheikh's house; they should not even put in foundations for it. After completing the work and establishing the headquarters, friends Lieutenant Ali, Falakadin Kakayi and Rashid Arif supervised and led the headquarters. Then we divided the headquarters into areas, from the Darwo, the Goyezerash, and the Malawa to be brought in. In fact, opening the headquarters and having leadership friends in the area was an important step for merging with the public, our friends and our arrangements in the cities.

In Burkem one day, God forgive him, Hamo came to us for a while and had some demands, and there was no possibility of a time when we could meet those demands, so we did not say what he wanted to hear. Finally, when I said no, he said, "Or. I said yes." He took the gun and wanted to go. He said, "if I was in your positions, I would be able to look after one million peshmerga". One day they caught some fish, and he sent a few with one of his peshmerga, and told the peshmerga to 'take them to Mr Masood, because they have nothing. Let them eat fish.'

After establishing the leadership headquarters and determining the duties of our friends and completing our affairs in the region, we went to Iran on 2nd December 1982, to carry out our affairs in the political bureau. Late at night, we arrived at the headquarters of Mohammed Khalid Bosali, who was in Gadar. The weather was very cold, and snow was up to our knees. Some peshmerga built a fire outside the headquarters, and I asked what the reason was they were sitting in the snow, but they said they felt they had no place. We started walking, and a strong storm hit us on the border, and it was by God's will that we were saved, because it was at that time in the house, Kawa Sheikh Latif and Lieutenant Tahir were trapped in the snow and martyred.

In 1983, the media department developed significantly, and with the appointment of a number of experts, and significant cadres, the level of work and activities of the media department increased, so this period is considered an important stage of the PDK's media and revolution.

For a while, Falakadin Kakei, in charge of the media department, had a major impact on his development because of his expertise and competence. There was media work. Later, Hoshyar Zebari, a member of the Central Committee, was in charge of the media department for the sake of improving the field of media.

The media department consisted of some talented friends and writers such as Hamid Suri, Dr Nasih Afur and Masoud Salihi.

The role of these friends in preparing and writing media topics was significant. After a while, several other friends were transferred to the media department, including Barzan Mala Khalid, who had a high hand in writing, despite being a spokesman for the Kurdistan Voice Station.

Fahmi Kakayi had been assigned translations.

The media section consisted of several sections:

Voice of Iraqi Kurdistan Station, which broadcast daily in the afternoon until late at night. Tahsin Dulamari, Qadir Hassan Agha, Barzan Mahla Khalid, Sabah Baytullah, Sdqi Hururi and Mahfuz Mai were the Kurdish section of the station. The Arabic sections were Abdullah Chalabi and Abdullah Khalo.

The topics and programmes of the station were news that was more devoted to the activities and bravery of the Revolutionary Army of Kurdistan, political speeches, interpretations and political investigations, the programme of martyrs' convoys, reviewing foreign magazines and newspapers (foreign and Arabic), memorials, national occasions, and national anthems, and many other topics and programmes based on the needs of the stage and situation.

Despite the intense confusion over its programmes, the Voice of Kurdistan station was the voice of the Party and the Revolution, and important in publishing and delivering the voice of the Kurdish people's struggle to the local public.

Technically, engineer and fighter, Haval Ahmed Briffkani, Dr Hamid Akrei played an important and important role, along with a number of assistants, tirelessly in their daily affairs of running the station effectively.

The Media Department's printing house was an important section. A number of loyal and active friends and cadres were responsible for managing the printing house, such as Rebwar Yalda, Jan Jabali, Tawfiq Salim, Hozan Brifkani, Dijwar Fayaq, Rizgar Muhammad Mustafa Dol Hamri, Muhammad Elias (Hazhar),

Ihsan Salim Bajloi, Ahmad Ghorhani Akri, Rizgar Maei, Ali Mushir (Ranjbar), who was then transferred to branch three and in Sharbazher, in 1985, he was a martyr; and Emad Salih Doski.

During this period, several publications were published:

Khabat was the voice of PDK, published monthly and continuously in both Kurdish and Arabic and occasionally in English.

Kurdistan News Weekly (Kurdistan News). In addition to the news and news, it contained many other topics and perspectives.

Printing and publishing statements, meetings, of the presidency and the political bureau in two sections of pamphlets and courses and publishing them on branches, areas, peshmerga forces and secret arrangements.

Archives and libraries were an important component of the Party's media department,

Hashim Ahmed Akrai and Hamza Rashid were tirelessly responsible for managing the archives, including a large number of sources, books, magazines and newspapers.

Anasat was an important area of the media department. It was distributed daily and regularly and distributed to the presidency and friends of the political bureau. Naji Argoshi, Rizgar Mai and Faraidun Kirkuk were responsible for managing them.

On 1st April 1983, in the village of Gurgadar in the Sharbazher area, Haval Jaza Ali Katib and five peshmerga were ambushed by PUK fighters and in a battle, Jaza Ali Katib, a teacher Mal Ghafur, a member of the Sulaymaniyah LN, Ahmed Mohammed, known as Ahmed Malajin(Sulaymaniyah), Hersh Omar, known as Hersh Amira (Sulaymaniyah) and Ismail Ibrahim, known as Khayat (Sharbazher), were martyred. Amanj Hama-Rahim, a Sulaymaniyah survivor, suffered severe injuries. Haval Jaza was a hero and a good member of our party. At that time, it was deemed necessary to be avenged and not to waste their blood.

Haval Fazil Mirani and forty peshmerga headed for Lolan and arrived at the political office in Lolan on 2nd April 1983. According to reports we received, thirteen PUK militants were killed in Sharbazher this day and a PDK peshmerga named Hersh Omar was martyred. Since 6th April 1983, we had been constantly informed that the famous criminal Saeed Hamo[1] was gathering Jash in Rwandese and intended to attack the borders of Barzan's forces and the political bureau. Perhaps he intended to catch the Garwa Snga, and there was a possibility of catching it.

On 19th June 1983, Mr Nadir Hawrami agreed with three hundred peshmerga to the Shler area, because after Iran attacked the area, it would provide our peshmerga with a better opportunity.

On 31st July 1983, Jash attacked the Kolaka area and thanked they was defeated, but unfortunately Ghafur Hussein was martyred. He was a great peshmerga, a good and competent man.

Between 22nd and 25th November 1983, the designated day for counting and reviewing the peshmerga list in Rajan, Silvana and the territorial one. On 10th December 1983, for the purpose of the counting and reviewing the affairs of the forces with Mr Fazil Mirani, we visited Shno.

On 14th December 1983, after completing the peshmerga counting, I returned to Silvana, where Mr Fazil Mirani was scheduled to visit the Khane in the morning for the peshmerga counting and the structure of the organisation. Between 24th and 26th February 1984, Shno forces were replaced, and Lieutenant Babakir Zebari placed in charge of the forces.

---

[1] An Iraqi military commander

On 27th April 1984, I saw Dr Seed Ahmed and Hali Dolameri plus about fifteen to 20 Barzan forces officials. I met with them for three hours, discussing the general situation in the area, peshmerga work, advising them, and deciding to follow the power system. The first force was formed and Salih Ozer became the head of the force and decision.

On these days, they would march to the south of Kurdistan. According to the programme, on 17th May 1984, he was fully responsible and the soldiers of the one, two, three, and other unit were called for this purpose.

The call was for a counting and a review of the structure and organisation of forces. After a long meeting, the work of the one, two and three units was ended, and it was decided that the forces system would be dismantled and reorganised. On 19th May 1984, we continued with counting and their affairs were completed.

According to the information, on 26th May 1984, a large number of Jash and regime forces advanced towards Mount Gara, and a commando force of the Turkish army entered the border of Branch 1.

According to reports, on 29th May 1984, fighting continued at the border of branch one, and the peshmerga heroically defended it. We hoped that Allah would be their protector and that the enemy would be defeated and humiliated. The news was that on 30th May1984, the war continued in the border of branch one and this lasted.

At 9:30 am on 13th July 1984, on the way to Kelashin a mine placed in the Hadka by Iraqi intelligence officials exploded in Abbas Ghazali's car, killing these civilians: Ghorbat Hassan, the wife of Abdulrahman Hali and his ten years old son Dilshad Omer;

30-year-old Zard Husseini, the wife of Khalil Hali and two of his sons, 10 and 12 years old, and Abdullah, three month; 25-year-old Siber Hussein; 20 years old Shamsi Khan Siso; and Najat Ahmed Mustafa aged 20 years.

On 3rd May 1985, we received a message claiming that Karim Khan had come with a special Iraqi force to Jara and Kani Kfri and Sari Spendar and captured all those areas.

On 6th May 1985, I met with Barzan forces officials to discuss a number of issues. The meeting, attended by Dr Saeed, discussed the general situation in the region, the latest changes and developments. After discussing issues, it was decided for them to prepare themselves to enter the Lolan area. They all liked the decision and after two days they went back.

I also sat down with Rashid Beshoni and Khalid Hamid Biri and they were warned to prepare themselves. We also sat down with Ali Khalil's forces to discuss our situation and discussed the problems.

On 6th May 1985, we received a communication that Sari Spendar not captured by regimes, and only the Kani Kifri was captured. A letter from Sheikh Akhr came late at night, claiming that Karim Khan had asked someone to see him and said they were obliged to go to the place and not go any further. I answered, "We don't mind. Come on." On 8th May 1985, Dr Saeed and Hali Dolmari agreed with 150 peshmerga to join the war front on The Sari Spendare, on 16th June 1985, new duties were assigned to the 3rd Unit forces and contacted their new mission. Then for this purpose we met with the Argoshi's forces to select their new task.

On 17th June 1985, In order to strengthen the Shno Frontline, Kelashin, we met with the heads of Unit one force, Haji Mirkhan,

Khalid Shali, Bahram Aziz and Hassan Charboti. After a detailed reading of the situation in general and Kurdistan in particular, new responsibility, duties and locations were determined, all were ready to fulfil their duties.

Unfortunately, on 25th June 1985, as a result of the collapse of a peshmerga barricade in Kelashin, Mr Hamid Shali was martyred, Bahram Aziz and another peshmerga were injured. On the same morning, we went to a people between Rajan and to visit the area. On 26th June 1985, the following equipment arrived: 750,000 Kalashnikov bullets, 30 RPG7 rounds, 6,000 Doshka rounds.

On July 12, 1985, Rashid Beshoni and Dasko Haji Berokhi forces, Lolan and the Barzan-affiliated Haso Kanialinji forces were sent to Dr Saeed Barzani. On the night of 12th July 1985, we slept very little, because we were all busy organising and Meeting with Hali Dolamari, Zakri Berokhi and Ramazan Mohammed, who gave us the necessary instructions and advice, and it was decided that the morning we would go through their tasks.

On 14th July 1985, Lieutenant Babakir arrived at Saqar to visit our forces, and most of our forces agreed to their locations. Hali to the right, Najmadin Goruni to the left, Barzan's forces to the Mergasor-Rwandese area, and we were on our way to Khanerat at night, because the attack was scheduled to take place the same evening. We arrived at twelve o'clock and went behind Lolan. It was a big fight. We didn't have any information about it.

On the evening of 20th July 1985, our forces in the Piran district were bombarded by enemy helicopters, injuring four Barzan peshmerga, as well as bombing planes from Piran to Sherwani. I received a message from Dr Saeed Barzani claiming that many people had come out, but had been blocked by Hussein Jangir's

Jash Force and not allowed to leave, and the Hayat area has been bombed by Iraqi forces.

On 20th July 1985, an Iranian Shinuk helicopter surrendered to Iraq.

On the morning of 29th July 1985, Hali returned to his forces and decided to open a main peshmerga headquarters in the village of Siran to help the war front there. One of the friends, Gulabakh, Hamid Argoshi, Tanjo Younis, Mustafa Gurni, mushir Guani, came to us from the Hassanbag front and talked in detail about the situation on the front lines of the war and the area in general the Hassanbag frontline.

On 30th July 1985, Khalid Taha returned by helicopter from Hayat (Gali Rash) and at 10 am on the same day, Dr Saeed Ahmed arrived in Hayat. Khalid also brought me a letter from Muhammad Khalid in which he asked for a strike on the Mergasor-Sherwan border against the Iraqi Army and he asked me to send Ali Khalil to him.

After the Zewa bombardment, the martyrdom of a large number of refugees and the injuries of others, we decided to improve our activities and make a bigger attack on our enemy. For this purpose, we visited the Sidakan area, during which time important activities were carried out by peshmerga and strategic events were carried out which influenced regime bases and strongholds.

On 4th August 1985, I visited the headquarters of the martyr Khoshwa's force, which was located in the back of Khnera, and we had a good discussion with Malham Mzhdin.

On 4th August 1985, Iraq heavily bombed our environs, and then we were informed that it had fired a large artillery shell near

Iranian artillery and that 120mm artillery had been fired at the 120mm cannon placed in the Garowi Sinee.

On the night of 6th August 1985, I met Rashid Bishooni, Khalid Hamid Biri and Dasko Berokhi, who spoke in detail about the front-lines of their battle in the Qalaandar area. I promised them that their forces would be replaced within fifteen days. We had selected several forces to replace them within the specified period. At the same time, the enemy heavily bombarded our place of residence.

According to a message from Dr Saeed Barzani on 7th August 1985, a bomb exploded in the hands of Habib Mahmud Kaklayi, killing himself, his three sons and three others, while five people were injured.

After visiting Daraveh, Ahmed Osman returned and apparently threatened the Iranian guards who had gone to the Communist Party headquarters and threatened to evacuate the area. Ahmed Osman said they spoke very arrogantly at first, but after they didn't give up and threatened to put their goods in the ground, they slowed down. It seemed that they had seen two Hezbollah peshmerga on the way and had taken them with them, then sent them back with their belongings to them and even humiliated them.

In the meantime, we commissioned Sergeant Ahmed to open a headquarters there and for the Communist Party peshmerga to return to their places, but they seemed to have done a wise job, saying we would not return so that there would be no problems. It was important that they understood very well that they were not given the opportunity to interfere in our affairs of their own will, and the guards' officers begged for a day to question their officers and demanded that it not be a problem.

On the same day, I saw Haji Majid Saidaki Tatra, a local expert who said that, on the 6th and 8th August 1985, Iranian artillery bombarded Iraqi positions, particularly in the region of the Sidakan and the Iraqi artillery in the Hajar Valley.

On 19th August 1985, I returned to our headquarters in Lolan. On a relative scale, the heights were as follows:

Garoi Khrene about 2,000 metres, the Garoi Spi 2,300 metres, Gadar 1,750 metres, Darwai Jeman about 1900 metres.

On 1st October 1985, the political bureau informed us with a 1969 letter that Zakri Yahya Khan Berokhi had been martyred in hospital and, because of his injury, this made him the third brother to be martyred in his family. Two other brothers were martyred before.

On 15th November 1985, a Barzan air strike bombarded four of their forces' headquarters, injuring several people and three horses. There was also we received a letter from branch one that the headquarters of branch one had been bombarded, but thankfully no one was harmed.

On the same day, branch one announced that the commander of Jolamerg brigade was asking for a meeting and we agreed. It was deemed necessary to insist on the peace and tranquillity of the borders.

On 19th November 1985, we received news of the failure of the enemy's attack on Ghalboke. Six helicopters, three armoured vehicles and Jash forces from Jaafar Besfki, Khalid Dobardani, Jaish al-Shaabi, and two special forces units were involved.

On 4th February 1986, we met Mushir Agha of Ruvia on 22nd February 1986, according to the Barzan force's letter. In their meeting, he promised to help and serve all kinds, Mushir Agha, the basic regiment are on Mount Qalaandar.

On 22nd February 1986, peshmerga forces in branch one heavily bombed the headquarters of the 38th Zakho Division, targeting several trucks and military vehicles on the same evening on the public street.

On 7th October 1986, we decided to release 37 regime soldiers who were captured on the front lines of the war, in light of our enthusiasm for humanitarian values and respect for international law. They were taken over by the peshmerga forces.

After we reached the border of branch one, the regime made every effort to intensify its attacks on the area on the one hand, preventing the proliferation and development of peshmerga activities and attacks on the other, during which time it launched several large-scale attacks on the border areas of branch one. In late 1986, it intensified attacks on headquarters in both Zakho and Duhok, where heavy fighting broke out. There was also heavy fighting in the Shekhan and Amedi areas, in many places, and there a battle between peshmerga and regime fighters took place.

The regime was not able to prevent us from being in branch one, while the peshmerga forces' activities were not prevented, and on the contrary, it became a strong point for the brave peshmerga. During this period, despite a heroic defence on the frontlines of the war, they were able to record the great epics Deraluk, striking the regime with a crushing blow, causing heavy damage to the Ba'athist forces. With these epic victories, they proved that the regime could be beaten in spite of all its weapons. The huge force was unable to confront the peshmerga forces.

At 6:50 am on 5th June 1987, eight fighter planes heavily bombarded the headquarters of one branch, but the difference between the bombardment this time was the use of chemical weapons and mustard gas.

On 7th August 1987, Adil Haso and Khaziran Salih were injured by a bomb in the Peyman area and Adil lost a leg.

On 28th October 1987, I visited Shno to visit the refugee forces and discussed the situation in the area, revolutions, and problems in an interview with the peshmerga. Later, we visited Mohammed Khalid in Bemzorta.

On 22nd October 1987, Hamid Afandi returned from Karaj and decided at a meeting that Lieutenant Younis Rozhbayani, Lieutenant Babakir Zebari and Lieutenant Colonel Yaqub and Lieutenant Colonel Yaqub would visit Mariwan to solve the problems there. It was decided for them to move to the location of their tasks as soon as possible.

On 26th November 1987, we held our last meeting with the friends of branch four: Hamid Afandi, Said Salih, Izzadin Barwari, Mala Haji Deloi and Mahla Hassan Shaqi, and after a discussion, it was decided that they would visit Shno in the morning, as well as friends Abdul-Muhayman and Lieutenant Babakir Zebari, to go with them to Sina, Saqqez, Dzli, and Zaeem Ali to stay in Shno for a while with the aim of reviewing and reorganising our forces.

On 28th March 1988, we met with our military commanders to take appropriate measures. For this purpose, on30th March 1988, all peshmerga officers were invited and the latest changes and developments were discussed at a meeting. It was decided to prepare for all these new developments and tasks. In order to review the peshmerga's structures and as preparations for the next phase, it was decided to reorganise the structure of the peshmerga of seperate organisations and forces. For this purpose, on the 2nd and the 3rd April 1988 in Razga village, the process of reviewing and reorganising the military forces of Salih Ozer, Chawshin Khano and Haso Kanialanji, Mergasor district committee and peshmerga of Barzan forces headquarters and Ahmed Mustafa Kanilenji was conducted and their work was successfully completed.

At 2 pm on 11th April 1988, four planes conducted a major bombing campaign, martyring Mr Jalal Khoshnaw, the heroic peshmerga of branch two and Haji Karimi of Rajan.

On 12th April 1988, in the village of Mirawe, Mustafa Abdullah's force structure was reorganised, and a new structure was set up.

On 13th April 1988, we reorganised the Silvan force, its structures and affairs. For the night, we had a meeting of the Kurdistan Front at the political bureau headquarters. The meeting resulted in good results and was successful.

On 16th April 1988, we went to Khre village to review and reorganize Haso Mirkhan Dolameri's forces. On 17th April 1988, a review of the structure and arrangement of the Political Bureau's forces (Darwesh Safti and Darwesh Argushi) was conducted, and new structures were established. A good and new arrangement was set up for both forces. On 18th April 1988, in Nare village, a new working arrangement was also set up for the Azadi District Committee. On 20th April 1988, in the village of Nove, the re-structuring of the forces (Khalid Biri, Mahla Abdullah Zewaie, Hamo) took place.

"I'm not afraid of the government," said Mohammed Amin Biayi.

As we continued to review the affairs and structures of the forces, on 19th and 21st April 1988, in the village of Nari, we ended the work of the forces of Jali Dulameri, Salih Biri, Hassan Jasim, Martyr Sabri Nerwai and Sarif who brought dervishes.

On 23rd and 24th April 1988, in the villages of Dukan Awa and Razga, the review and reorganisation of the forces of Rashid Beshoni, Dasko Berukhi, Yassin Berukhi, Martyr Zikri, Rasul Faqe, Hassan Samad and Rashid, the Slevani were successfully completed.

On the days 26th, 27th and 28th April 1988, we were in Shno to reorganise the forces of Lieutenant Babakir, Ghazali Zhazoki, Mirkhan Muhammad Amin, Gharib Akrayi, Ahmed Shango Akrayi, Zaeem Ali and the headquarters of branch four.

In the afternoon, we visited Bemzorta, and then we returned to sleep.

In order to complete the review of the forces' work, we were reviewing the refugee force on 3rd and 4th May 1988, at the Headquarters of branch two in Shno. Also, news was sent to Khnera and Khwakur forces to review their settings and come to Shno.

According to the communication from two and three branches on 6th May 1988, chemical bombardments once again hit the Shwan and Koya, killing 100 people and injuring hundreds more. After staying for several days to review the forces' arrangements, at 4 am on the night of 6th May 1988, we returned to Silvana.

On 14th and 15th May 1988, in Razga village, we were reviewing the reorganisation of the second list, numbering about 400 people, and four organizations were established, and the review work for Ahmed Malaswari's forces was also completed, then I visited Hlach Village where there is immortal Barzani and Kak Idris Srine (Graveyards)

On 19th June 1988, preparations were made for the return of Salim Asaad and Qadir Salih to Selke. The next day, Mullah Muhammad Amin came to us. In the meeting, the situation in the area, the people and the problems of the area were discussed, and it seemed that the people of the area were in a bad situation.

On the morning of 10th September 1988, I met with the Barzan forces and discussed in detail the general situation and their problems.

At 5 pm on 10th September 1988, we went to the Benara people before we went home. I went to the graves of the martyrs of Zewa.

On the 13th and 14th September 1988, friends Mr Nadir Hawrami and Mr Azad Qaradaghi came to us. At a meeting, they discussed how to escape. On the morning of 16th September 1988, I met with a number of citizens who had left the country, that evening I met Hamarash Rasho and the situation was discussed.

During this period, the regime attacked Kurdistan and most of the areas were bombarded with chemicals which caused the martyrdom and injury of a large number of civilians. Many citizens escaped these regime attacks by going across the borders of Iran and Turkey.

On 27th and 28th August 1988, dozens of wounded and chemical weapons victims surrendered to Turkey in the Arosh area of Chale, including Faruq Abdullah Abdulaziz, Abdullah Faruq Abdullah, from Mae village; Najmadin Rashid, Mahmoud Rashid, Fatima Muhammad, Nasima Rashid from Shirna; Haji Ahmed Muhammad, Amin Ahmed Muhammad from Banavi village; Muhammad Ababakir Musa, Tahsin Hussein, peshmerga and people from Ekamale village; Shamsaddin Mustafa, Salim Mustafa, Bashir Shamsaddin, Nazir Shamsaddin, Kurdistan Omar, Nazdar Muhammad, Randak Jawzal Doman Jawzal Abbas Ahmed, Sardar Abbas, Amir Shamsaddin, from Warmel Village. Unfortunately, Naif Abdullah Hussein Kestai in Shafraza area and a daughter of Akram Noah Ekamalai died and they were buried.

I visited Zewa on the evening of 19th September 1988, to welcome people and families from Iraq. In a speech, I spoke to them about the general situation and the area, and they were thanked for their patience and defence. Because of the funeral of the martyrs of Khwakurk, this programme came forward. On 28th September 1988, I visited Zewa to visit and welcome the families of our nation, and in a meeting with our patient audience, the latest event occurred.

The struggle of our people for freedom was discussed.

On 29th September 1988, I visited Bemzorta to visit relatives. It was decided that friends Muhsin Dzaie, Shukri Nerwai, and Babakir Zebari should cross the merchant border into Turkey to visit our refugee camps, but Turkey reneged on its promise and did not allow it. On 3rd January 1990, we had a series of meetings and concluded, that we could manage the following:

1. We met with military officials; the meeting discussed the new situation, the latest developments, changes, and the way aid was distributed to those who carried out their duties and were on duty, if possible, and would be distributed to others and the proposal was accepted.

2. I met with field phone cadres who had a lot of complaints about their administration. I told them to gather and send me their suggestions.

On 5th February 1990, at the Rajan village mosque, a military conference was held for all branches, in which the situation in the region was discussed in detail, along with the latest developments, changes, the situation in our Party and the revolution. Reorganising peshmerga work and reviewing the military structure were also discussed. We agreed that the military department had the necessary guidance and advice, and this was sent to all branches.

At 3 am on 12th February 1990, Mr Hamid Biri, a close friend, and friend of Mr Barzani, died. Hamid Biri was an example of loyalty throughout his years at the struggle. In the cemetery and at the time of Mr Hamid's burial, we received news that Shokri Ziti was dead.

At 10 am on 12th February 1990, the loyal peshmerga Haji Darwesh went hunting and did not return. They conducted a search, hindered by storms and fog, especially on the heights, to look for him, but he was not found.

On 13th and 14th February the search for Haji Darwesh continued, and there was no sorrow. On 15th February 1990, Mr Jawhar Namiq returned.

Once again, on 16th February 1990, Zewa residents searched the mountains to find Haji Darwesh. There was a high probability of disappearance, falling into a rock, or being thrown, or if the wolf had attacked. Storms were a danger in this capital season, and the police, or guards, were likely to be weak protection.

On 26th February 1990, Pirot Ahmad returned from Italy and said Italy had agreed to take 25 wounded and sick people to treat them, or to receive four refugees from Turkey.

On the 10th and 11th March 1990, Saddam issued an apology that was:

"In the name of God, the most Gracious, the Most Merciful"

Revolutionary Leadership Council
14ᵗʰ March 1990, Decision number 140

Based on section A of Article 42 of the Presidency Council Law, Revolution decided:

1. General amnesty for all Iraqi Kurds abroad and stopping all legal procedures against them for all crimes and acts, provided they will return home during the issuing of this decree.
2. Crimes of intentional murder, theft and crimes not related to the events in northern Iraq are not subject to this law.
3. This law will be applied from 11th March 1990 to 11th May 1990.
4. Expert ministers and relevant parties are implementing the articles of this law.

Saddam Hussein
President of the Leadership Council of the Revolution

On 20th March 1990, I spoke by phone with Diyarbakir camp officials who were friends: Saado Korki, Akram Mai, Said Nayef,

Nayef Musa, Saeed Kestai, Salih Haji Hussein, Hussein Chalki and Osman Qasim. There was a complex problem with the election of the camp's management committee, so we had to mediate and form a committee for them at their own request. They also promised to maintain their unity and harmony, and the three were appointed, Akram, Saado and Salih, who would oversee the camp, and then all the officials would come together and agree, informing us of what they were asking for. In the phone call, Akram said:

- The human rights movement had been very strong in Turkey.
- In memory of the Halabja disaster, large demonstrations should be held in all cities such as Istanbul, Ankara, Azmir and Adana, and all Kurdish parties should participate, especially in Diyarbakir. On the anniversary of the Halabja disaster, ten people in Diyarbakir, and three hundred in Jazire and Slopi were arrested.

On 1st July 1990, Dr Kamal, along with 75 peshmerga, advanced on the Khalil Road near Jerme to branch one, first going to the village of Shaktane in Turkish Kurdistan. We had been busy with them for six months until these friends were present, and we held several meetings with the cadres of the branch, as well as a large number of peshmerga and cadres of branches two, three and four returning, which was an important step in itself.

On 29th July 1990, loyal and advanced cadres of both the September revolutions, Gulan and the peshmerga of Qarman Ali Akbar Hidayat, from Khanaqin, were martyred between the villages of Hodan and Chwarkalaw.

On 16th September 1990, branch one of the letters informed us that each of our friends: Mahdi Tyar Osman (Dilbrin) and Idris Abdullah Ahmed Doski who were in the wounded branch head-quarters were sent to Iran for treatment, after Turkey refused to allow them to take them, but they were later martyred because of severe injuries. In that time, we always said the Turks had a saying, "No one has eaten Turkish food for free and no one will ever eat for free". Majid Bagi also said, nothing is in his hands, which meant he had no power.

He didn't come and couldn't do anything, and the only advice was to get the forces back.

On November 20, 1990, 40 brave peshmerga returned to branch one. Their officials were friends Sdqi, Shukri Nerwai, Younis Dotazai, Sharif Abdulrahman Urai, Salih Chiaie. I spoke to them and wished them success. It was decided that they would go to the border of branch one and not return, and we were certainly proud, and we would go after them in the land of our homeland.

On 4th December 1990, fighting continued fiercely in the Guli area. In order to persuade Iraq, Iran's 28th division seemed to have put a lot of pressure on branch four, and it seemed to be the same from then on.

CHAPTER SEVEN

Peshmerga's Impressive Battles

Peshmerga's Epic Stories

THE BRAVE PESHMERGA had been active at all stages and eras, attacking Ba'athist bases and institutions, and did not hesitate to threaten, force, or enter into danger. They also carried out partisan activities in the depths of the enemy's territories and during the Gulan revolution, with peshmerga active in different areas and places.

Separately, they have recorded great historical epics:

1- The Sharansh Battle:

At 5:30 pm on the night of 18th August 1976, on the main road between Sharansh and Dasht-e-Takhte in the Qala Salmani area of Sindi, a regime force fell into the ambush of our brave peshmerga and after the conflict 12 regime gunmen were killed, including an officer in the rank of captain and one first lieutenant, a sergeant and several other officers were among the dead. Kalashnikovs fell into the hands of the peshmerga.

2- The Sharsten battle:

One of the most famous epics, in which the heroic peshmerga bravely confronted the enemy, was the epic of Sharsten. On 26th December 1976, two military regiments were moving towards the villages of Seder and Sharsten, while a peshmerga force from the Second Interim Leadership Region, led by Dr Kamal Kirkuki and Nasreddin Mustafa, faced them. The fighting lasted several days, although 11 helicopters supported the regime's forces and as a result, more than 163 regime soldiers and officers were killed, many wounded, and three helicopters shot down. Seven peshmerga and 14 civilians were martyred in the fighting, and 52 civilians and peshmerga were injured. Kamal Kirkuk was one of them.

3- Belmber's battle:

Another major and important activity of the brave peshmerga against regime forces is the famous Belmber epic in the High Barwari area. After the enemy felt the presence of peshmerga forces in the area, on 25th May 1977, a force of 500 soldiers, backed by nine helicopters, attacked the peshmerga headquarters from three sides, and a fierce battle ensued between the two sides. Peshmerga Mardana faced the enemy's huge force.

According to the statistics, 45 enemy soldiers were killed and 30 wounded, but unfortunately, this story was recorded with the bright blood of 14 martyrs whose bodies fell into the hands of the enemy. Zorab Aziz Pishtiwan, known as Anwar among the peshmerga, was from Khanaqin, and he, and nine other peshmerga were injured. On the second day of the battle, the brave peshmerga, Haji Qado Gravy, was also martyred.

The participants of the story were Ali Ibrahim Hururi, later martyred, Muhammad Khalid Bosali, Lieutenant Muhammad, and Muhammad Gawda's forces, who shot down a helicopter with an RPG.

4- Attack in Zakho:

In 1978 in a unique activity, friends Musa Sharif and Abdulrahman Salih were able to attack the enemy in Zakho region and cause great damage, but unfortunately, in this heroic activity, our party's talented cadre, Abdulrahman Salih, was martyred and gave his life to Kurdistan.

5- The Qasrok Battle:

Another important story in 1978, recorded by our enemy in bitterness, was the heroic peshmerga attack on enemy bases in the Qasrok area. Many regime fighters were killed and a number wounded in the operation. The regime's institutions suffered a lot of material damage, but unfortunately, in this tragic epic, our brave peshmerga, the skilled PDK cadre, Hamid Hafizullah, were martyred, and after a great deal of pain, his holy body was delivered to the village of Blanc in the District of Mreba and he was assigned to Kurdistan.

6- The Kani Sef Battle:

One of the great and historical epics, the epics of Kani Sef and Chomerasi and Qocha mountain on 20th October 1980 on the road SaidSadiq - Penjwen was recorded by the brave peshmerga.

Although the regime had launched a large number of forces in the area by helicopter, the peshmerga launched a major blow to the enemy. In the story, a large number of enemy soldiers were killed and many wounded. An officer named Pilot Captain Ahmed Ismail Aqili was captured by the peshmerga, but unfortunately, after the victory in this story, a PUK force attacked our peshmerga from behind in the Kani Manga area, resulting in two peshmerga named Muhammad Wardawala nd Azad Sheikh Qadir were martyred.

7- Haji Omaran Battle:

After assessing the situation, we decided to attack Haji Omaran. We wanted to test ourselves and try to save Haji Omaran. The Tamerchin Heights were under the control of the Kurdistan Democratic Party of Iran, which was an obstacle in the way our forces.

On the night of 17TH and 18th October 1980, Democratic peshmerga, backed by Iraqi artillery, attacked the military base at the house, which was rarely heavily attacked, but it turned out that the team's commander, Sarhang Maham, was a brave commander, because he resisted all the pressure. Then the Democratic Forces evacuated Tamerchini, and after that, we sent our forces to the heights and surrounding villages. We asked Iran to help us save Haji Omaran, and they agreed, but their promise was not applied properly.

On 5th November1980, I met with all peshmerga commanders to prepare, and after the discussions, the duties were as follows:

Ali Khalil, Sabri Nerwai, Ali Shaaban and Najmadin Goroni were to go to the Valley of Ena and Maran and put pressure on the Choman Haji Omaran road. Ali Khalil was in charge of the area.

Lieutenant Ali and branch two were to go to the village to get down Rayat Road.

Hamid Afandi, Sergeant Yassin, branch four, Tahsin Nerwai and Abdulrahman Taha were to go to the Shadow Valley east of Haji Omaran.

Haso Zhazokiwas placed on the head of the Shewa Rash.

The branch two forces, Rasul Faqe, Abdullah Qado, Faizo Salim Khan and Mala Rasul, were on the streets from Tamerchin.

Haji Birokhi and Rashid Isomeri remained in Qamtara as reserve forces.

Friends Dr Rozh Nuri Shawis, Rais Abdullah, Azad Barwari and Fatah Agha were commanding and supervising the front.

On 11th November 1980, all affairs were complete; our forces moved and confirmed in their places.

We agreed with Iran:

- to support our forces with artillery.
- Helicopters should be used logistically and to transport the martyrs and wounded.
- In the event of enemy helicopters coming and our forces being bombed, Iran would enter the war with fighter planes. Iran promised, but it wasn't enough. If not for the bravery of our commanders and peshmerga our forces would have been destroyed.

In that war, we realised that the situation of the regime's forces was stronger and greater than we expected because according to the information we received, the enemy was weak and unable to defend itself. The biggest obstacles were snow and cold, and then we realized that it was a big mistake to attack in this season and in such a cold and high land.

On 15th November 1980, the peshmerga attack began. Before the attack the Iranian artillery bombarded it, but it was not as expected as it was to destroy our forces. Omar Osman, who was responsible for directing the artillery, disagreed and asked for the artillery to stop, because they didn't hit their target and they were in danger of hitting our forces.

In the Dolseber area, three important and strategic locations were captured by the peshmerga and five soldiers were captured.

Peshmerga also went from Shewa Rash to Haji Omaran, but were in a difficult situation at the heights due to snow and storms. Although peshmerga had not fought such a big military engagement for a long time, they showed bravery, surprising Iran and the people of the area.

Dariush Foruhar, who had visited the area and was with us at the time of the attack, frankly, told Sarhang Mahami, "The peshmerga attacked bravely, but we (Iran) made no promises to them, and this is a shame." He also said, "I will go to Tehran and personally say this to Imam Khomeini."

The fighting lasted 48 hours and many enemies followed the peshmerga, but we decided to withdraw, because there was a risk that roads would be blocked by snow and no one would survive. Iraqi forces had prepared themselves in Diana for a major peshmerga attack but was not defended in the situation they were in.

The casualties to the enemy were more than 70 soldiers killed and wounded, and five soldiers were captured, while some weapons and explosives were seized by our forces.

In the battle, several peshmerga were martyred and gave their lives to Kurdistan: Fatah Agha, Saeed Recordi, Faizo Salim Khan, Mala Rasul, Ali Surchi, Suleiman Charboti, Teli Khasraw, Suleiman Karim Barzani, Majid Toman, Jamal Bab Yazdin Badli, Ahmed Hado Barzani, Abdullah Mirza Barzani, Qadir Islam Bari Gara, Shaker Aziz and 26 peshmerga were injured.

I was worried and saddened by the martyrdom of these heroes, but regarding Fatah Agha, the day before the attack was planned, a message came to Mr Ali Abdullah that Abdullah Agha, Fatah Agha's brother, had arrived at the headquarters of the political bureau and had just left Sulaymaniyah and had contacted the revolution.

Whatever I did and tried, I couldn't persuade Fatah Agha to come back to the political bureau to see his brother Abdullah, he was martyred and did not see him.

In truth, attacking in the cold and snow was wrong, but it was a great experience for us, and a strong learning point, obviously we learned that it is generally harder to fight in snow and storms.

8- Soren Mountain Battle:

In 1981, our heroic peshmerga in the village of Banibnok in Mount Surin, Zalm and Karchal, in two great struggles, launched strong blows against regime soldiers. In these heroic epics, a number of enemy fighters were killed and wounded, and 124 soldiers were captured, while hundreds of pieces of weapons and military equipment were seized by the peshmerga. Unfortunately in this story Akram Hamarashid Banibnoki, Teacher Suleiman, Osman Penjweni, and the fearless commander AbuBakr Mahmud Banibnoki gave their lives to the holy land of Kurdistan and the joined the rest in the caravan of the immortals.

In 1981, the activities of the Kurdistan peshmerga against the Ba'athist dictatorship continued and developed, in a way that during the first six months of 1981, the brave peshmerga were more active and they conducted 238 activities.

The enemy's casualties included 1,251 deaths and a large number of injuries. Our peshmerga achieved a lot, but unfortunately, 48 peshmerga were martyred and gave their lives to Kurdistan, and a number were injured.

9- The Biara Battle:

Our brave peshmerga, led by Nadir Hawrami, launched a massive attack on regime bases and strongholds in Biara and Shram. In the fighting, the area was seized for several days, causing heavy damage to the enemy, leaving dead and wounded in the area, capturing 45 soldiers, and several pieces of weaponry and military equipment were seized by the peshmerga. This epic was recorded with the blood of Suleiman Shamirani, Majnoon Hawrami, Hassan Shiramari, and Omer Brakhas, while several peshmerga were injured.

On the 3rd and 5th January 1982, we received a communication from branches three and four regarding the participation of our forces in the Battle of Tawela and Biara, which was later controlled by Biara. At Tehran's decision, Iranian forces withdrew. The decision was surprising as Iranian forces withdrew after controlling the area, but Iran seemed unwilling to provoke Arab sentiment. On this day, we received information that the Great Sherwan district had been destroyed and its people had been transferred to the vicinity of Erbil, and that there was a possibility Iraqi forces would withdraw from that area.

10- The Sharazur Battle:

Sharazur's epic was another story recorded on 31st May 1982, in partnership with socialist and communist forces between Said Sadiq, Halabja, Zarayan and Darbandikhan. The fighting lasted three nights, killing dozens of enemy soldiers, and killing four peshmerga: Muhammad Quta, Barzan Salih, Muhammad Sarawi and Sirwan Saadun Karkuki.

11- The Siyana Gara Battle:

In order to expand the liberated areas and launch larger strikes on enemy bases, the leadership decided to send a peshmerga force deep into the area. On 10th December 1982, peshmerga, 30 kilometres deep, attacked Ba'athist bases and strongholds, including the Maghavir forces, and the Jash traitors belonging to Latoo and Arshad, in a heroic battle that lasted three days and nights. The enemy arrived, and the attack had a huge resonance in the area.

12- The Sharmen Battle:

Another epic that hit the Ba'athist and Jash fighters was a shameful battle. At 4 pm on 29th March 1983, the brave peshmerga of the Amedi, Akre, Shekhan and a leadership force attacked the Jashs of Latoo and Arshad in Sharmen and northern areas.

The attack hit all its targets until 6 pm and caused great damage to the enemy and Jashan, but unfortunately, our loyal and heroic brother, Shaaban Ghaffar Bedouin, was martyred and four peshmerga were wounded.

13- The Said Sadiq-Shanadari Battle:

On the anniversary of the founding of our Party on 16th August 1983, our forces launched a heroic attack on regime strongholds through Said Sadiq-Shandari, causing heavy damage to Ba'athist institutions.

Our peshmerga were initially unharmed, but unfortunately, after this victory, our peshmerga fell into an enemy ambush, and in a heroic defence, each of the talented commanders, AbuBakr Haji Osman and Ali Rasul, the deputy of the area, Jalal Muhammad Dolasuri and Shahab San Ahmed, were martyred and joined the convoy of the immortals of our people.

14- The Kanilenja Battle:

On 21st November 1983, the Barzan peshmerga force launched a heroic attack on enemy bases and headquarters in Kanilenja. This epic bears the bright blood of each of the martyrs Salih Omar, Anwar Khardnaei and Zuber Haris Mamiski.

15- The Akre Battle:

One of the activities that had a major impact was the attack on Ba'athist bases and headquarters in the centre of Akre in 1983. Friends Abdullah Qado, Suleiman Harni, Bilal Surchi, Abdulaziz Amedi, Sadiq Guzi, Ahmed Shahin, Raza and Shimal Zebari and Uncle Sheikh Surchi took part, although unfortunately most of them were martyred later.

They played a significant role in hitting regime bases, and some Communist Party peshmerga were involved in the attack. The operation caused heavy damage to the enemy and there was a lot of voting, but unfortunately, Maam Sheikh Ahmad Ibrahim

Surchi was martyred and Jasim Zebari and Ahmed Bahariki were wounded in the fighting. Martyr Maam Sheikh Ahmad Ibrahim Surchi was buried there, and Lieutenant Babakir and Hoshyar Zebari were also in charge of the plan.

16- Duhok:

In August 1984, the regime launched a massive and widespread attack on the Duhok District Committee border in the Mangesh area, in which peshmerga defended bravely and prevented Ba'athist advances. A large number of regime fighters were killed and many wounded in the fighting. in the battle between the two villages of Galnaske and Alandke Abdullah Zebari, the brother of You Zebari, was among the dead.

17- Sarsang:

In the spring of 1985, Adnan Khairullah Tulfah was scheduled to visit Sarsang, but before he came, his special guard cars were ambushed by the peshmerga, killing several people and capturing three quarters of the force. The bag of Adnan's special secretary fell into the hands of Peshmarga which contained many important documents.

18- The Qaradagh Battle:

Qaradagh was another of the most famous epics recorded in the area. According to a strong and careful plan, in June 1986, the peshmerga cleared the Qaradagh district centre of Ba'athists. The story was a major blow to Ba'athist repressive institutions across the border. The story was written with the blood of eight martyrs and many who were recorded injured.

19- Amedi:

On 8th October 1985, three regime positions and bases were seized by our heroic peshmerga in a heroic peshmerga attack, according to a Message from L.N. Amedi. There's a lot of captures and achievements. Then came another communication from the Amedi area, which seized three other barricades, including the servants of Mount Dewali Doski. The funeral of three Jashs remained, three of them captured, five Kalashnikovs, two wireless agencies (Laslaki) and one dictatorship were taken over by the peshmerga who were our heroes.

Unfortunately, the heroic peshmerga, Muslih Ni'mat Ghazi, was martyred and a peshmerga was wounded in the attack. Journalist Goin Robert, who participated alongside the peshmerga, recorded his entire fight with cinematic cameras and video. I congratulated the brave peshmerga on this victory.

20- Zakho:

On the night of 11th to 12th October, 1986, the enemy's offensive began towards the Zakho headquarters, blocking the Dilai heights, and severing ties in the Zakho area. The Duhok area reported heavy fighting on the border between the two areas of Duhok and Zakho. Fighter planes heavily bombarded our surroundings. According to Duhok news, Kani Poung village was bombed, killing an elderly man named Haji Nabi and injuring four women and children, one of whom was seriously injured. The village of Zewa was also bombed near the headquarters of branch one, where an elderly man was martyred.

On 13th October 1986, fighting continued in the border areas of Both Duhok and Zakho, and the Duhok area sent us news that the enemy had taken control of the Zakho headquarters, and planes were continuing to bomb the area. At 4 pm on 14th October 1986 that the Jashan forces were on the Zakho and Duhok fronts.

21- The Terpaspian Village Battle:

After the start of the Golan Revolution, the peshmerga had a strong presence in the Erbil plain, and they were troubled by the enemies and, in number, they defended the existence of the PDK in the area, especially in the Erbil plains, and recorded many great and visible epics, one of the great epics of the village of Terpaspian in the border of the Qushtapa district.

After feeling the presence of peshmerga forces in the area, the regime started moving its own forces to the area to surround and destroy the peshmerga and in the short term delivered a large force to the area, numbering about 4,000 Jash and soldiers, with the support of storms, armoured vehicles, helicopters, Pilatu planes, and hundreds of military vehicles to surround the peshmerga forces who were in the village of Terpaspanda.

At 12:15 am on 27th October 1986, there was a fierce fight between the regime forces and the PDK peshmerga who were involved in the Qarachuk and Shamamk organizations Baranati and Didawan. It began with an attack on the Erbil Plains Committee, led by the martyr Khidir Swara, Jamal Murtaka, and a revolutionary intelligence force that separated from Hask. regime planes and helicopters.

They began shelling the area very heavily. The regime moved more forces from Erbil, Mosul and Kirkuk to prevent peshmerga from rescuing them. The fighting continued fiercely until late at night, and after a heavy fighting of several hours, peshmerga forces were able to break the enemy's siege and leave the village and escape. More than 100 regime soldiers and armed men were killed and hundreds more wounded in the fighting. Two helicopters were shot down, with several vehicles and much military equipment being broken and destroyed. Unfortunately, in this heroic battle, two peshmerga named Qahar Aziz in the itjahi movement and Farhad Ahmed Aziz, the cadre of the Erbil plains, were martyred and gave their lives to Kurdistan's land and were buried in the village. Four peshmerga were also wounded in the Erbil plain, including Ako Qurmushwi, who was later martyred, plus Zirak Sabir Betel, Zirak Zamara, and Ammar Majid, known as the Mountaineer.

22- Bastek:

At 4:30 pm on 20th December 1986, the brave peshmerga in Zakho heavily bombarded the Bastek community. The land of the Kurds and the original people of the area had been expelled, filled with imported Arabic people. That was the day we met with the residents of Spindari village in Barwari district.

Their problems and the situation in the revolution and the region were discussed in general. On 22nd December 1986, during the enemy's attack on the area, Barvan, deputy director of Muhammad Tahir's organization, and Izzat Taib, head of the main unit, and Amin Safar, a member of the Shekhan area, entered the enemy lines, according to a message, in the Duhok area.

The enemy surrendered, alongside Hikmat Najman, who had fought against the peshmerga.

23- The Ahmadawa Battle:

On 1st July 1987, the Battle of Ahmedawa and Hana Qol was recorded by our brave peshmerga. In a heroic attack, the headquarters of a Jash regiment, the regiment's army regiment, and the Saraya headquarters of the Sha'abi Army were seized. Hundreds of regime fighters were killed and many wounded in the fighting, and nearly 220 were captured. More than 1,000 weapons and large quantities of military equipment were seized by our peshmerga. The area was in the hands of the peshmerga for two days, before they withdrew. Unfortunately, in this story, Sardar Haji Hussein, Sheikh Kamel Friasi, Gharib Dolasuri, Ali Mala, Kawa Darbandi, Qadir Jabbar and Hassan Marf were martyred and joined the immortal convoy.

24- Atrush:

According to the LN- Duhok message service, on 4th January 1987, a large enemy force came to the Sarsnag and Bamarn, and blocked the road between the two towns. Nearly 200 Eva military vehicles appeared to have arrived in Deraluk and brought a large number of forces to Shekhan. Then a communication of Shekhan and Akresh areas talked about a lot of enemy movements in the North, around Atrush, Corett Gavana, Bagera and Swaratuka

On 5th January 1987, the enemy attacked the Shekhan area and branch one headquarters in the area of Barchi, Goharze, Sargali, and Kani in the Atrush area.

At 7 pm, we received news of our enemy's defeat in the area. It was easy to hear the sound of Doshka and artillery shooting,

The fighting continued until late at night, and the enemy failed in their attacks.

According to a letter from the Shekhan area on 6th January 1987, three enemy attacks on the Kanika citadel were overcome in the Atrush area. On the same day, the enemy began attacking and advancing from our north to the Battle of Merge, and because of the heavy bombardment of the area, all the families, women, and children were evacuated from their villages and took refuge in Mount Gara, a mountain with cold and harsh weather, and a week of inclement conditions is not good for people.

Despite the cold weather, fierce fighting continued on the Shekhan front on 7th January 1987. Enemy attacks continue from the Atrosh areas towards the Fortress of Kanika, Bewze and Hasnaka towards the Shekhan area. According to messages from the Shekhan area, helicopters attacked more than 20 battlefields last day, forcing hundreds of families, women and children to evacuate their villages and head to and around Gara Mountain. In that war, there was a lot of damage to the enemy.

The previous day, through suicide bombings, Jash and the Mughavirs infiltrated Kanika Citadel and a peshmerga from the Communist Party of Iraq was martyred and his body fell into the hands of the enemy. On the same evening, the enemy arrived in Hasnaka. A regiment of Maghavir – a special regime force, alongside Jash and Jash advisers, participated in the attack. The damage to our peshmerga was the disappearance of Atto and the injury of Hassan Abdullah. The peshmerga of Shekhan area showed heroic resistance and patience and were able to defeat the enemy. In that defence and struggle, the peshmerga of the Zakho and Duhok committees participated in the battle alongside the Shekhan forces.

On 8th January 1987, fighting continued fiercely in the Shekhan area. Duhok forces reached the border to support Shekhan forces, as well as Said Salih and Slo Khidir, with forces on their way to Shekhan and Zakho. According to the communications in the Shekhan area, Jash withdrew from the Meroke area to our north, leaving many belongings and fleeing. The night before, peshmerga fighters in both Shekhan and Duhok attacked and destroyed Jash, killing a large number of them. The bodies of some of them and eight living Jashs were captured by our forces, whose names are: Izzat Muhammad Mustafa Hetuti, born in 1969; Qasim Elias Qasim, from Duhok, born in 1961; Mushir Jamil Abdullah, born in Barbir village of Kani Masi; Jamil Abdullah Younis, from Barbir village in Kani Masi district, 1965; Fahmi Sabri Salim, a Sarzer resident, 1963; Sabah Mohammed Hassan, from Shekhan, born in 1967; Emad Ahmed Suleiman, born in Duhok, 1968; Khalid Mohammed Hassan, from Duhok, born in 1967.

In these battles, eight Kalashnikovs, one Brno and one RPG were captured through the achievements of the brave peshmerga. Unfortunately, peshmerga and Garaman wireless operator, Zahir Haji Yahya, was martyred in Zakho and Younis Ali Ni'mat in the Shekhan area, where his brother Hassan Ali Ni'mat was martyred in Halgurd in 1969. Muhammed Hassan Hasanaki, a national defence man, was also missing. It seemed that the forces of Duhok and Zakho had arrived on the front lines of the war in Shekhan,

The situation in the war improved in the interest of our forces. What is true is that the Shekhan forces were tired, but they fought a heroic battle. At the time of the war, the caves and mountains in this unpleasant situation, the cold and cruel weather, war was the only noise for the displaced people, hundreds of families, hiding in it with women and children.

The incident painted a shocking and heart-breaking scene.

According to the news, on 9th January 1987, the enemy was completely destroyed in the areas of Spindari, north and Hasnaka. There was only one force left in the Kanika citadel and would be expelled with God's support. According to messages and news from the Shekhan district committee, the enemy's damage was as follows: there were 40 killed in the Kanika area, two of them in major and wireless ranks, and five soldiers had been captured by the peshmerga. 32 soldiers were killed and wounded in the Spindari area. Four bodies and eight captives had been captured by our forces. 30 people had been killed and wounded in the Hasnakash area, and the enemy's damage was certainly greater. According to a message from the political bureau, dictator Saddam's remarks were answered at the station. Thank God the enemy's attack in all Shekhan areas was completely broken, only the Kanika citadel remained, and Muhammad Salim received the citadel's shoe.

On 14th January 1987, fighting continued the Shekhan front. The enemy launched a massive attack on the Kanika and Spindari fronts and was able to reach the land, heavily bombarding the area with planes, artillery, and tanks. A peshmerga in the Duhok area was martyred and 11 wounded, but many others were killed by the enemy, according to an urgent message from the Shekhan district committee. Our forces had their place and position in the Series of Sedra and Barane and included Kani Mazi.

On 12th January 1987, a helicopter was targeted and crashed in Atrush. On the night of 11th January 1987, peshmerga in the Duhok region launched a heroic attack in the centre of Duhok and many of the enemy's locations, bases, and headquarters were targeted.

Unfortunately, after a heroic battle, on 15th January 1987, two beloved brothers in the national defence, Ghazi Ismail Saad and Tahir Qeshuri, were martyred. Shimal Zebari, the head of the Shekhan district committee, also helped those forces and pesh-merga who had a major role in the fight.

After a fierce battle, the enemy arrived at the Shekhan and Akre district committee headquarters, although we had not yet received enough detailed information, but according to the news on the night of 15th to 16th January 1987, the enemy returned to the previous location on the Shekhan front.

On 15th January 1987, enemy forces reached about 150 metres from the Shekhan area headquarters but were forced to withdraw and break as a result of peshmerga defence, according to a joint communication from Slo Khidir, Said Salih, and the Shekhan district committee on 17th January 1987. Between 13th and 15th January 1987, fighting continued and the peshmerga defended bravely, and the Communist Party and Dawa were with them. Eventually the enemy failed. The Jashs committed great crimes and burned and looted all the villages they entered; Bebade, Karava and Agush were among the looted villages. We promised that if Allah gave us a chance, we would avenge this burning and we would plunder them.

According to the Shekhan district committee's communique on 23rd January 1987, on 21st January 1987, the brave peshmerga of the martyr Amin Nasiri's and Martyr Mahmud Yezidi organizations in Shekhan area and Shorsh organization in Zakho region bombarded Arshad Zebari with 120mm cannon, attacking several criminal bases and strongholds in Sharman. This peshmerga activity made me very happy.

25- Bamarne:

On the night of 26th May 1987, our brave peshmerga was able to strike a strong blow against the regime and record a great story in a rare activity in the Bamarne district.

In this encounter, 13 barricades, Bamarne airports, border regiment headquarters, and 140 regiments fell into the hands of the peshmerga, although the attack was delayed one night because of the betrayal of the Jashs, because they had promised to help, but then they changed their mind.

In this action, the enemy was severely harmed, including the killing of more than 100 people and the capture of 58 others, and the acquisition of more than 215 pieces of weaponry with more than 1,500 different bullets.

Unfortunately, this great story was recorded with the blood of the brave peshmerga Fawzi Ramazan Rasho Skarini and Abdulstar Salih Murad Banavi, and the injuries of three peshmerga.

These forces participated in this historical story: the Amedi, Duhok, Shekhan and national defence committees.

In the attack, 32,000 dinars were seized at the regiment headquarters. In a courageous moment, peshmerga and officials made the money a gift to the families of the martyrs; this was a show of respect and loyalty, this made me happier than all the successes.

All praise be to God, who changed the direction of the battle.

26- The Basrea Battle:

On the night of 27ᵗʰ July 1987, the brave peshmerga of branches three and four launched a massive attack on the base of the Basra regiment, which soon destroyed the regiment and caused great damage to the enemy. 152 people were killed in the attack, 70 people were captured, and, at the headquarters of the regiment, all the Rabayas and barricades were destroyed. A large number of weapons, bullets and military rifles were also seized by the brave peshmerga. Unfortunately, in this story, two peshmerga sacrificed their lives to the victory.

27- The Kani Masi Battle:

On the night of 13th September 1987, according to an advanced military plan, the brave peshmerga of branch one of the three districts launched a major attack on regime headquarters and strongholds in Kani Masi and soon liberated the area. Peshmerga of branch one recorded a historical story with this victory.

In this story, more than five regiment headquarters and an area of 70 square kilometres were liberated. The enemy was badly damaged, and the killed and wounded amounted to more than 100. A number of regime soldiers were captured by peshmerga. Several destroyed military vehicles. The peshmerga made great gains in this victory.

Unfortunately, in recording this story, seven peshmerga and two of the national defence gave their lives to Kurdistan. The epic of Kani Masi is considered one of the great moments of the Gulan revolution and is recorded with gold ink on the pages of the history of the Kurdistan Liberation Movement, because it was a story at the level of war between the two countries and in terms of the forces, weapons, and military technology of the era, there was no balance between the peshmerga and the regime's fighters, but what changed the balance of power was the power of belief in the struggle for freedom and the defence of rights. It was the righteousness of a nation.

Following the recording of Kani Masi battles and the success of the brave peshmerga, I sent a message of congratulations and appreciation to the brave peshmerga and the participants of these battles in which they made history. The letter read:

Struggling friends and activists,
The brave peshmerga of Kurdistan

I congratulate you on your great success, the liberation of Kani
Masi district and its surroundings. It is truly an honour-
able historical story in the history of the Kurdish liberation
movement. With this epic, you have given peace to the pure
souls of the martyrs and the hearts of their families, and
you have raised the morale of the fighters of the Kurdish and
Iraqi revolutions, and encouraged towards the struggle.

The struggle proved that the steely will of the People
of Kurdistan and the Revolutionary Army of
Kurdistan has reached a point where it will hurt the
hearts of the fascist regime and its hired people.

I warmly salute the sacrifice of all the peshmerga,
the head of your branch and the district committee.
Each person who participated in the war with selfless-
ness, the people of our nation looking forward to it. You
have sacrificed, and you have been heroic.

Greetings to the pure souls of the martyrs of this story, the
martyr of the PDK and the revolution, Muhammad Salih
Suleiman, head of the Amedi district committee, who was
indeed the symbol of a fearless and orderly struggle.

Greetings to the pure souls of the other martyrs of the
Kurdistan Revolutionary Army, Wasif Salman, the

head of the Revolution Organization, Yusuf Salih, Salih Salim, Said Yassin Ahmed Ghafur, Nabi Waisi, Ali Shukr Jawhar, and all the martyrs of the national defence and the innocent citizens of this historical story.

Greetings to the brave peshmerga from all sides and the forces who participated in this victory in some way.

Thanks and praise to the local public for their support, as well as to all the national defence forces and all the men and women who helped to succeed in this war.

Dear friends,
Brave peshmerga

Your success has been recorded in a very detailed and sensitive historical moment of the Kurdish freedom movement and the struggle of the Kurdish people, strengthening this success will change the amount of power in the interests of the people and the struggle.

Indeed, you are the heroes of saving hundreds of square kilometres from our beloved homeland, while Saddam's regime carried out a brutal attack to destroy Kurdistan. While displacing its people, while implementing another phase of displacement and annihilation of our people, this victory is the greatest epic so far in the sovereign history of the 1976 Gulan revolution. It is another pride on the page of the Kurdish revolution, our Party, and Barzani's immortal struggle. This victory is an honour for the Iraqi people and all the national forces and parties of Kurdistan and Iraq, by taking a step. It is important to bring us closer to the day of liberation from Saddam's fascist regime and its annihilation so that the Kurdish people and all the Iraqi people can be saved from that regime and a democratic national government will be formed in Iraq and the Kurdish people will achieve their legitimate national rights.

Dear brothers, try to strengthen your great success, do not let success make you arrogant and work on your affairs. Today, more than ever, you must try to unite your ranks in the political and military fields and continue to protect the people and their interests. Let this success be the basis for greater success. Our nation's revolution has a long way to go. You have a great war ahead of you. Let this victory be the beginning of your success, bigger and more permanently in the future.

Brothers, we believe in you and the awareness of the brave peshmerga and the patient masses of our nation, that they will continue their struggle, strengthen the spirit of co-struggle with the struggling national forces and strengthen the relationship with the people in order to clarify the path and bring your struggle to the end.

We have the ability, self-confidence, and aspirations to succeed in the endless support of our nation and the difficult roles, those around the flag of our Party,

the revolution, the Kurdish freedom movement, and
the movement the Nation of Iraq has gathered.

I congratulate you once again, and I hope that the epic of Kani
Masi will be the leader of all the brave peshmerga of our Party.

So forward,
Regards
Masoud Barzani
The president of Kurdistan Democratic Party of Iraq
17 on 18th September 1987

28- Amedi to Deraluk:

At 4 pm on 11th January 1987, a large number of bullets were shot by our forces in the Rashava valley. From Amedi to Deraluk, they blocked the main road and severely hit the enemy and the result was as follows:

1. The breaking of an 82mm cannon, two military tankers, one armoured vehicle, a pickup truck and the burning of the headquarters of the Deraluk regiment, the Ba'athist headquarters, and the security forces.
2. 2The situation of the Shekhan and Akre fronts was very good and in the interest of the peshmerga. All forces that had gone to help arrived and were scheduled to launch a major attack on the Atrush-Kanika area.
3. At 12:30 pm, two Iranian planes flew over us, and the Tehran station announced that they had bombarded the Amedi area.

29- The Qaradagh Battle:

On 20th April 1987, branches three and four, Hasha and Hask forces launched a massive attack on Garadagh district, according to the branch three message. After heavy fighting, the district was liberated, with more than 100 soldiers killed, and 100 captured by the peshmerga. peshmerga also seized light weapons, two vehicles, military vehicles, wireless and military equipment. In this battle, three brave peshmerga were martyred and a number of all parties were injured.

30- Deraluk:

On 3rd May 1987, the sound of weapons used in the fighting in the Deraluk-Amedi area was heard. We were informed that about 2,501 Jash had contacted the peshmerga on this side.

5th May 1987, a holy and great day. Thank God for a great day. At 3 am on 5th May 1987, the Amedi district committee forces and three of the Gulan District Committee, two branch one organizations and a national defence force launched a large-scale attack on the Headquarters of the Light Regiment (Khafifa). Of the 111th adviser, Sheikh Nuri Barzinji. After fierce fighting, the headquarters of the regiment, 81 barricades around the peshmerga, were seized.

38 people were killed and more than 40 were captured by the peshmerga. Among the captives were the first lieutenant, Abdul Hamid Khatab Abdullah, Amerfawj, three soldiers, one Naib Zabat (officer) and 30 Jashs, while 16 more Jash surrendered to the peshmerga. Also, a vehicle, a driver and nine military vehicles were burned, 200 pieces of Kalashnikov, Brno, RBK, one 82mm, one 14.5mm, one Greenoff, fourteen wireless agencies, a large number of bullets, bullets, RPG bullets, etc., fell into the hands of the peshmerga.

After the attack at 1 pm, planes bombarded the area and pesh-merga bases and headquarters, but peshmerga between Tashish and Grka fought back with Sam seven missiles. A helicopter landed and seven soldiers on board fell into the hands of peshmerga forces, two of whom are known, pilot Colonel Hamid Saeed and first lieutenant pilot Nizar Adnan. Friends Dr Rozh Nuri Shawis, Lieutenant Ali, and Saeed Salih led the major attack, and all offi-cials and peshmerga played their part. The damage of peshmerga was only the injury of three peshmerga, but unfortunately after the end of the battle a peshmerga of Gulan area committee named Satar Orai was martyred.

In order to contact and thank the brave peshmerga, on 6th May 1987, we went to Gara, and because of the Betel (field phone), we were able to contact the Amedi front.

Their morale seemed to be high and strong, especially after the helicopter was shot down. A lot of artillery was heard in Amedi, Barwari and Deraluk, because Mr Ali Salim Bajluri, who was in charge of the revolutionary artillery, sent him to Slo Khidir to bombard enemy bases and strongholds between Deraluk and Sheladze. They did it and saw a significant success.

31- Hiran:

On 16th and 17th August 1987, on the 41st anniversary of the founding of the PDK, a major activity was carried out against regime fighters in the Hiran Valley and they suffered great damage. Unfortunately, seven peshmerga were martyred and 20 injured in the operation. A French journalist, alongside the peshmerga, recorded the story in pictures and published it in the Figaro newspaper after return-ing to his country. In his writing, he described the peshmerga as: "They were brave like lions, they were fast like tigers in the mountains of Kurdistan."

32- Deraluk:

On the night of 11th January 1988, according to the peshmerga's plan the heroes of branch one in the Deraluk-Shiladze area launched a massive attack on regime strongholds and headquarters. The attack, which was carried out by the committees in Amedi, Shekhan, Akre, Zakho, Gulan and the forces of branch one headquarters, caused heavy damage to the enemy. The attack began at 9:30 pm. According to the news, the enemy's damage was as follows: 112 barricades and enemy strongholds in Nizar and deep head and Kane, Deraluk and Shiladze were seized.

Peshmerga entered the centre of Deraluk and took over the city, and all the city's institutions fell into the hands of our heroic forces. There was only little defence left in the city and a number of regime intelligence-led protesters. Otherwise, the headquarters of the Regiment of Ahmed Kalhe Rekani, Ali Abo, the headquarters of the Ba'athist Party and the Security and Intelligence Organization at the base were captured.

In the attack and victory, two brave peshmerga, Burhan Ismail, who was in charge of the Pirs organisation in the Amedi area and appeared as the lion of Mount Matin and the head of all the attacks in the area, arrived at the immortal convoy with Ahmed Ghazi Skrini and recorded a historical victory. By the time the news reached us, 41 captives had arrived at the headquarters of branch one. On that day we could say that Kurdistan was happy with these heroes; that peshmerga were the heroes who sing the nation into being with the blood of the flag, for freedom.

Despite the region's overcrowding, the fighting continued, and the brave peshmerga of branch one continued to advance until 13th January 1988, when Deraluk was released and all regime institutions fell into the hands of our heroic peshmerga, and both bridges between Deraluk-Amedi and Deraluk-Shiladze were taken over by the peshmerga. The captive crew were transferred to the headquarters of branch one. 53 members of the Ba'athist Security and Intelligence Forces were killed in Deraluk.

According to a branch one message on 14th January 1988, due to snowfall, cold and freezing conditions, and because the attack had achieved all its goals, it was decided that the peshmerga would withdraw. In order to counter any possibility of revenge by the enemy, the peshmerga took important strategic positions before withdrawing.

The result of this great attack was as follows:

Destroying the headquarters of the Ali Abo regiments, Ahmed Kalhe Rekani, Kadhim Omer Khan, and the intelligence regiment, which is 70 percent of the headquarters of the Regiment of Muhammad Kalhe and 50 percent Ali Shaaban's regiment was destroyed; more than 550 regime gunmen were captured and more than 1,300 were killed; 67 different military vehicles of the regime burned, and more than five enemy attacks were destroyed. peshmerga's achievements in this major attack were:

Two armoured vehicles, three 14.5mm cannon, 1,000 light weapons, 120mm mortar, three advanced wireless facilities and a large amount of weapons were captured.

Unfortunately, 11 martyrs recorded the story with bright blood, and 15 peshmerga were injured. The martyrs were Burhan Ismail, head of the Pirs organization; Khasraw Hussein, Head of the

Shrin Organization; Saadi Muhammad al-Kishki, Head of Media Organization; Karim Saeed Shanwali, Deputy Media Organization; Aswad Ismail Kani Sarki, media organization; Lazgin Yassin Siri, Tiari organization; Izzadin Ismail Sharif; Salim Abdulkhaliq, Gulan District Brotherhood Organization; Ahmed Gazi Skarini, Lt Amedy; Saeed Hussein, Wireless Lt Akre; Karam Yazdin, Deputy of the Zmnako Organization.

Tehran's station unjustly published the news, which was propaganda and untrue, and misled by saying that Malik's team allegedly attacked the martyrs' graves and the 75th Muzafar team, and that PDK forces helped them. The truth of the story was recorded with the blood of PDK peshmerga.

On 16th January 1988, branch one sent a message, saying that because all their goals had been achieved and the peshmerga were tired, they wished to end the attack, and their request was accepted. 27 wounded were recorded with the blood of 11 martyrs.

On 23rd January 1988, we received the news that at 11 am, a military spokesman from Baghdad radio said:

In the name of God, the most gracious and the most merciful.

While major general Abdul Aziz Ibrahim Hadisi, commander of the 5th Legion, and several Legion officers were conducting and carrying out their duties, at 5:20 pm on Friday night, 22nd December of 1988, their plane crashed due to technical problems near Shwan village in Tamim province, so we asked the employees of the National Defence Regiments and Kurdish citizens to facilitate and assist the military forces working in the area, to find the bodies of the victims and the plane.

On the night of 28th January 1988, the enemy bombarded the headquarters of branch one, which martyred four people.

33- Zakho:

On 8th January 1988, the brave peshmerga of the Zakho Regional Committee entered the Arabized Bastek community in a courageous activity, causing heavy damage to regime strongholds and closing the international road for several hours. In connection with this activity on 10th January 1988, the Tehran Station published a warning message from the Kurdistan Democratic Party (KDP) to foreign countries and companies regarding their bravery in traffic on the Zakho international route, but the station inadvertently and unjustly transmitted the news.

34- The Mandil Battle:

On the night of 10th to 11th January 1988, the third branch heroes bravely attacked the headquarters of the Sixth Special Regiment in Mandil - five kilometres from Chamchamal - and completely took control of the headquarters. In this attack, a large number of captives and military rifles were seized and this was an achievement for the brave peshmerga.

The battle on the Chamchamal border was as follows: With the participation of the Chamchamal, Shwan, Bazian, Kalar, Ranjbaran organization and a third branch headquarters force, the attack on the sixteenth regiment headquarters in Mandil - five kilometres from Chamchamal - began and the regiment headquarters was seized within forty minutes. As a result, 14 Jash and a regime gunman were killed as captains. Although no full census of the achievements was carried out, the enemy's material damage was as follows: the explosion of the regiment store, the burning of 40 military tents, the burning of three Toyota vehicles and two military Ivas, in addition to capturing 37. Dale and a transportation car in Nurasot village, Greenofi transport car, four Kalashnikovs, two Nissan pickups, one Toyota Crona and one LandCruiser, two remote-looking, six RPG number eleven, a large amount of equipment from the Regiment headquarters, 40 bullets, an RPG, one Arbika and a battle telephone.

In recording this historical and revolutionary epic, four peshmerga sacrificed their lives and, with their bright blood, became the strong wall of their country, including the martyrs: Martyr Salih Muhammad Sattar, known as Rebwar, at the branch headquarters. Martyr Rizgar Hamid, from L.N. Chamchamal. Martyr Jabbar Ghafur, known as Dewana, belongs to L.N. Shwan, the Khalkhalan organization, and Martyr Salih Muhammad Salih, known as Mam Salih of L.N. Duz. 13 brave peshmerga were injured.

On 9th January 1988, a regime Sikho fighter plane was shot down on the border of the Gulani Suhr district committee in the Qafni branch. The pilot, captain of the plane, Salih Jadua Sajar, from Ramadi, the governor of Anbar province, was arrested injured and after a while, he died of his wounds.

35- Balisan:

At 7 am on 26th February 1988, in the Bethwata and Khalifan areas, the enemy launched a massive attack on the Balisan Valley. Although the attack was carried out with the help of planes, artillery and tanks, we heard of the enemy's defeat on that side on the evening of the same day. Unfortunately, a heroic PDK peshmerga, Hassan Avdal, known as Dr Ashti in Erbil, and two

PUK peshmerga were martyred in the attack and gave their lives to Kurdistan.

36- Zakho - Batofa:

On 26th February 1988, our brave peshmerga struck the enemy on the Zakho-Batofa road, according to a message from Zakho. 34 people were captured in the attack by peshmerga, including Deputy Sheikh Sadiq Briffkani and Lieutenant Jumaa, a name from Samarra, in captivity, with dozens of deaths and injuries by regime fighters. It was on that day that the news of the enemy's attack on PUK headquarters.

On 6th March 1988, Ansat's publication was quoted by Tehran's intelligence agency that the Turkish newspapers admitted saying that seven large truck vehicles were disabled due to an activity carried out on the night of 24th February 1988 by peshmerga from the Shekhan district committee.

37- Attack on the Halabja area:

In early 1988, it seemed that the balance of power and the Iran-Iraq war was in the interest of the Baghdad regime. Therefore, it was thought that an easy and peaceful road would be provided for the Garmian and Qaradagh areas. At that time, there were a lot of peshmerga forces, parties and there were also a large number of Armed Shia organisations in the area.

For this purpose, discussions and consultations were held between the PUK, PDK and other parties, and then with Iran, which had originally made their final decision, to attack the Halabja and Sharazur areas.

After the discussion and exchange on the plan, it was agreed that:

- PDK, PKU, socialist, Islamic movement forces, and a force affiliated with the Supreme Council for Islamic Revolution in Iraq (Baqir al-Hakim) would participate.
- Each side had tasks specified.
- It was decided not to enter the centre of Halabja city centre, in any way, to protect the lives of the people.

The attack began on 12th March and was a major success from the beginning. Many of the peshmerga followed, and Iraqi forces broke down and fled. Unfortunately, a number of PUK military officials and Iranian guards violated the agreement and entered the centre of Halabja. They prevented people from leaving the city and immediately appointed mayors and employees to enter the city. They did not hand Halabja to the peshmerga from other parties.

When Iraq felt the morale of its forces in the area had collapsed and would not tolerate another attack, it committed a major historical crime on 16th March 1988. The city of Halabja was bombarded with mustard and sarin gas. With this bombardment, a major disaster occurred in a short time, nearly 15, 000 were affected: 5,000 were martyred and 10,000 were injured. Most of the victims were children and women. In terms of military tactics, the regime with this inhumane crime, could attack and save its forces, but it was unfortunate that the crime was committed and ignored by the whole world.

On 17th March 1988, a message from the PUK's political bureau and a letter from the fourth branch came, describing how big the disaster was. "We have tried hard to warn those who have reached out to our friends and conscience that they will not commit this great crime."

Iran opened its borders to the people and took the wounded, and it did not hesitate to help the disadvantaged, but it was a huge disaster, and the wounds could not be treated in any way. Many families were martyred. Omer's picture Khawari became a symbol of the disaster.

On 22nd March 1988, Dickoyar, secretary-general of the United Nations, condemned the crime and accused Iraq of gassing Halabja. According to reports received on 20th and 21st March 1988, the level of casualties and losses in Halabja was very high, and we sent a message to the Political Bureau of the Patriotic Union of Kurdistan, Socialist, and Communist Party of Iraq that a solution must be found and that in order to convey the voice of our people abroad, this situation requires unity and harmony. There was a union of parties.

In response, we received a message from Nawshirwan Mustafa expressing the PUK's readiness for all cooperation.

On 22nd March 1988, Abdul-Muhaiman and Haji Haji Braim returned to Mariwan to investigate information from branch four about Iran's behaviour and attitudes in Halabja.

On 23rd March 1988, from early morning to 4 pm, the enemy launched five attacks on Mount Glazard and Darbandikhan, and according to messages from branches three and four, all of which were destroyed and forced to withdraw.

On 24th March 1988, the enemy's attack on Mount Glazard continued, all the way to Darbandikhan. peshmerga and forces defended it bravely, although Communist Party and Islamic movement forces evacuated their positions, and enemy attacks were destroyed. Unfortunately, the enemy heavily gassed villages around Darbandikhan (Sewsenan). 68 civilians were martyred and 53 were wounded, and the village was destroyed.

Until Iraq invaded Kuwait, the great powers were indifferent to the unprecedented catastrophic crime, and other countries ignored the wrongdoing; some countries even defended Iraq, alleging they had not committed the acts in Halabja, some accusing Iran of the crime instead. In fact, after the fall of the regime in 2003, the United States and Europe were very concerned about this issue.

After the invasion of Kuwait, countries said aloud that this was a major crime, genocide, and punishable by all laws. Many European companies helped Iraq to create chemical weapons. Unfortunately, this was covered up.

In 1989, I asked a German journalist, Dishner, the author of The Book of Ahfad Salahuddin, how we could file a lawsuit against several German companies that helped Iraq build chemical weapons? He said, "Is there evidence?"

I said "We have fully verified information."

He said, "If there is no evidence, you may be charged in court!"

This is strange.

The role, selflessness and bravery of journalist Gwen Robert, who risked his life in search of, find, and take samples of land in the chemical attack sites, was later confirmed in foreign laboratories and was an important reason for informing the outside public about the fact that Kurdistan had been gassed.

I must point out here that we, as Kurds, have not been able to use the regime's great crime well for the benefit of our people, to investigate the criminals continuously and legally, and to compensate the victims of the Anfal and chemical weapons. Now there is room, we need to be more scrupulous and investigate the crime further because the Iraqi governments after 2003 are heirs to the Ba'athist government and need to take their legal and ethical responsibilities.

On 25th March 1988, the enemy invaded areas such as the Faqra and Watershed. At 6 pm, the brave peshmerga were able to capture all the areas the enemy had taken over in a counterattack, but in that successful action, Saeed Salih was lightly injured.

38 –

On 30th March 1988, branches three and four warned us via messages that the enemy had attacked Bazian, Sangaw, Darbandikhan and Glazard, and that heavy fighting was continuing. In the afternoon, we heard that the enemy had arrived in Qaradagh, and we warned branches three and four to defend, but if they were obliged to do so, to think about withdrawing and to make the necessary decisions in cooperation with other parties.

39 -

On 25th June 1988, the enemy tried hard to advance from the Mergasor front. There was a fierce battle, and the peshmerga defended bravely. Unfortunately, in this defence, Khano Arab, Ibrahim Shekhomer Kanialanji, Saeed Hussein Mamoli and Ali Khidir Ibrahim Shahid reached the convoy of the immortals of our people.

40- The Sutke Regiment 143 Battle:

On 13th March 1988, branch one told us with an urgent message that in a heroic attack, the peshmerga seized the headquarters of the 143rd Jassim Slevani regiment. Lieutenant Colonel Kamal al-Majid was killed in the attack and 30 were captured. Unfortunately, three brave peshmerga were martyred and nine others were injured in the activity. On 26th March 1988, branch one warned us via a message that the enemy was planning to attack the headquarters of branch one. The third and fourth branches told us that it had been decided and agreed with the PUK and socialist parties to withdraw to a new line.

On 27th and 29th March 1988, enemy attacks on the Qaradagh area continued, and apart from the Sharazur and Darbandikhan fronts, they attacked and advanced on the Kadoshi mountain, and there was heavy fighting and many enemy attacks were destroyed.

Sotke

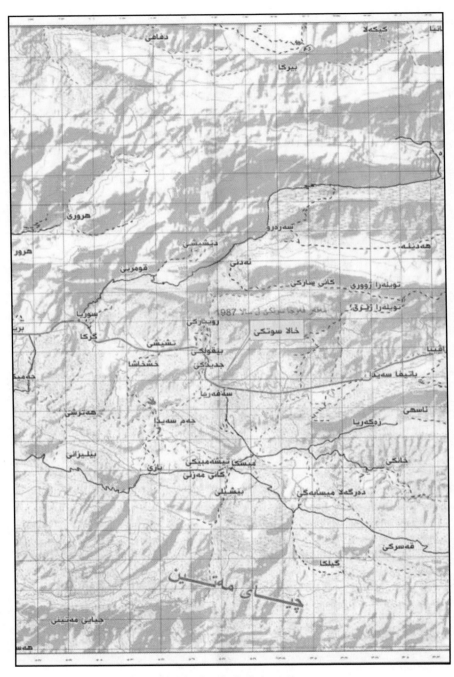

Geographical – Sutke's Location map

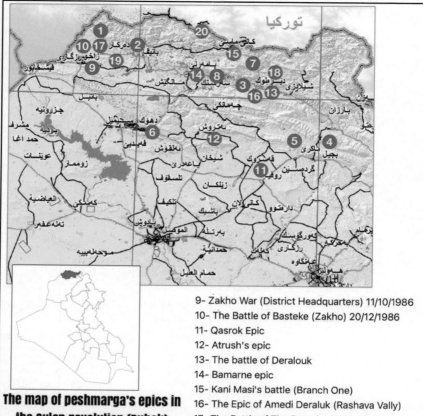

The map of peshmarga's epics in the Gulan revolution (Duhok)

1- The War of Sharansh 18/08/1976

2- The Epic of Belmbere 25/05/1977

3- The Syani Gara Battle 10/12/1982

4- Akre's Epic 1983

5- Sherman's War 29/03/1983

6- The Duhok War August 1984

7- Amedi War 08/10/1985

8- Sarsang Battle Spring 1985

9- Zakho War (District Headquarters) 11/10/1986

10- The Battle of Basteke (Zakho) 20/12/1986

11- Qasrok Epic

12- Atrush's epic

13- The battle of Deralouk

14- Bamarne epic

15- Kani Masi's battle (Branch One)

16- The Epic of Amedi Deraluk (Rashava Vally)

17- The Battle of The Basteke (Zakho)

18- The battle of Deralouk

19- Batufa War (Zakho)

20- The Sutke's 143 Regiment War

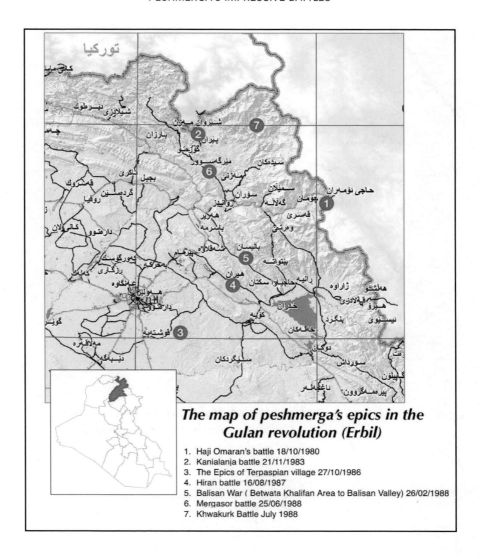

The map of peshmerga's epics in the Gulan revolution (Erbil)

1. Haji Omaran's battle 18/10/1980
2. Kanialanja battle 21/11/1983
3. The Epics of Terpaspian village 27/10/1986
4. Hiran battle 16/08/1987
5. Balisan War (Betwata Khalifan Area to Balisan Valley) 26/02/1988
6. Mergasor battle 25/06/1988
7. Khwakurk Battle July 1988

The map of Peshmarga's epics in the Gulan revolution (Sulaymaniyah)

1-The Epic of Sharsten 26/12/1976
2-Kani Seif's epic 20/10/1980
3-Soren Mountain War 1981
4-Biyarea's War 01/1982
5-Sharazur's epic 21/05/1982
6-The Battle of Shanadar (SaidSadiq) 16/08/1983
7-Qaradagh Battle 07/1986
8-Qaradagh War (Branch 3,4) 20/04/1987
9-Ahmadawa Epic 01/07/1987
10-Baasra War (Branch 3,4) 27/07/1987
11-Battle of Mandil (Branch 3) 10/01/1988
12-Halabja War 03/1988
13-The battles of the (Bazian, Sangar, Darbandikhan, and Glazarda (Branch 3,4) 30/03/1988

Peshmerga political and partisan activity

Between November 1979 and August 1980, peshmerga carried out 180 activities against the regime, killing more than 850 officers and soldiers, injuring 2,880, destroying 49 military vehicles and disabling ten artillery pieces.

In total, the activity of the branches was as follows:

Branch one (32 activities)

Branch two (28 activities)

Branch three (8 activities)

Branch four (7 activities)

Branch three and branch five (1 activity)

Branch three, branch four and branch five (2 activities)

Branch three with leadership force (1 activities)

Branch three and branch four (1 activity)

Barzan force (24 activities)

Bradost force (19 activities)

Branch five (8 activities)

The peshmerga acquired weapons in these activities, including: Grenades 92, Doshka 2, 81mm bullet 50, Brno 37, doshka bullets 2500, Kalashnikov 7, Greenoff's bullet 1000, Greenoff 3, Russian bullets 29000, Dictatorship 3, Brno Bullets 4000, Howitzer 1, RPG rocket 44, 60mm Howitzer 2, Rain coat 50, RPG 2, Kalashnikov part and many other items 45, Car 1, Field telephone 3, Military Telescope 5.

During these military activities, 38 brave peshmerga were martyred and 28 peshmerga were injured. The number of martyrs and wounded in the branches is as follows: Branch one 9 martyrs; branch two 11 martyrs and 17 wounded; branch three 7 martyrs and 2 wounded; branch four 5 martyrs and 6 wounded; branch five 5 martyrs and 2 wounded; Bradost force 1 martyr and 1 wounded.

A group of peshmerga were prepared to return to the border of branch one with supplies. On 9th January 1980, we visited Zewa to attend their leaving ceremony. Then we visited the training ground on the 57mm anti-tank ball, which was the first to open this course and take advantage of such a weapon. The 57mm ball is a strong weapon and in the activities and actions of the enemy's strongholds it was going to be effective.

In August 1980, our peshmerga carried out more than 29 military activities against Ba'athist bases and headquarters as follows:

1.   Branch one 23 activities
2.   Branch two 4 activities
3.   Branch three 2 activities

More than 189 regime militants were killed and 33 wounded in the operation. The peshmerga also gained a lot of military equipment. Unfortunately, in these activities, three peshmerga heroes were martyred, and three others were injured.

In the face of the chauvinist and racist policies of the Baghdad authorities against the people of Kurdistan and in their revolutionary attacks, the Revolutionary Army of Kurdistan, fought on 26th May 1980, and 78 were martyred for the sake of the holy land of Kurdistan.

In 1984, the brave peshmerga undertook these activities:

1.   629 revolutionary activities against the forces and bases of the Iraqi regime.
2.   194 revolutionary activities in cities.

3. 671 political and mass activities
4. 46 joint revolutionary activities of the Jud front.

The enemy's casualties included the deaths of more than 1,492 people and the wounding of 1,830 others.

In these activities, 60 brave peshmerga were martyred and joined the immortal caravan.

From 23rd June 1983 to 1st January 1984, the peshmerga of the Kurdistan Revolutionary Army were able to conduct 233 activities against the Ba'athist regime's revolutionary bases and institutions, including:

- 15 successful activities of capturing Rabaya and seizing their belongings.
- 31 activities against hundreds of army convoys and regime fighters
- 63 activities in the city and forced camps
- 65 activities hitting enemy bases and barracks
- 11 joint activities with Jud forces
- 19 activities to eliminate the regime's hired men.

The peshmerga seized the following in these activities: Kalashnikovs 132; grenades 483; Rashash Bekasi 5; bullet cartridges case 392; bullets 28210; sniper rifles 8; ARPG 9; 60ml Howitzer 9; field telephones 7; anti-aircraft weapon 1; military vehicles 3; Various pistols 9.

In these activities, the enemy's damage included the killing of 680. 15 captives were released of various ranks, 65 captives taken, and two helicopters were shot down.

During this period, 190 peshmerga officials and friends sacrificed themselves for the success, and 41 civilians, including women and children, were martyred. 53 peshmerga and 24 civilians were also injured.

Between 1st March and 1st May 1984, the brave peshmerga were able to carry out 130 activities against Ba'athist bases and institutions, killing 281 people, injuring 140 and destroying various military vehicles. The peshmerga succeeded in capturing 22 Kalashnikovs, 2 RPG, 2 60mm cannons, and 3,650 bullets.

During this period, seven brave peshmerga sacrificed themselves for their success, ten civilians, mostly women and children, were martyred, and 22 peshmerga and 16 civilians were injured.

In March and April 1985, the brave peshmerga carried out the following activities:

140 revolutionary activities against enemy forces, convoys, bases and barricades.

16 revolutionary activities in cities. 122 political and mass activities Two joint activities with Jud's sides.

The enemy's casualties were: 152 killed, including eight officers, 174 wounded, 26 captives, 21 vehicles, one armoured vehicle, fourteen barricades and five bases captured.

The peshmerga succeeded in capturing 91 Kalashnikovs and two cars.

Six peshmerga and nine civilians were martyred in these activities.

On 14th October 1985, a detachment of our peshmerga visited the area between the villages of Ahmedawa and Golpda, but they fell into an enemy ambush and after a fierce defence, a number of peshmerga were wounded. Brave peshmerga Anwar Haji Osman was among the wounded and remained wounded for three days. Unfortunately, in the battle, Shakhawan Hussein, Muhammad Faraj, Arkan Muhammad Sharif, Nawzad Muhammad Sharif, and Kafia Mala Omar, the wife of martyr AbuBakr Bani Bnoki, were martyred.

In general, in 1985, 413 activities were carried out by the brave peshmerga, including 94 activities in the central cities and joint activities.

As a result of these activities, the enemy's casualties were 760 killed, 645 wounded and 98 captives. There was material damage to 97 different cars, 6 armoured vehicles, 69 barricades and headquarters. The peshmerga captured Kalashnikov 131; mixed FN MAG 17; small SAMOVAR 3; ARPG 8; military vehicles 12; field communication Bakelite telephones 6.

In these activities, 65 peshmerga were martyred and 79 were injured.

The total number of brave peshmerga activities in April 1986 was 38 activities, including 11 in the cities. The enemy's casualties included the deaths of 64 people and the wounding of 12 people, more than 23 military vehicles and 18 barricades were destroyed, and a large amount of equipment was seized by the peshmerga. Unfortunately, in these activities, two peshmerga were martyred and gave their lives to Kurdistan.

In 1987, a total of 656 military activities were carried out by brave peshmerga and local organizations, in which the enemy was harmed as follows:

1. Killing 3423 regime soldiers, including many officers with ranks of majors, colonels, lieutenant colonels, pilots and lieutenants were among the dead.

2. More than 3,281 people were wounded.

3. 1527 surrendered.

The peshmerga seized the following: Howitzer 35; ARPG 126; FN MAG 63; ARPK 28; BKC 16; rifles 4; Kalashnikovs 1943; Brno 312; sniper rifles 8; Kalashnikov FAS 4; Road mines 3296; military phones 87; field military phones 36; Gas and anti-chemical masks 55; typewriters 10; Anti-aircraft weapons 7.

In these activities, 180 peshmerga, 12 national defence force members and 187 civilians were martyred, 281 peshmerga and 228 civilians were injured. 80 members of our party were executed.

Capturing foreign engineers

Although a number of foreign engineers and experts had fallen into the hands of peshmerga forces several times, our policy had always been never to hold foreigners and treat them as hostages. The arrest of foreigners was not planned, but by accident, or by mistake, and after their arrest, they were tried to protect their lives and reach their families and to be formally handed over to their countries.

We had a bitter experience with this. In 1979, a Pakistani engineer and an Egyptian were ambushed and arrested, later released, but killed by Ba'athist institutions, and the regime was spreading propaganda to accuse the peshmerga of killing engineers in order to mislead public opinion.

The ambush was originally set up for regime fighters and was not intended by foreigners, but in 1982 three Austrian engineers were arrested in Erbil province. After their arrest, an Austrian named Hiner Bishler visited us and sent a letter to Kraiski to free the hostages.

He was misunderstood, and they thought they had to bargain with us, and the hostages would be released with after the payment of a ransom. I was sad with this understanding and told him: the engineers had fallen into a minority that was considered wrong by the regime's fighters.

It was a setup, unfortunately, and the engineers were involved but the incident was accidental. I said that I would make it better. The detainees were protected by us, but Turkey and Iran would not allow them to be handed over inside their territory. I asked if they could persuade Iran to transport them by helicopter from Hayat, as we were ready to hand them over there, or by convincing Turkey to allow an exchange on the Shamzinan border, even if they persuaded Iraq and some civilians came to the rescued areas. We were ready to hand them over.

We also told them that we are afraid that if they were liberated in Iraqi territory they might be killed by Iraq and to put the killing on the shoulders of the peshmerga, because we have a bitter experience with the regime in this regard and I gave him the examples of two Pakistani and Egyptian engineers.

After much effort, on 25th and 26th December 1982, Turkey agreed to take engineers on the border, but on the condition that Austria's representative and the peshmerga's representative were not present on Turkish soil. We responded by declaring we had released him unconditionally, but the Austrian government must decide that they agree to hand over the engineers to Turkey without their representatives on the border.

According to the information, on 26th December 1982, Turkey agreed to the presence of Austria's representative, so on 28th December 1982, our friends and engineers agreed to be at the

Turkish border, at eleven o'clock on 31st December 1982, in order to hand them over. The Shamzinan area handed over the engineers.

On 10th May 1984, we were informed that on 14th May, a delegation from Switzerland and Syria was scheduled to return two Swiss and Italian engineers to the Chale border; we warned the first branch to do whatever was necessary to co-ordinate this and ensure the necessary measures were taken.

On 15th May 1984, branch one informed us that for the second time, two Swiss and Italian engineers had crossed the border, but no one was ready to take them back and they were not allowed access to the borders.

Efforts continued to free the hostages. In this context, on 17th June 1984, we received a letter from Papa Kraisky and George Marshm. The letters were related to the release of French engineers, and the engineers' mother wrote a letter to my mother. It seemed that an expert had guided them and allowed them to leave, and they should take advantage of this opportunity.

Heiner Bishler, an Austrian journalist, brought the letters to Tehran, but returned to Austria because his mother had died. He sent me a cassette recording with his voice. In the cassette, he detailed his departure to Paris at the request of France and explained how he came. He also mentioned France's readiness to offer humanitarian aid and assistance and provide time studying for our students.

In the same cassette, he asked for a representative to go to France and talk about it.

He also claimed that a French minister had told him that the Iraqi government was talking about our detainees every time and had not shown a clear stance. Once they said that 57 people were only 21. Then they said ten were killed and afterwards they claimed none of them were alive.

The cassette is protected as a document.

Heiner Bishler arrived in Wrme on 5th July 1984, to take back foreign experts who were with our forces. We sent Uncle Hoshyar to Wrme, because the Iranian government did not allow him to come to us and sent a man named Younis with him in the Security Council to monitor him. Although he did not have the opportunity to speak freely, the representative of his government, Younis Nazari, visited me and told me that the council of ministers had been asked to also demand the release of some Iranian prisoners.

On 6th July 1984, Hoshyar visited Bishler, responding to us that a representative of the PDK and the International Red Cross should come to the Turkish border to take back the detained experts. Their speech seemed to have grown, and their conversation was tense and threatening, and when the warning was answered, he withdrew. Then he contacted Austria's foreign minister at the hotel, and after a while, he went to Turkey through a businessman. We asked for a press conference to be held before they were released, as our goal was to show our policy and attitude toward arresting experts.

He requested that necessary measures be taken as soon as possible.

From right, Jawhar Namiq Salm, Karim Shingali,
Mahmood ezedi and lieutenant Ali, 1978

Karaj, 1978

Mawana, 1979

Kawparr, 1979

June 1979, Kani Spi - Dashta Beale

Heasmawa, 1980, With branch four and a group of
the peshmerga in the Sulaymaniyah region

from right, Reis Abdullah, Masoud Barzani, Mustafa
Abdullah and a group of the peshmerga, 1980

Establishment of artilleries headquarters, 1980

October 1980, top of the Dolatu

Zewa, 1980

Shno, 1980

Kawparr, 1980

With a group of Branch four peshmerga, 1980

Haji Berokhi Headquarters, 1980

Khrena, 1985

Branch two, 1981

Berkm, August 1982

Berkm, 1982

Berkm, 1982

Lulan, 1985

Slivana, 1985

Lulan, 1985

Slivana, 1982

Kherena July 1982, from right, Nechirvan Barzani
and Masrour Barzani were on the visit.

Kelasheen, July 1982

With a group of branch One peshmergas 1983

Hamreen force headquarters, 1983

Lulan, 1985, Bringing the good news of the Victory of the brave Peshmarga

Zaweta, spring 1985 Branch one ambush success

Zaweta, spring 1985 Branch one ambush success

In May 1987, in the Nerwa area.

Immortal Barzani's Special guards. From right: Hasan Khal Hamza, Muhammad Issa, Dr Saeed Ahmad Barzani, Aziz Muhammad Dolhamri, Muhammad Amin Dulhamri and Mala Ibrahim Babaker Sitting: Mustafa Abdullah and Hajke Cheme.

CHAPTER EIGHT

Media and financial situation and development in the Gulan revolution

The Voice of Kurdistan Radio Station

AT THE BEGINNING of the Gulan revolution, our media was not enough to get out our message, due to a lack of necessary facilities and equipment available to carry out any media processes such as printing, publishing, etc. However, the role of cadres, loyal members, and internal arrangements cannot be disregarded, because they played a heroic role in spreading messages and delivering information about the revolution to the public. The lack of facilities was due to the collapse of the revolution as a result of the Algerian agreement when all the media facilities were lost and consequently, we endeavoured to obtain the right media tools and begin working again. This would be announced in all areas.

After a short time, we found printing and publishing tools, such as a hand printing house and a communication facility. In this way, with these basic and simple tools, the news of the revolution was published.

One of the things we considered was getting a broadcasting station. We asked Dr Hamid Akrayi and the engineer Ahmed Briffkani, who were in Austria, to find such a station. After a while, in 1977, we bought modest broadcasting facilities with the money being borrowed from Dr Ahmed Chalabi.

The station was delivered to Qamishlo in Syria. Engineer Mr Darawan Namiq, from Sulaymaniyah, who lived in the Netherlands, and was a patriot, and returned to become a peshmerga. They arrived in Qamishlo with essential broadcasting equipment, and at that time we had a PDK office in Qamishlo. Through the office, the bases and equipment were delivered to the village of Karab Rashk on the Syrian border against the northern Kurdistan Jazeera and later, with the help of loyalists and patriots of the Turkish Kurdistan Democratic Party, the station was delivered to Julamerg, where it was transferred by friends to the Basia area on the Turkish-Iraqi border. Haval Karim Shingal, a preacher, was one of those who brought the station. He was with us until Jazeera, when he joined our forces.

Shukri Nerwai received broadcasting facilities. Later, along with Izzat Amedi, who was unfortunately martyred, Mr Ahmed Hassan Aunam and Mr Darawan, with the help of the people of the villages of Arshe, Shulk, Harkash and Jarmande, transferred the station into southern Kurdistan. The situation was difficult at the time, and they were often forced to physically carry the equipment by hand. Tired and suffering a lot until they eventually arrived at Mr Jawhar and Mr Karim Shingal in Kurdistan. The history needs to be discussed, the key to the success and arrival of the station in Kurdistan, the great help and assistance of Mr

Majid Behg Chale, who was the chief of the Panyanshi tribe. It was decided that the station would be transferred to the border of Region II, because the area was mountainous, and it was better for broadcasting.

For this purpose, the village of Harke (located in Barzan area in Mergasor district) had been selected. Friends took a hard road and arrived at the destination after much pain in late 1977. In this way, Harke village became the first location of the Voice of Kurdistan station in the Gulan revolution, Mr Ahmad, a name for the people. Northern Kurdistan monitored the technical condition of the station.

After a while, the station began publishing its programmes. Friends Shamal Hawezi and Aso Karim, two skilled cadres, scientists and peshmerga, possessed the necessary technical expertise, and they supervised the station and succeeded in their work. Their talented friends, Fathi Akrayi, martyr Izzat Amedi and later Syamand Banna, became the announcers of the station. The operation of the station was a huge achievement for the revolution and had a significant impact on the dissemination and delivery of the voice of the revolution in and around the country. Mr Azad Barwari was in the station and Mr Sami Abdulrahman himself supervised his work. He announced that Mr Syamand Banash would be the director of the station.

The radio station remained in Harke until the ninth congress, then moved to the village of Zewa and was later transferred to the village of Shaqlawa, near Halaj, where Barzani's holy grave lay.

On 28th September 1980, the Kurdistan Voice station commemorated the evil plot of September 1971, which featured a long-running programme and report on the attempted assassination of Mr Barzani.

On 29th February 1981, we held a press interview with the Kurdistan Voice agency about the general situation in the region, the latest issues, and changes.

Then, in order to broadcast and publish the programmes and voices of the station on Kurdistan's land, and get closer to the brave peshmerga and the masses of our nation to avoid the pressures and excuses of Iran, we decided in 1982 to transfer the station to Kurdistan's land; first to the region Lolan and relocate after a while.

After a lot of efforts to develop our media, especially the station, we bought a another and arrived in Syria. On 28th June 1983, Osman Gazi came through the Syrian embassy in Tehran, before arriving in Tehran and later in eastern Kurdistan. The station was authorized by Aristotle and indeed, the handover of my station was very surprised, I was not expecting it.

On 25th April 1984, there was a strong presence at the station, which caused us concern because the programmes on that day were dedicated to covering student demonstrations. Despite the situation preventing the message from supporting them fully, the news indicated that student uprisings were taking place.

In mid-February 1984, Haval, Nissan Ushana Hitu, was martyred in Nahla district of Akre. This martyred media worker, in delivering the voice of our nation to the local and foreign public opinion through the radio station of Kurdistan, played a significant role.

Ahmad Dashti and Shukri Nerwai worked as anchor-men at the station for a while, and then from 1983 to 1984, the station's anchors were Barzan Mala Khalid, Masoud Salihi, Tahsin Dolameri, Sabah Baytullah, Masoud Nerwai, Abdullah Chalabi, Qadir Hassan Agha and Nissan Ushana Hitu who was a Christian. Ibrahim Mustafa and Hemin Hassan were long-time anchors, engineer Ahmed Breifkani was the director of the station, and Hashim Ahmed Akraish completed the technical team.

My visit to the media department in Khrena in 1983

The technical cadres were Ismat Rajab, Talib Saeed and Saifadin Hussein. The writers of station were Masoud Salihi, Dr Nasih Ghafur, Dr Rizgar, Hamid Soori, Falakadin Kakaei, Rebwar Yalda, while Fahmi Kakaei and Barzan Mala Khalid were for a while members of the staff of station writers.

On 10th June 1985, Paul Mobik and his family visited The Raids and took large photographs of the camp, holding a two-hour press conference with us.

On 8th November 1985, Shawkat returned and talked about the film that Goin had taken to Mustafawi and was sad about it. I sent a letter to Mustafawi asking him to meet, as I meant to resolve the misunderstanding.

On 1st April 1988, journalist David Hertez arrived in Rajan and two days later, on 3rd April, we interviewed him about the general situation in the area, and we answered all his questions. The meeting lasted more than four hours. On 2nd May 1988, I received an invitation to participate in a press conference in Tehran which was an ideal, fruitful moment.

On 19th July 1988, a German television delegation came to us. On that day, Hamrin forces attacked the enemy and as a result of the attack, 23 people were captured by Peshmarga, two of whom were officers.

On 18th August 1988, we published a message through the radio station regarding the situation in the region and the struggle of the Kurdish people.

On 4th September 1988, we held a press interview with Raza Khairi and a team of Iranian television and newspaper representatives. On the afternoon of 10th September 1988, journalists Murad Gonash, Jawad Kurkafir, and Ihsan visited us for a press conference and, in an interview, we talked about a lot of topics for a long time.

On 19th October 1988, we held a press conference with Goin Roberts and, following this interview, had an interview with an Anatolian news agency reporter.

On 28th October 1988, we held a press interview with Goin for the second time.

On 10th November 1988, I went to visit friends of the political bureau. I met Goin Roberts at the political office and held an English-language meeting.

On 11th November 1988, Goin returned and sent Jamshid and Syamand to us .

On 22nd November 1988, Paul Mobek and his family visited and held a press conference with us. They asked us a lot of questions. On the same day, London Television released footage of Goin's film, and on 23rd November 1988, Channel Four showed Goin's film for four minutes. The film seemed to have a huge impact. The film showed that the fact that the land samples they had taken with them had traces of mustard gas and this was confirmed by British laboratories. It produced and broadcast several clips of the Khwakurki war, and that the Canterbury Oscillator condemned Iraq's work on television. It's appropriate to remember that after our meeting, Mobek, went to Tehran and had problems.

At 7 pm on 24th November 1988, Goin, Hoshyar Zebari and seven British parliamentarians had a press conference in parliament. Goin met with foreign ministry officials and confirmed that Iraq had used chemical weapons. Although Iraqi Ambassador Mohammed Mashat denied that, Goin's insistence once again brought strong controversy over Iraq.

On 2nd January 1990, we held a special meeting with friends of the media department to ensure they were aware of the demands, situation, and living conditions of our media friends. The problems of their lives, livelihoods, and their assistance were discussed. Their assistance consisted of 750 dinars and needed to be increased, and a new press agency would be provided and more attention would be paid to work. This would be announced.

For the same purpose, two days later, 4th January, we gathered to better manage media affairs which were divided as follows: Haval Falakadin Kakayi, Rebwar Yalda, head of the department. The administration, Masoud Salihi, would also monitor the station's programmes and schedule. Hamid Al-Suri will go to the media, to transfer Zebari's gas from the media and Barzan Mahla Khalid would remain if he works. Salvation from the media existence.

In a meeting with the political bureau, after evaluating the affairs, it was decided on 8th January 1990 that he would prepare a project simultaneously on the way of work, authority, duties, quantity, quality and purpose. He would outline the overall spending necessary.

On 21st April 1990, journalist Majid Gorboz visited me in Turkey's Hurriyet newspaper and discussed a number of issues in a press conference. In that meeting, the general situation, the region and Kurdistan were discussed.

On 24th October 1990, Yasser Ahmed Farahat, journalist in Egypt and the director of the Cairo office of the Muslim newspaper arrived in Rajan, and it was night in Silvana when we held an interview about the situation in the region and the Kurdish issue and on a number of different topics and issues. We had an intense conversation.

Then he talked in the name of Egypt and Saudi Arabia and asked for opinions and viewpoints. I had my views, and I told him very frankly: "Our problem is a political problem and needs a political decision. We are ready for any step and we must be guaranteed that we will not be sold out or betrayed. We would be supported militarily and financially." I stressed that Turkey should be satisfied with the opportunity to move and not put pressure on us.

On 25th October 1990, we met with Yasser Farahat again, but this time it was recorded in a video. In part of the meeting, he repeated several times that Both Zakaria Azmi and Mustafa al-Faqi in Egypt were important personalities and influences, so asked them to be contacted.

On Friday, 26th October 1990, Ansat published a news release about Saddam Hussein's visit to Sulaymaniyah and his meeting with the Kurds, where he called for national reconciliation. At the meeting, Saddam asked for a five-year license and insisted that if Kurdistan had not been rebuilt during these five years, then the Kurds could seek refuge in their weapons.

Prints and publications in the Gulan revolution

Although the situation after the setback was sensitive and dangerous, we, along with our Party friends in the interim leadership, tried our best to print and publish our Party's publications according to the possibility. Especially the Khabat newspaper, our PDK vocal source.

Although there were no tools or equipment available for this work, after much effort, Khabat newspaper No. 527 was published in Arabic on 1st July 1976, under the name "The September Convoy Is Advancing". In this issue, on the occasion of the Gulan revolution, the text of the KDP statement was published on 25th May 1976, under the name of the Interim Leadership. The other editions were published in Kurdish, during which about 84 were printed and published by letter and typing agencies. The number 527 of Khabat newspaper is counted as the first edition of Khabat in the Gulan revolution led by Mr Jawhar Namiq Salim.

In May 1979, a special run of Khabat newspapers were published in Kurdish, dedicated to Barzani's immortal death. The newspaper was decorated with the headline: Immortality for Barzani, victory for the Kurdish people.

After holding the ninth congress in 1979, Mr Falakadin Kakayi was given the responsibility of the party's central media department, the editor-in-chief of the struggle and the Voice of Kurdistan station for a while.

In the Gulan revolution, apart from publishing Khabat newspaper as our PDK voice, a number of other newspapers, publications, and magazines were published in different stages by the central media department and PDK branches:

- Sada-e Khabat: An occasional newspaper published by the KDP's foreign committee, the first issue was published in November 1976.
- Zagros: Published in two stages by the PDK branch in the United States and Canada:

1. Zagros magazine: The first issue was published in July 1978, and after stopping for a while, two editions (8 and 9) were published together in Kurdish and Arabic in 1984.
2. Zagros newspaper: The first issue was published in February 1990 and published five editions in Arabic, and an appendix was published in Kurdish. Zagros newspaper is counted as a successful newspaper that Teacher Falakadin Kakayi had significant participation in.

- Kurdistan News: It was a political cultural publication, published by the PDK media department in Kurdish and Arabic, and which was widely spreading peshmerga news and activities, and played a significant role in presenting different aspects of the revolution, the first issue in Kurdish and Arabic in March 1980 opened and a special number was published in Persian.

In general, about 250 Kurdistan newspapers were published and counted as the complementary newspapers of Khabat. Because of the technique they sporadically dispersed Kurdistan's news and this counted as the full content of all the events that took place between 1979 and 1989.

- Sadeh Kurdistan newspaper: by democratic party office Kurdistan was published in Arabic from Beirut, Lebanon. He was rich in publishing a wide range of topics in the United States and Canada. The first issue was published at the beginning of 1983 and after Number 34 has also been suspended.
- Country magazine (Gavery Walat): The European branch of PDK was published in Arabic and the first issue was published in March 1982.
- Kurdistan Today Magazine, published by the seventh branch in English in the United States and Canada. The first issue was issued in January 1987.
- Matin: Published by a party branch, it is still ongoing and is considered a successful magazine.
- Azmar Magazine: A political cultural magazine published by The Four Branches, the first issue was published in mid-1984.
- Rizgari Publication: Published by branch eight, the first issue was published in the early 1980s.
- Safin: The magazine of the 2nd branch of the Kurdistan Democratic Party appeared without interruption in the September revolution.
- Baba Gurgur magazine: a political cultural magazine published by the third branch of the Kurdistan Democratic Party. The first issue was published in August 1984.

- Students and young people, it was a encompassing publication.
- The struggle was the publication of the Jud Council.
- The first issue of Student Voice magazine was published in August 1978.
- Martyrs magazine was a periodic publication by branch 3 and 4 of our Party; it was published in the Kurdish language.
- Peshmerga magazine was a seasonal magazine, by the sixth branch of the PDK and published in English.

Other publishing activities included:

- The law of the Revolutionary Army of Kurdistan.
- Party organizing and activity pamphlets with several pamphlets for cadre institutes
- The pamphlet of some advice for our Party cadres.
- The Khawan booklet of the weapon.
- The booklet of Handsa and army minority refugee proverbs.
- The words of their ancestors' values.
- Poetry Poster Diwan (Waiting).
- Internal Educational Bulletin (Organization Department), for the proper application of principles of organization, centralization of democracy, criticism and self-criticism, collective leadership, revolutionary democracy.

The pamphlet was another cultural publication published by the political bureau's media department.

The documents were published in Arabic in two parts of a pamphlet in Europe by branch six, which included important letters and documents.

Several pamphlets were published, such as pamphlets of some explanations about the International II Group, meaning Social Democrats, pamphlets, for perpetual foresight and more progress, the pamphlet, (From Messira), Historical Barzani, (1945-1958), Historical Walk to the Soviet Union, Booklet: Jarida (Hurriyet) Dialogue of the President of Our Party, Booklet: Freedom of the Press and Freedom Press, Booklet: The Turkic Invasion, 26/5/1983, Namilikhi Dehengy Kurdistan, Voice of Kurdistan, Issue (4) First, Haziran 1983, Booklet: Resumption of Iraqi-American Relations, Internal Bulletin, on the Results of the Meetings of the Iraqi Opposition Forces in Damascus to Form an Iraqi Front.

Kurdistan Democratic Party announcements were also made via the station, newspaper, and magazine, and the publications, during this period, played a significant role in delivering the news of the revolution abroad in peshmerga activities, internal arrangements, and relations, especially the visit of our Party delegations abroad, and the announcement of PDK played a major role in raising awareness and for enlightening friends, people, and peshmerga of Kurdistan.

Radio and the relationship between the revolutionary institutions

Radio has always played an important, effective, and major role in regulating relations between revolutionary agencies, and transporting and exchanging information and news. It played a role between the revolutionary and leadership institutions, even as a factor in the success of the war-fighting activities. According to the leadership, radio has always been of particular importance, and in the sensitive field of revolution is considered vital. There is never disdain for strengthening and improve communication work through radio broadcasts.

After the 1975 setback, the radio department was quickly reorganised in terms of institutions, cadres and structures and put in the service of the revolution. After the arrival of the political bureau headquarters for Rajan, we found some radio institutions for regulating relationships and establishing a network between revolutionary institutions.

Mustafa Amedi, Abdullah Darwesh and Shamsaddin Muhsin were radio primary cadres and played significant and historical roles in re-establishing the network via radio broadcasts.

On 23rd December 1979, we held a detailed meeting with a number of experts and technicians in the field of radio and communication. This was a great success and a pleasure.

At that time, the revolution had a complete network of communications, under Mustafa Amedi, Abdullah Darwesh, and Mullah. Suleiman Mawlud Nankali and Shamsaddin Muhsin, as early Betal cadres, participated after the setback.

Following our meeting, a full effort was made to re-operate and work with radio communications, and shortly thereafter, the efforts were made.

After the 1975 failure, the first radio connection in the revolution was held at 8 am on 13th January 1980, between branch two stations in Kawpar and the political office station.

According to my experience, the existence of a radio network in the revolution was an important factor to advance changes and successes. After these efforts, relations developed and improved. Daily relations between the institutions, headquarters, and leadership were getting more secure.

On 25th February 1980, the Apple Branch was contacted by radio, which was a great achievement and good news in the situation.

On 26th February 1980, as a result of the tireless work of the talented cadres in the field of communication, the first contact with branch one was made, which was a great success and we were able to be aware of all the activities and topics through radio broadcasts from Zakho to Khanaqin. This was an important achievement.

After the radio network was established, new and advanced cadres were attempted to open a training course in wireless and oscillation. For this purpose, four radio cadre training courses were opened, three of which were held in the headquarters of the political office and under the supervision of Suleiman Mawlud, Zakri Habib, Mustafa Amedi and Abdullah Darwesh.

75 students participated in all three courses in the political bureau headquarters and were armed with advanced and modern science and art in the field of radio and communication. After the end of the courses, they were divided into stations and played a significant role in connecting the establishments and institutions of the revolution during the Gulan revolution.

The fourth round of radio cadre development opened at the border of branch one. Six radio cadres participated, then dispersed into branch border stations.

Cadre Development Course

After the 1975 setback and the start of the Gulan revolution, the issue of cadres' development took on a more formal framework. In a key section of the Party's internal programme and procedure, section 9 of Article 8 and Article 26 of the PDK's internal procedure, the opening of the course of the Party's Cadre Institute was discussed. The first round of cadres, after the failure, was opened by decision No. 3907 of 28th December 1980, of the political bureau, the seventh round of cadres. For this purpose, it was written that all branches were to be opened to send students to participate in the course.

The conditions for accepting students were: 1. The age of the student should be between 20 and 30 years. 2. Their degree of literacy should not be less than primary six. 3. The period of receiving from the party would not be less than three years. 4. That they participated in the September revolution, or Gulan. 5. They would receive a test to take in the course.

After the nomination of students by the branches, the arrival of the names to the political bureau and the conduct of the exams, by decision No. 1119 of 5th March 1981 of the political bureau, the 40 candidate students were approved and they were one student body. The course enrolled on 1st April 1981, and began on 7th July 1981. When complete, 39 students participated and 35 successfully finished the course.

The course involved studying six days a week with four lessons a day, each of which lasted 50 minutes, with a ten-minute break between the lessons. The course was held in Rajan village, the death-prone area of eastern Kurdistan, and Mr Hamid Soori was the course's supervisor.

In the fifth decision of our Party's central committee in November 1985 and the implementation of that decision, the eighth round of cadres was set up in writing no. 10337 on 2nd November 1985.

This course began on 30th November 1985, and ended on 4th April 1986. 45 students participated in the course. The division of branches was as follows: Branch one had 19 students, branch two 6 students, branch three 6 students, branch four 5 students, while the district committee and the departments of the political bureau put forward 9 students.

On 10th April 1986, the political bureau announced the success of the course by decision No. 909, which took place in the village of Rajhanin in the death zone of eastern Kurdistan.

The financial situation of the revolution

After the collapse and the evil plan of 1975 in Algeria, at the time of the Gulan revolution, the revolution did not have a specific source or significant income to manage the affairs of the revolution financially, but the leadership of the Gulan Revolution benefited from it to manage the affairs of the revolution.

It received the following sources:

- At the beginning of the Gulan revolution, the revolution benefited from the amount of money left for it in the September revolution to manage its affairs.
- The unique and loyal cooperation of the Kurds of the north, east and west.
- Local loyalist assistance
- After the reorganisation and development of the revolution, especially in terms of military, peshmerga, attacks, and major military activities, a region of Kurdistan's territory was liberated, thus relying to a great extent on the interior and linked to managing revolutionary affairs financially.
- After the fall of the Shah's regime and the victory of the Iranian people's revolution, the Islamic Republic of Iran helped the refugees living in Zewa and the families of the

struggling peshmerga who were in Kurdistan and provided them with financial assistance.

It had greatly relieved the situation of the revolution.

- Although Syria and Libya helped us with weapons, they did not help the PDK financially.

CHAPTER NINE

The role of Mr Idris Barzani in the Gulan revolution

In 1987, while we were busy with our activities, and meetings in the midst of the revolution, our patient crowds, the liberated areas, and the brave peshmerga, there was a sudden unpleasant event. On the evening of 29th January 1987, news sources reported the Urmia bombing. As our children were students in Urmia, we asked the political bureau to ensure their safety and asked them to leave Wrme. Mr Idris is scheduled to return to Tehran and Silvana on 30th January 1987. Mr Idris on 31st January 1987 in Karaj, arrived safely in Rajan and Silvana and the evening of the same day, Kak Idris passed away.

On the morning of the 1st February 1987, I was praying, and I greeted my prayer. Hamad Faqo, the guard, came in and gave me a package.

This was a communication from the political bureau. I read the letter, and I didn't believe it. Was I dreaming? The world was dark in my eyes, I saw nothing, and my soul felt fragile and poor. I didn't know where to go, this was a huge and sad shock. It was a moment that would never be erased from my memory.

Mr Idris's death was sad. It was a great loss, not only for us, but for the Kurdish liberation movement in general, and the political forces and parties in Kurdistan and the regions in particular. On 1st February 1987 I wrote this in my daily note:

In the name of God, the Most Gracious, the Most Merciful.

We belong to God and to him we shall return. Nothing will happen to us except what God has written for us.

Unfortunately, dear brother, I wish I was in your place. I am pleased with the fate of Allah, but did we not promise to leave each other? I'm sure you didn't have it in your mind, otherwise, you would not have left me. Again, our wounds have been unhealed, (did we not promise?) once again in sorrow and our pain is going to pass.

Brother, your father seems to be thinking about you, and you certainly have a job, but we needed you more. The caregivers of the poor and the needy, the education, and the change of your father. By God, you were an example of morality, loyalty, purity, and truth. The people have no chance, otherwise, you would not have left them. Do you know that every loyal Kurd in Iran, Turkey, and Iraq, and Syria, and wherever they are, will mourn for you, they send you condolences?

On this sad occasion, the political bureau also issued a message discussing Mr Idris's role and influence in our nation's liberation movement, particularly in establishing unity and harmony within our people's ranks.

Mr Idris was a key caregiver of the refugee brothers who had fled to Iran and was closely helping them, and he was constantly trying to solve their problems.

After the 1975 setback, despite a sensitive and difficult situation and the emergence of the ideas, names, and rumours that spread, Mr Idris Barzani fully believed in protecting a unified identity within the liberation movement. There were Kurds, and they attached great importance to multi-party life. These two factors were the main reasons for providing opportunities for public reconciliation in 1986, which led to the title of general reconciliation engineer, which he was awarded in recognition of his peacekeeping.

Historian Jarjis Fethullah says: "After I went into the revolution and got to know him, I understood that Idris Barzani was much older than his age in terms of thought, and understanding." At this stage, writing letters, and sending reminders to parties, diplomatic groups and international organizations, and in particular, he was recognized by the International Red Cross.

Idris Barzani secretly supervised the return of political and military cadres to Syria to prepare for their return to Iraqi Kurdistan, particularly a large number of cadres and peshmerga who were sent to Kurdistan.

Despite all the hardships, Mr Idris considered the need to work to protect Kurdish unity and harmony important, so he met with everyone and parties, even those who were different to him.

Political work and activities in Iran were not easy, as security agencies, particularly SAVAK, had put intense surveillance on Mr Idris. Despite the fact that political and party activities were secret, he again devoted most of his time to reading and investigating the political activities of the party and the cause for our nation.[2]

Many peshmerga detachments and political cadres returning to Kurdistan at the beginning of the Gulan revolution received orders and advice on their traffic and activities from Idris Barzani.

Mr Idris made great efforts and was the main reason for stopping the bloody war between the Patriotic Union of Kurdistan and the Kurdistan Socialist Party. The war that began in the summer of 1982 with the attack of Patriotic Union of Kurdistan forces on socialist forces among the Shela people of Warte in the Rwandeze, and a lot of blood, from both sides, was lost. But because Mr Idris was very eager for unity and harmony to exist among the Kurdish people, he always tried to protect and strengthen the relationship between the Kurdish parties and political parties and called for strengthening the struggle of the Kurdish nation. He did this for the sake of the revolution and the Kurdish people.

Mr Idris was known for his peace and tranquillity. When the Iraqi regime acted to remove 8,000 Barzani in a catastrophic act in 1983, he was patient and prevented grief from being overwhelming and he had a heart for them all.

In 1986, Idris Barzani visited Tehran to meet with Iranian parliament speaker Akbar Hashemi Rafsanjani. In Tehran, he met With Jalal Talabani, and after Jalal Talabani's return from Tehran, at the request of Mr Idris at the end of November 1986, a delegation of our Party visited the PUK leadership headquarters

---

[2] See document number 5.

in Yaksamarri, including Fazil Mirani, Franso Hariri, Haji Haji Braim and Abdullah.

Mr Idris played a key role in the success of the Iraqi People's Cooperation Conference held in Tehran at the end of December 1986 for the Iraqi opposition. In the congress, Mr Idris insisted on destroying the Ba'athist regime and the unification of the Iraqi opposition.

The relationship between Immortal Idris and Barzani was a special one. It is rare for any son or father to be like this. It was a spiritual connection. He revered his father and was blessed, even though he had his own opinion, but without appeal he fulfilled all his father's commands. Mr Barzani took his opinions very importantly and cared about him and considered the request, and how he behaved.

Mr Idris had full experience in the content, behaviour, and policies around him, from state politics to opposition parties. He had strong relations with the Kurdish and Iraqi parties. He could successfully contact them and be ready to take important steps step by step. This experience made him able to work at the level of Iraqi, Arabic, Iranian, and European diplomacy at that time, and to carry out significant activities to defend Kurdish rights.

At our ninth Party congress and after Barzani's farewell, Mr Idris became a strong supporter of all sides. He was trying to accept all the problems within a proper limit that was in the interests of the Party congress' success.

At the Iraqi People's Cooperation Conference in Tehran, Mr Idris openly expressed the Party's stance on the political system and governing style in Iraq and stated that the Kurdistan Democratic Party of Iraq supports a free and public referendum in Iraq in order to govern the country's future. Regarding the results and outcomes of the possibility of a free and general election in Iraq, he defended the voice of the Iraqi people and stated: "We accept the views and demands of the people, even if they are contrary to our point of view."

Mr Idris worked with a spirit of progress, invention, and high morality to restart the armed revolution after the 1975 failure. Mr Idrissi's sense of responsibility and, as a person responsible for the events, he worked.

Mr Idris had a strong, serene, thoughtful personality and an outright awareness. He insisted on solving people's problems and knew that he had great responsibility for his father's morals and behaviour in his life because he would neither give up nor get tired. That's why wherever he was, the Kurds would gather around him. He would listen to their complaints and hopes.

In terms of relations, Mr Idris not only had a strong relationship with his people in the South, but also his political relations.

He linked the Kurdish people to Iran, Turkey, and Syria, and took advantage of those relations to pave the way for national and political work before the resumption of 26th May. He had a strong relationship with all the nations, religions, and sects within the Kurdish community. He was a strong supporter of Iraqi opposition groups and the Brotherhood of Kurds and Arabs.

Mr Idris always reminded the young people who went out and said," I don't care where the Kurds live, it's important to be Kurds, but those peshmerga in the mountains of Kurdistan, they have made themselves shields, just as you are young."

He believed in success and confirmed that even though the leftist days had afflicted us with this great disaster, the Great Lord would never accept injustice. We were oppressed and betrayed, but God would keep us going. He was sure that Kurdistan would be saved, and we must take lessons and lead this time's revolution to success. Of course, we must avenge ourselves against our enemies. This great disaster should not be ever forgotten, and a lesson must be taken from it.

Mr Idris, who made great efforts to improve relations with Iranian institutions after the victory of the revolution, knew one of the established figures of the Revolutionary Leadership Council: Ayatollah Talaqani. "I am afraid of the government, said Abu Musab. "I am afraid of the people who are not going to be able to do anything about it." Even at a meeting, one of the attendees said:

"Mr Barzani appears to be carrying out a lot of propaganda against you and being accused of belonging to some countries." Mr Idris said it was true. At first, Talaqani responded and defended Barzani and his revolution, but Mr Idris said:

"Thank you, Mr Talaqani, for your stance, but let me answer. We do not belong to any party or nation. We have been denied the ability to restore that right, and any party that helps us will receive it, but you, who are an Islamic state and whose constitution is the Qur'an, and my father was a great religious scholar. I will prove to you that we were not men. Now there are about 180,000 refugees in Iran who can hand them all over, kill us, tear us apart, but we will not be sure of anyone's man. You are Muslims, and we are a Muslim nation. Come and help us. Give it to me."

Of course, after Mr Idris's speech, everything changed.

Mr Idris was a great man, and his greatness stemmed from his understanding and maturity, which led to his gentleness. He was a forgiving and earthly person. He forgave and did not think about retribution. He often considered ordinary and poor people to be a member of his family, whatever their shortcomings, which led Mr Idris to take his place in the hearts of people and all classes who considered him as a protector and saviour. Despite all the dangers, Mr Idris often protected the wounded and peshmerga in his own home and saw treating them as his duty.

July 1982, Kelasheen

Kunalajan valley, 1983

August 1985, Lulan

July 1987, when we returned from the branch one
after the death of Mr Idris Barzani

CHAPTER TEN

Mass organisations in the Gulan revolution

Establishing and reorganising mass organisations

O NE OF THE decisions of the ninth congress was the establishment and maintenance of organisational and professional work. After the ninth congress, a determined effort was made to reorganise, and hold conferences based on circumstances and time. With that purpose in mind, groups for students, youth, and women, were organised.

After the 1975 failure, the resurgence of the arrangements did not last long, and for the first time in Zakho, Haval Rebar Mullah Hussein Avdal began liquidating the secret arrangements of the Student's Union on 20th June 1975, with the help of friends Salim Ahmed Jasim, Nayef Abdul-Rahman Eminki and Tariq Jamil Jasim. On 16th December 1975, Haval Rebar became the head of the Kurdistan Student's Union in Zakho. Unfortunately, the night of 20th to 21st April 1976, Baghdad regime spies seized their homes and found publications in them.

As a result, he and his nephews and relatives were arrested and transferred to the regime headquarters in Zakho, where they endured three days of resistance in the most brutal forms of torture. On 23rd April 1976, he was martyred and joined the immortal convoy.

The first secret organisation of the Student's Union was founded in Erbil province in 1976 under the name of Shirin, and it played an influential role in the resurgence of student arrangements.

In Newroz in 1978, both Brotherhood and Duhok Industrial High Schools held a large and significant demonstration in the centre of Duhok. Revolutionary and national slogans were raised: peace, freedom, long live the nation's revolution, martyrs, new and blue martyrs and ... etc. The regime responded by deploying a large number of armed forces who, by using force, making arrests, and organising pursuits, ended the demonstration.

As the refugees arrived in Iran, Abdul-Rahman Hamid, Ibrahim Abdul-Karim, Jasim Ahmed and Dilshad Barzani began organising their students, first on behalf of the Iranian organisation and later for the Iranian committee. The Iranian committee later became two branches: Iran branch and Duhok branch (Kurdistan Students' Union).

After the establishment of the Kurdistan Democratic Youth Union, and the development of the arrangements, an interim committee was established in 1980 to lead the Youth Union in Iran and some friends for the committee were selected.

On 18th February 1980, on the anniversary of the founding of the Union of Students and Youth, the Kurdistan Democratic Party,

KDP, was holding a party in Zewa, and I went there to participate in the commemoration. Unfortunately, near Razga we returned because of the accumulated snow and the ice on the roads. Many cars were stuck. It made me feel bad by being deprived of this memory. We are obliged give the news to the committee we had sent to the Zewa area and apologized to them.

The Kurdistan Democratic Youth Union held its first conference in 1981. In that conference, a legitimate leadership was elected and because of this the Democratic Youth Union of Kurdistan continued again and reopened both their work and activities.

The Kurdistan Students' Union in Iran held its first conference in 1981 and was elected as the head of the refugee branch and given legitimacy. They approved a new programme that suited the situation at that time. The Awara branch issued two magazines called "Student Voice" (in Persian).

The situation for the Women's Union was different and more difficult. After the 1975 failure, particularly between 1975 and 1983, and due to the unstable and sensitive situation, women rarely carried out significant activities.

In 1983, a review and reorganization of women's organizational work was carried out in exile. For this purpose, the High Committee of the Kurdistan Women's Union consisted of friends: Minister Pir Dawd, secretary; Razia Hassan Khatab, a member of the Supreme Council; Pir Dawd, a member of the Supreme Council High Group.

The Student Union played a significant role inside the country, especially in managing and supervising the uprisings as:

- On 10th May 1982, they attacked the Ba'athist student head-quarters in Qaladze.

- On 10th May 1982, they held a large demonstration in Masif Salahaddin, publishing pictures and posters of the Party.
- On 4th June 1982, when the regime forcibly sent students to battlefields on the Ankawa road, students staged a large demonstration.
- On the night of 19th to 20th July 1982, Zakho Student Union published several pamphlets.

In 1982, the second refugee branch conference in Karaj was held and a new leadership was elected, and its work and activities went to a more advanced stage.

According to local reports, on 24th April 1984, students from Salahaddin University and Duhok students launched a multi-party demonstration against the regime, as a week earlier, the regime took forms into school centres to register students to participate in the war.

Duhok students who had travelled to the Zanta people of Akre district for tourism began protesting against the regime and supported the Party.

On the occasion of their establishment, I congratulated the Kurdistan Students' Union:

To the Kurdistan Students Union – Iraq

Revolutionary greeting,
Your letter number 27 arrived on 3rd February 1984.

It is true that we do not have time to celebrate this holy memory, so I congratulate you on your private magazine on behalf of myself and all members of the political bureau.

*Students have always been the pioneers of our
Kurdish people's revolutions and have sacrificed
a lot for the rights of our Kurdish people.*

Regards,
Masoud Barzani
The president of Kurdistan Democratic Party

I also congratulated the Kurdistan Democratic Youth Union:

*For the Kurdistan Democratic Youth Union,
the Iranian branch is a fighter*

Revolutionary greeting

*Your letter no. 124 arrived on 5ᵗʰ February 1984, and
this is the answer: On the occasion of the 31st anniversary of the founding of the Kurdistan Democratic
Youth Union of Iraq on 18ᵗʰ February 1953, an introduction on behalf of myself and all members of the
political bureau congratulate you all for the memory.*

*Your struggling Union has always been the flame of the
brave Kurdish people's revolutions and the strong support of our Party and the Kurdish people's revolutions.*

So forward...
Masoud Barzani
The president of Kurdistan Democratic Party

On 1ˢᵗ July 1983, the third conference of the Student Union's Refugee Branch was held under the slogan "Science and Struggle for Democracy for Iraq and Autonomy for Kurdistan", "Death, Disgrace and Extinct for Imperialism, Zionism and Old-Fashionedness". 46 representatives attended the conference and it lasted three days.

In the early 1980s, friends Abdulrahman Hamid and Abdulrahman Haji played an influential role in developing the arrangements of the Kurdistan Democratic Youth Union, refugee branch. Because of this, the refugee branch made great progress. In 1983, the officials of the Awara branch, friends Fryad Barzani, Ahmed Zakri and Hoshyar Zakhouli played an important role in the development of youth organisations, activities and arrangements in all Iranian cities (Kurds and refugees). Also in 1983, the branches of the Youth Union (Sulaymaniyah, Kirkuk and Erbil) developed a wide range of activities.

Both the Duhok and Nineveh branches of the Students' and Youth Union played a very good role, and friends Abdulaziz Taib, Nechirvan Ahmed and Martyr Simko Amedi played an important role in leading the two branches.

In order to further develop the work and activities of students and young people within branch one, the office of mass organizations was established to supervise both branches of Duhok-Nineveh students, youth and Nechirvan. Ahmed was appointed in charge of the office.

The Patriotic Union of Ba'athist students was expelling their smart students from Salahaddin University. On 7ᵗʰ April 1984, the Kurdistan Students' Union confronted them and there were several martyrs, such as Sarkawt, Nizar, Kamal, Najia, Najat, Falah, and Bestun.

On 10th April 1984, the Salahaddin University directorate asked students to join the Popular Mobilisation Forces, and the students refused. On 13th April the university presidency decided to expel 200 students. The university's decision sparked protests by teachers and a large number of students, who participated in the strike, confronting Ba'athist chauvinist policies. After the beginning of the uprising and demonstrations of the students of Salahaddin University in Erbil and Duhok schools, we announced a statement that reads:

*Masoud Barzani and the political bureau for
the unrelenting masses of Kurdistan*

For several days, revolutionary students at Salahaddin University in Erbil and schools in Duhok have rebelled against the bloodthirsty Aflaqi regime. As immortal Barzani said, students are the spearhead of the movement. Indeed, the great Barzani knew the importance and role of students very well and today his assumptions about them has come true.

While we warmly congratulate these brave students, we also call on all Kurdish people – the people of the cities and villages – to support these struggling students and not to let them be alone in this barricade of honour, all of you. Give and protect them.

We also call on all the heroic peshmerga and members of our Party, who with all their might, together with the other brave forces of Jude, tried to reach and help the uprising students, as soon as possible in the institutions of enemies of all Iraqi peoples and humanity.

We are with you with our hearts and souls, and all the liberals in the world are with you. Indeed, your tireless struggle is an honour for all those who strive, and success is for our people.

25th April 1984

At the invitation of the Iraqi Communist Party, on 29th May 1984, Mr Izzadin Bahrawari and the delegation of the Kurdistan Democratic Youth and Students' Union visited Lolan to participate in the organisation's multi-party meeting.

In order to further promote the work and activities of mass organisations, the Unity committee was established in 1984, consisting of Miqdad Ali, Rebwar Yalda and Ibrahim Mustafa. The committee belonged to the organising department in the political office and supervised the affairs and activities of students, youth and women.

In mid-March 1985, a delegation of secretariats consisting of friends Miqdad Ali, Rebwar Yalda and Ibrahim Mustafa visited the borders of branches three and four. The visit had a significant impact on reorganising its arrangements, students, and youth union, re-establishing their own organisations and areas.

A large part of the Students and Youth Union joined the peshmerga and gave many martyrs to defend their land and people. Examples of these martyrs are: Soran Muhammad Faraj, Muhammad Abdullah, Peshraw Abdulsalam and Salam Sheikh Kamil, Aram Sheikh Mustafa and Soran Ismail, head of the student and youth area, and Nawzad Hama-Najib, head of the student and youth branch. They gave their lives to Kurdistan.

On 21st April 1985, we held a multi-party meeting with a large number of members from the Youth Union's Zewa organisation.

I talked to them about the general situation in the region, Kurdistan and the revolution. At the same time, the role and influence of mass organisations in general and young people in particular in the revolution was appreciated. They were also encouraged to organise and strengthen their local areas.

On November 28, 1986, I welcomed a large number of students and youths. The meeting highlighted the general situation in the region and Kurdistan in particular. In the meeting, students and young people had encountered problems which they presented.

1st to 3rd June 1986, at the Communist Party headquarters in Lolan, the High Committee for Cooperation between Students and Youth of Kurdistan and Iraq was established in these organizations:

- Kurdistan Students' Union.
- Kurdistan Democratic Youth Union.
- Kurdistan-Iraq Socialist Youth Union.
- Students' Union in Kurdistan.
- The Iraqi Democratic Youth Union.
- The Democratic Youth Union in Iraqi Kurdistan.
- The General Student Union in Iraqi Kurdistan.

The representatives of the Kurdistan Students' Union were: Abdulsalam Muhammad, Miqdad Ibrahim Shaswari, and the representatives of the Kurdistan Democratic Youth Union were:

Fryad Barzani, Ahmed Zakri and Hoshyar. Zakhoyi and the two delegations were supervised by Mr Izzadin Barwari.

With the slogan "Towards uniting to overthrow the regime and end the war, so that we can study peace and democracy", the Kurdistan Students' Union and the Kurdistan Democratic Youth Union held a joint conference between 28th and 30th August 1986 in the village of Khnera in the Sidakan district in the liberated areas of Iraqi Kurdistan. 77 representatives attended it.

After the seventh congress of the Kurdistan Students' Union, the August conference was the first to be held in a multifaceted manner. The most important decision was to unite the two unions in a new and co-owned organisation programme with rules governed under a joint leadership.

At the August 1986 Conference on Students and Youth, the 15 members of the Executive Committee were elected: Rebwar Yalda, Kurdistan Pir Dawd, Haji Abdulrahman and Ibrahim. M Mustafa, Abdullah Khalo, Simko Amedi, Fryad Shafi'barzani, Tayar Saleem, Ahmed Mala Qasim, Adil Ali, Dzhar Faiq, Rafat Saeed, Nawzad Muhammad Najib, Ehsan Abdullah Amedi and Rizgar Kamki.

After the return of the Executive Committee of the Union of Students and Youth on 2nd September 1986, at the political office headquarters in the presence of Mr Idris Barzani and Fazil Mirani, the secretary and members of the secretariat were elected, including Rebwar Yalda, Secretary and Haji Abdulrahman, Ibrahim Mustafa, Fryad Shafi'a Barzani and Abdullah Khalo, members of the secretariat.

At the Joint Conference between the PUK and the Union of Students and Kurdistan Democratic Union, a number of important decisions were made:

Pave the way for the reunification of both organisations. issuing a central magazine in the secretariat's office called Progress. Caring about the angle of the mass and professional organization in the voice radio Kurdistan.

Drafting and preparing a regular programme to pave the way for students and youth associated with the revolution.

Encouraging and caring about various seminars, and courses in the liberated areas of Kurdistan, particularly among the peshmerga ranks.

On a National Level:

- Supporting the Gulan revolution and helping the struggle of the parties of the Jud Council and all the democratic and national forces of Iraq to overthrow the regime.
- Expanding joint struggles with other Kurdistan organisations, such as women, teachers, and all other mass organisations in Kurdistan and Iraq.
- Advocating for Iraqi identities for the Faili, Goyan, Umrian and Assyrian Kurds.
- Trying to remove the traces of Arabization, Ba'athist policies, and forced relocation for the reconstruction of Kurdistan.
- The conference also made several other decisions at the student level and around the world.
- On the occasion of holding a student and youth conference.

I sent a letter direct the to conference participants to the following text:

To friends of the student conference and youth,
The Democratic Kurdistan of Iraq is constantly striving.

Greetings of struggle and revolution

We were willing to attend your conference, but by staying
away from the conference area, considering the work of the
Party and the revolution at this time, we were unable to par-
ticipate in the conference. But with this letter, we will shake
the hand of your students and youth from afar, and we hope
that your conference will be successful and will be at the level
of responsibility for this historical stage that our nation is in.

It's going to pass. Every step in your conference, that we will
take freely should be in the interest of your people and country,
and steps should be taken towards an informed and free soci-
ety, to overthrow the fascist regime of Baghdad and to establish
a voluntary government of the Iraqi nation that governs.

To ensure real Zati for the people of Kurdistan,
for sovereignty for Barzani and all the mar-
tyrs of Kurdistan, and success for our nation.

Masoud Barzani's signature
25/8/1986

On the anniversary of their founding, we sent this communication to the Unions.

To the committee of unions belonging to the organizing department of PDK

On the occasion of the day of the founding of the struggling Kurdistan Union, I warmly congratulate your struggling committee and through you, present it to the struggling Kurdistan Union and the base.

I hope that God will help us all in the service of our poor and oppressed people.

On this holy occasion, I ask you to strengthen the unity of your ranks and intensify your struggle. Alongside the high committee of cooperation between democratic organizations of students and youth in Kurdistan and Iraq, in light of the certificate of the National Democratic Front of Iraq (Jud)

The fighters will develop a struggle to overthrow Baghdad's fascist regime and achieve democracy for Iraq and real autonomy for Kurdistan.

Your brother Masoud Barzani
President of Kurdistan Democratic Party 1986

In order to support the deprived children of the liberated areas, supervise schools, and advance the education process in areas under peshmerga control, a committee to do so was decided at a meeting of the Central Committee.

This consisted of: Ehsan Abdullah Amedi, head of the Students' Union/Officials; Zuber Abdulrahman, member; Tofiq Hussein, member; Muhammad Tahir Tofiq, member; Jalal Hussein, member; Ibrahim Mustafa, member.

The committee's tasks were:

- To open schools and provide needs.
- To organise meetings of the council of parents and teachers in villages
- Solve of school problems sending them to the district committee.
- Raising monthly reports on school conditions, education and problems.

At the beginning of 1987, friends of the Secretariat Office of the Union of Students and Youth established headquarters in Balisan village and were organising and establishing the district committee and their organisations. For this purpose, friends Rebwar Yalda, secretary of students, Abdullah Khalo, Ibrahim (known as Kurdo) and Haji Abdulrahman, supervised the reorganisation, and after that step, the Erbil branch of the Union of Students and Youth opened in Balisan. Haval Adal Botani, head of the branch and Azad Mawarani, media officer, and friends Rasul Jalal and Taib, a member of the area and Haval Kamal Aqubani, were in charge of the city area. Friends of these two organisations had significant activities, even participating in military activities. They were peshmerga.

On 8th January 1988, in Silvana, I welcomed a large group of Barzani students from the city of Naghada. Striving for their nation and the importance of their enthusiasm was the main topic of the meeting. At the same time, the importance of organising work was discussed in the student class.

On 5th February 1988, I met with the Naqada Students' Association, which included a large number of students from the city. The meeting discussed the Party's agenda and policy, the general situation in the region and Kurdistan, and the latest developments and changes. The purpose of these meetings was to pay more attention to the students and young people, plus their education and development as the next generation of our nation. In the meetings, students were encouraged to strive for their people.

Importantly, organising work within the school class was another aspect of the meetings.

Prints and publications of mass organisations

The Kurdistan Students' Union and the Kurdistan Democratic Youth Union published a large number of prints, pamphlets, magazines and cultural topics, the most important of which were:

Student voices published by the Kurdistan Students' Union's refugee branch and the Youth Hope magazine by the Kurdistan Democratic Youth Union's refugee branch. Duhok branch - Nineveh of Kurdistan Democratic Youth Union (Rozha Youth) and Gazia student and youth magazine and Zakho committee published a student and youth magazine.

Several publications and magazines were published by both student and youth organizations such as:

- Exhibition (Mountain - 1987): After the Joint Conference on Students and Youth in 1986, it was published as the organ of both organizations, the first number was issued in January 1987, until the 2007 uprising.

- Fidelity, loyalty, traditions and festivals, March 1989.
- Rebwar's Novel was translated into Kurdish from Persian.
- Programme project and operating bases.
- The documents of the Joint Conference of Students and Youth - August 1986.
- Several poems
- Youth Day (Mountain) 1983.
- Gazia Student and Youth, (Mountain) 1983.
- 42 issues by the professions of branch one were printed and published.
- The voice of students and youth magazine Iran-Karaj magazine, 1985, was jointly published by the Youth Union Refugee Branch and the Iranian Branch of the Student Union.
- Hiwa Magazine of Students and Youth - Karaj - Iran 1986. After the August 1986 conference, it was issued by the Refugee Branch of the Union of Students and Youth, and number 1 was published in the fall of 2686 in Kurdish with 32 pages.
- Karaj-Iran Appendix (Hope of Students and Youth), 1987.
- Bayan magazine, Mountain 1987, was a political and cultural magazine, the organ of the Kirkuk branch of the Union of Students and Democratic Youth of Kurdistan of Iraq. The first issue was published in the spring of 1987, only one was published.
- The 1988 Mountain, the organ of the Erbil branch of the Kurdistan Democratic Youth and Students' Union, published

9 issues, the last number 8 and 9 in January 1990 and on 14 pages.

- Shamale magazine Wrme/ Erbil 1989, in the secretariat office

The Union Student was published in Kurdish and Persian by students Gohdar Ismail and Rizgar Saeed in the eastern Kurdish city of Urmia.

- The Progress newspaper, which was the language of the organisation. The development of culture was another publication published by students and young people.
- In 1983, Gazia was published by the Zakho district committee of the Kurdistan Democratic Youth Union and published 8 in the mountains.
- Student Voice magazine (Karaj/ Iran) was published in 1979, only 29 editions were published.
- In 1982, a local publication was published by the Iranian branch of the Kurdistan Students' Union, publishing 19 editions.

Kurdistan Islamic Scholars Union

After a short period of time following Algeria's ominous agreement in 1975, the public and professional organisations began organising and doing professional and public work. The Kurdistan Islamic Scholars' Union, like all professional and popular organisations, soon began organizing and religious teachers gathered around the Union of Scholars.

The teachers were: Mullah Muhammad Mzuri, Mala Ali Mullah Omar Doski, known as Qazi Shorsh, Mullah Muhammad Gori, Mullah Abdulrahman Mir Sardari, Mullah Abdulkarim Khoshnaw,

Mullah Jubrail Biri, the head role. They had a vision of organising the Union of Scientists.

It is worth mentioning that teachers' organisations contacted many religious teachers in different cities and regions of Iran.

Meanwhile, Kak Idris Barzani played a significant role in organising the Union of Islamic Religious Scholars in exile.

Even if it hadn't been for the role of Mr Idris, the arrangement and regrouping of teachers would have been very high in the short period of time.

After contacting the teachers and providing a suitable environment in 1980 in Zewa camp, the preparatory committee of teachers was formed, consisting of:

The late Mullah Muhammad Gori; the late Mullah Ali Doski; the late Mullah Muhammad Mzuri.

After the establishment and announcement of the preparatory committee for religious teachers in all different cities and towns of Iran, they contacted the Teachers' Union, as well as a large number of religious teachers inside. They contacted the committee from Kurdistan.

Between 1981 and 1988, a number of religious teachers contacted the committee and joined the Ranks of the Islamic Religious Scholars Union: Mullah Wali Ahmed, Mullah Sarhan Hussein, Mala Fazil Yassin Dri, Mala Rasul Sheikh Rasul, Mala Saeed Gardi, Malatha Sham Zini, Mullah Ahmad Mala Yusuf, Mullah Muhyadin Mohajer, Mullah Mamdouh Mzuri, Mullah Shafiq Khalil Edlibi, Mullah Islam Ibrahim Bazid, Mullah Mahmood Dershawi, Mullah Malam Muhammad Salih, Mala Ali Shukari, Mala Asmat Guharzi, Mullah Fatah Nerwai, Mullah Muhammad Palo, Mullah Muhammad Tahir, Mullah Zaki, Mullah Sheikh Jami Zebari, Mullah Sheikh Yassin

Zebari, Mullah Abdulwahid Rashawai, Mullah Saeed Nerwai, Mullah Tahir Chalki, Mullah Ali Tatarkhan, Mullah Abdullah Guli, Mullah Majid, Mullah AbdulGhafuri Kuri, Mullah Issa Rekani, Mullah Muskin Edlibi, Mullah Asmat Rekani, Mullah Muhammad Amin Warty and Mullah Ahmed Awa.

After years of work and struggle, in order to elect a new group in 1989, the Union of Scientists completed its conference at the Headquarters of the Union of Scientists in the Zewa camp with the presence of more than 50 religious teachers.

At the conference, they discussed the work, duties, and programmes of the Union of Scientists. At the end of the conference, due to the widening of the active boundaries and the increase in the duties of the Union of Scientists, a new group of teachers was selected to become members of the preparatory committee, which included:

Mullah Muhammad Gori; Mullah Muhammad Mzuri; Mullah Mamdouh Mazuri; Mullah Abdulrahman Mir Sardari; Mullah Fazil Yassin Dari; Mullah Mahmood Dershawi; Mullah Islam Ibrahim Bazid; Mala Asmat Goharzi; Mullah Taha Shamzini; Mullah Muhammad Amin Warty. Mullah Mahmood Dershawi was elected president of the Islamic Religious Scholars' Union at the conference.

At the conference, the Islamic scholars' union's programme was approved as it was and it was decided to publish without delay. Khabat Printing House was also responsible for printing.

The most important work and activity of the Islamic Religious Scholars Union was:

1. Reopening religious schools in the Zewa camp, where 200 to 400 students would study religious lessons throughout the year in the morning and evening.

2. Solving the problems of society according to Islamic law.

3. Managing marriage and divorce affairs.

4. Continuous attendance at funerals and ceremonies for refugees, martyrs and special occasions.

5. Visiting refugees from different parts of Iran to provide the necessary advice and instructions.

6. Participating in the war alongside peshmerga struggles, especially in Khwakurk's historical epic, even Mullah Bahri Shukri Majid Dri was martyred in this great epic.

7. Issuing and publishing statements and notes to the country and international organisations to support the rights of our people.

8. Visit the liberated areas, especially after the chemical attacks on different areas of Kurdistan.

9. Necessary preparations, appropriate programmes, and significant participation in the uprising of our people against the Ba'athist duplicating institutions.

CHAPTER ELEVEN

Iraq-Iran war

THE DIFFERENCES BETWEEN Iraq and Iran, their history, and the background of the eight-year war between them significantly affected Kurdistan. There was a great sensitivity between the two sides, their relations contained ups and downs and developed, over time, at different stages.

In 1968, when the Ba'athist party took control of Iraq through a coup, conflicts between Iraq and Iran arose. Following this incident and in 1969, the King of Iran broke the 1937 agreement between them. At the end of 1969, Iran tried to produce a coup d'état in Iraq through Abdul-Ghani al-Rawi, but this failed. Many officers and civilians were executed when they were found to be involved in the attempt.

Saddam's strengthening in Iraq's political theatre was an important turning point in the region. From the beginning, he became the first person in the decision making process. His entry into the leadership of the Ba'ath Party and the army was strongly opposed, but until he strengthened his party and military position, he decided to stand by Ahmed Hassan Bakr.

Then, on 1st July 1979, Ahmed Hassan al-Bakr was forced to give up power. Consequently, Saddam became the first and absolute ruler of Iraq.

In addition to the Algerian agreement on 6th March 1975, relations between Iraq and Iran were complicated and the disputes between them were not resolved.

Of course, the Ba'athist regime did not want the Islamic revolution to succeed, because they considered the shah to be more suitable, even trying to persuade the shah to expel Khomeini from Iraq. However, they did not believe this would happen and did not expect the situation in Iran to change in this way. When the revolution succeeded, Khomeini was looking for excuses for conflict with Iraq. At the same time, Saddam sought a reason to cancel the Algerian agreement, because he felt a great deal of failure, shame, and betrayal at losing Shatul Arab and a significant part of Iraqi territory whilst breaking the agreement in Iran's interest. The execution of Said Muhammad Baqir Sadr and his sister Bint al-Huda demonstrated that Khomeini clearly had a strong attitude against Ba'athist regime.

The victory of the Iranian revolution was a golden opportunity for the Iranian people and even the Kurdish people, as it led to the collapse of one of the region's conservative regimes and a major part of Algeria's ominous agreement, so we were pleased with the destruction of the Shah's regime and the success of the Islamic Revolution of Iran. After the revolution's victory, we tried to have a friendly relationship. After their success, we had contacts with many Iranian officials and leaders, officials of the Islamic Republic of Iran and in particular Imam Khomeini.

They gave us good help and assistance, especially in the time of the return and burial ceremony of Barzani's holy body.

This was a good opportunity to return most of our refugees from central and southern Iran to the cities of eastern Kurdistan, which had a major impact on development of revolutionary affairs.

It is worth saying that although we had relations with the Iranian authorities, these associations were not in any way based on accountability, or compromise on our principles; political, strategic, or national goals, but on the basis of friendship, respect, and protection in order to build common interests and understanding.

The attack on the U.S. Embassy and the hostage-taking of all embassy employees on November 4th 1979, for 444 days, had a negative impact on the relationship between Iran and the United States and even the entire West, because the incident created a new crisis.

Mahdi Bazargan's interim government faced a major crisis, as US-Iran relations began deteriorating and other problems emerged with western countries. The incidents led the West to support Iraq against Iran and they even encouraged the war. The situation between the two sides became increasingly complicated and tense.

In May 1980, clashes broke out in different locations between the two sides.

On September 10th 1980, Iraq announced that it had liberated several villages on the border from Iran, and on September 17th 1980, Saddam announced that the Algerian agreement would be terminated.

At 2:30 pm on September 22nd 1980, the Baathist Revolutionary Leadership Council issued a statement saying the Iraqi army had been given the power to attack military targets inside Iranian territory. Iraqi air strikes were launched on most of Iran's military bases and air bases. Iraq announced that most of Iran's aircraft had been bombed, such as Tehran, Isfahan, Abadan, Ahwaz, and Tawrez airports. Because of the bombardments, Iranian forces were harmed in many places, but here was no way to discard Iran's power and capabilities.

Iraq intended to repeat Israel's attack and experience, which in 1967 destroyed the Egyptian Air Force in its first attack. Bani Sadr, Iran's then-president, said: "Saddam has repeated a failed imitation of Musha Dayan." On September 23rd 1980, Iran launched multiple airstrikes on Baghdad and several important places in Iraq. Of course, both sides had multiple successes and were doing each other great harm.

After Iran's airstrike, Iraq launched a multi-day attack 800 kilometres on Iranian soil. At the beginning of the attack, Iraq succeeded, entering 20 to 60 kilometers, invading the depths of Iran's territory including many cities and towns.

At the beginning of the war between them, Iraq was able to capture much of Iran's territory and cause great damage to Iranian forces, because Iraq was prepared, and it had not been long since the victory of the Iranian revolution. Consequently, its forces were scattered, in disarray and not adequately organized.

Iraq was able to take advantage of the opportunities and strike Iran to some extent, imposing its supremacy on the frontlines of the war, but what was remarkable and even led to the withdrawal of Iraq was the patience of the Iranian people, who changed the balance of power in the war, and the Iranians showed great sacrifice and selflessness. Even the son of the Shah of Iran (an F5 fighter pilot) sent a message to the Iranian authorities saying he was ready to defend his country against Iraqi attacks. A response that Iraq did not expect and contributed to Iraq's despair and hopelessness was the attitude of the Arabs of Ahwaz, most of whom stood against Iraq.

After a while, Iran reorganized its forces and reviewed the war fronts and the situation, changing the balance of power and the situation of the frontlines. Iran was able to save most of its cities and towns from Iraq. Many times the fronts and cities were seized between the two sides and each time by one of them but the fate of the war was not decided by any party.

Instead of overthrowing the Regime of the Islamic Republic of Iran, the war, on the contrary, strengthened it, as all the Iranian people defended their country side by side.

On 23rd and 26th September 1980, everyone's eyes were on Iran and Iraq, closely monitoring the situation. At the beginning of the war, Iran was dominant in the sky and the sea, but on land, Iraq was more successful, and in fact, no one expected how strong the Iranian defence would be.

According to information, on 24th September 1980, Iraqi planes bombed the Zewa camp, killing one woman and injuring 12. We had already warned the public to evacuate Zewa, but some chose to remain. The behaviour reiterated a clear indication of the Ba'athist morality. Iraq, despite being in a major war with another country, had not neglected the killing of Kurdish women and children. During this time, Iran's planes bombarded Dore refinery which was a strong blow to Iraq.

On 28th September 1980, Mukri, Iran's ambassador to the Soviet Union, announced that Iran had four conditions for stopping the war:

- Saddam's resignation.
- To put Basra on Iran.

- Referendums would be held in Iraqi Kurdistan so that Kurds could choose a path, join Iran, or be given autonomy.
- The Iraqi army would surrender.

However, as the war broke out, much effort was made, and several parties played an arbitrary role in ending the Iraq-Iran war. The committee's most important group for this purpose was Yasser Arafat, head of the Palestinian Liberation Organization, Ahmed Sikotori, president of Kenya, and Matran Hilary Kapochi, who visited Baghdad and Tehran several times. Despite their efforts and visits, the results were inconclusive.

At the beginning of the Iraq-Iran war, we were in the Kawpar area, located between Piranshar and Sardasht.

On 11th October 1980, Both Mala Hassan Rastgar and Fatah Kawian, members of the leadership of the Kurdistan Democratic Party of Iran, came to us at the request of Dr Qasimlu.

The purpose of the visit was to negotiate and agree with Baghdad, claiming to have made federal promises, but it was later revealed that the Ba'athists were arrogant, unremorseful, and dishonest.

Four days later, on October 15th 1980, Iraqi planes bombarded the Kawpar area and our headquarters, but thank God there was no harm.

On October 17th and 18th 1980, we travelled from Tarkashawa to see the bombardment of Khane military base, and I rarely saw such intense bombardment, and it was strange that they were able to stop. The aim of the bombing seemed to be to pave the way for the Democratic Party's attack. I expected the military base to be easily captured but this failed after much effort. Sarhang Maham, commander of the Khane team, seemed to be a brave and skilled officer and he did not allow his military base to be captured.

By the end of 1980, Iran was able to stop the Iraqi attack with all its might, sacrifices, and then came independence and this changed the course of the war.

Iraq occupied Iranian territory of approximately 800 kilometres (20 to 60 kilometres) wide and took control of several cities and towns. In early 1981, Iran launched a counterattack, and its defence line was strengthened.

One of Iran's major victories was the breaking of the Abadan blockade in September 1981.

On June 7th 1981, Israel targeted a nuclear plant near Baghdad and struck Iraq with a major blow. At the time, Iraq was expected to have nuclear weapons after two years, so it was a major aid to Iran — even if it was not in Iran's hands. Iran lost several of its commanders that year, which was a major blow to Iran. The command of Iran being in the hands of:

- Mustafa Chamchaman, defence minister.
- Waliallah Falahi, chief of staff.
- Fakuri , commander of the Air Force
- Koladuz, deputy commander of the Pasdaran army.

In 1982, Iran launched a major attack on Iraqi forces. On March 22nd 1982, a massive attack on the Iraqi Army's Fourth Legion on the Central Front and the Dezf was launched, causing heavy casualties and loss of military equipment, forcing it to withdraw 100 kilometres long and 20 kilometres wide. It was a great success and somehow raised Iran's morale.

On May 3rd 1982, Algerian Foreign Minister Mohammed Sadiq Yahya's plane was shot down by Iraq, while he flew to visit Tehran for arbitrage, killing him.

After Iran's victory in the Fatih attack, on May 26th 1982, the city rescued Khoramshahri from Iraqi forces. After Iran's successes, Iraq announced on June 20th that it would stop the war unilaterally and withdraw from its international borders by June 30th, but Iran refused and demanded a hundred and fifty billion dollars in compensation, whilst demanding two more - the trial of Saddam and allowing Iranian forces to enter Lebanon and fight Israel!

On June 13th 1982, Iran launched the largest offensive to capture Basra, but failed and suffered major setbacks. Although it initially succeeded, Iraq took all its places in a counterattack, causing major damage to both sides.

In 1983

On February 6th 1983, Iran launched a major offensive on the Ammara front, advancing well and invading several areas and locations, but Iraq in counterattacks removed some areas from them.

The situation on the front lines remained the same, with no major change, as a result of counterattacks between the two sides.

According to reports published by the end of 1983, the damage to both sides was as follows: Iran: 120,000 killed, Iraq: 60,000 killed

In 1984

On the night of February 15th to 16th 1984, Iran launched two attacks, Fajri Five and Fajri Six, which sought to prevent Basra from entering Baghdad, but these failed. A fierce battle between the two sides continued, but no party was settled again. Iran was able to capture the oil-rich Majnoon valleys, all Iraqis effort was to retake it but all failed until 1988.

On March 8th ,1984, Iraqi planes bombed the Piranshar house, killing 20 civilians.

On February 5th, 1984, Iraqi planes heavily bombed the city of Bana, killing more than 1,000 civilians.

In 1985

In this year, fighting with planes and Scud missiles began fiercely between the two sides, in which Iraq was dominant. The number of Iranian planes was decreasing day by day due to the lack of repairs, as the United States had blockaded Iran. On the contrary, Iraq was buying weapons from both the west and east, and the Gulf countries were paying for it. Iran occasionally targeted Baghdad with Scud missiles that they were getting from Libya, Syria, and North Korea.

On March 8th, 1985, Iraq heavily bombarded the military bases of Khana, Paswe, Jalidian, and the centre of the city of Khani, which resulted in 150 civilians being killed, and one refugee, Hassan Ibrahim Khalani, was martyred.

On the night of March 11th to 12th 1985, Iran launched a 15-kilometre-long attack on Qurna in northern Basra, advancing 14 kilometres deep, but then led Iraq to the ground. The attack captured and recovered the lost areas.

On March 14th to 16th 1985, Iran targeted Baghdad with Scud missiles and two missiles hit at Rafidain Bank.

On March 18th 1985, Iraq issued a statement no. 1774 stating that Iranian offensive forces had destroyed Horlhwez. Between the March 26th and 31st, the beatings and bombardments of each other's cities continued strongly. Iran bombarded the Koraki Mountain Tower by plane.

On 25th April 1985, the assassination of the Emir of Kuwait was attempted, and Baghdad announced that Saddam had led a military and political meeting and that Iranian cities had been heavily bombarded.

In 1986

On February 10th 1986, Iran launched a major attack on Fawi under the title Walfajri Eight, and on February 11th it announced the capture of Fawi and attacked Iraqi forces from the Majnoon side, causing heavy casualties, military and morale damage to Iraq. With these successes, Iran's spirits rose greatly. Iran announced that in the Fawi attack, a lot of weapons fell into the hands of their forces and they have caused great casualties to Iraqi forces.

On 13th February 1986, heavy fighting broke out between Fawi and the Basra Road, where Iraqi forces suffered heavy damage, but Iraq prevented Iran from attacking by using chemical weapons. On 25th December 1986, Iran launched a major attack on the fronts of both the 3rd and 7th Legions, but on 27th February 1986, Iraq announced in statement No. 2503 that it had broken the Iranian attack, Karbala IV, causing considerable damage to Iran, which did not count.

The battle was led by Lieutenant General Mahir Abdulrashid.

In 1987

In 1987, the war between the two sides continued fiercely. On the night of 8th January 1987, Iran launched a major attack on Shalamcha and the 3rd Legion, which it said in a statement had caused serious casualties and material damage to Iraqi forces. Baghdad also announced that it had stopped the Iranian attack and caused great damage to Iranian forces, but it seemed that Iran was in power in the attack. Iran also announced that on 11th January 1987, it had targeted Baghdad with missiles. On 14th January 1987, Iran launched the Karbala Six attack, saying that several Iraqi tanks and artillery had been destroyed and that it had released the names of Iraqi military units that had suffered heavy damage. In turn, Iraq acknowledged that Iran had launched a major attack, but the Iraqi Army's 2nd Legion under the command of Lieutenant General AbdulsattarAl-Muaini, in a counterattack, attacked Iran.

In the battles of Karbala Five and Six, both sides exaggerated a lot, but indeed, both sides suffered great material and spiritual damage.

On 22nd January 1987, Iraq announced that, apart from the frontlines of the war, it had launched 568 airstrikes against Iran, including against the cities of Qum, Tawrez, Isfahan, Hamadan, Dzfoul, Khoramabad, Malayar. Poldukhter, Zanjan, and several Iranian military bases.

On 23rd January 1987, a large number of Basra residents came to Duhok because of the heavy fighting in the region, and we asked branch one to advise our people and to respect those people.

Iraq issued a statement no. 2551, rescuing several locations around the Al-Asmak River.

Saddam did not attend the Arab Summit meeting held in Kuwait on 26th January, but Izzat Duri represented him.

Rafsanjani announced at Friday prayers on 31st January 1987, that Iraq had 194 brigades, of which 124 had been sent to the war front in Basra, and that all brigades had been harmed and captured. They hit 50 brigades with great blows.

On 19th February 1987, Iraq and Iran announced that they had stopped fighting in the cities.

Iraq announced that on 17th February, Saddam welcomed Masoud Rajawi. Rajawi allegedly calling on Saddam to stop attacks on cities.

On 20th February 1987, Khamenei announced that, as a result of Iraq's attacks on Iranian cities, 135 people were martyred and 11,500 civilians were injured.

On 26th February 1987, Iran announced that it had ended the Karbala Five attack under political pressure.

On 31st March 1987, Muhsin Razaei announced in a television and press interview the result of a year of war as follows:

Three large and small attacks were carried out, resulting in:

- The capture of 8,000 people.
- 200,000 people were killed and wounded.
- 150 planes and seventy helicopters were shot down
- Destroying 1800 tanks and large military cars
- 200 different military vehicles damaged over four hundred regiments (20 % - 100 %).

On 7th April 1987, Iran announced that it had launched an attack on the eastern side of Basra, destroying Iraqi forces and advancing significantly. On 9th April 1987, they launched another attack under the title of Karbala Nine on the middle side of the Zahaw and Qasre Shirin, and achieved great success, and they caused great casualties to the Iraqi forces.

On 11th April 1987, Iraq announced that, in a counterattack, the Persian forces, led by Lieutenant General Hussein Rashid, had liberated all areas which Iran had seized in Karbala Eight.

On 15th April 1987, Iran announced that, with the help of PUK forces in the Mawat and Chwarta areas, they had taken control of a wide area and liberated the villages of Galala, Olaghlu, Maluma and Gapilon. They stated that 200 people had been captured, and that the number of killed and wounded in Iraq had reached 1,000. Although there were several major battles and attacks between the two sides in 1987, no party was able to resolve the war.

In 1988

According to local information, Iraq punished several officers on various charges, including Brigadier General Tala Duri, Brigadier General Rahim Taha Duri, Brigadier General Ali and Brigadier General Tariq. On 27th February 1987, Iraq issued statement No. 3035, saying that Iraqi planes had launched a major attack on the Tehran refinery.

On 6th April 1988, Iraqi planes launched a brutal attack on the village of Silvana and its environs where our house was located, using an Anqudi bomb. Unfortunately, 18 people were killed and 60 were injured. Following the Iraqi attack, Iran also announced that Baghdad and Basra would be targeted by their missiles in the next few hours, after which fighting and shelling of cities began, with Iraq more powerful due to it being helped more by the international community.

In 1988, the balance of war against Iran changed, and in fact, the forces of both sides were completely exhausted, but the international stance changed the situation in Iraq's interest.

On 3rd June 1988, Iran bombarded Saddam's house with four Phantom aircraft. Meanwhile, in retaliation for Iraq's continued bombardment of oil carriers, Iran also attacked several Saudi and Kuwaiti oil carriers in the face of Iran's attacks. Gulf countries generally entered the war and Saudi aircraft of the Type F15, shot down an Iranian F4 fighter jet; the United States destroyed two

Iranian fighter ships, and on 3ʳᵈ July 1988, the U.S. Navy shot down an Iranian passenger and killed 290.

On the frontlines of the war, there was a better opportunity for Iraq, and there was complete information about the despair, hopelessness, and tiredness of Iranian forces.

On 17ᵗʰ April 1988, Iraq launched a major offensive on the Fawi region, engulfing the island after heavy fighting. Iranian forces suffered military and moral setbacks and losses, but Iraq did not stop by doing so, carrying out other attacks under the title "Taukult-e-Alialla One", which resulted in the attack on Tauktult-e-Alialla II and captured all Majnoon islands.

Iraq launched attacks on Iranian forces in many areas, and frontlines of the war, capturing many of the zones it had previously lost. The dramatic changes forced Iran to approve Security Council Resolution 598 on July 18, 1988, which was specific to stopping the war. Imam Khomeini was concerned and upset by the approval of the Security Council's decision, but the military and political commanders told him, the situation was bad and unstable and that they would no longer be able to fight, because it had changed from war between Iraq and Iran and had become a war between Iran- the United States, the West and the Gulf.

On 20ᵗʰ August 1988, Iraq and Iran formally agreed to stop the war and agreed on the following five points:

1. Stopping the war.
2. Withdrawal to international borders.
3. Exchanging captives.
4. The start of peace talks.
5. Reconstruction of both countries with international cooperation.

Although Iraq was dominant during the eight-year war between them, Iran succeeded in the peace talks.

The discussions took place on 25th August 1988, and if it is considered deeply, what was the result of this eight-year war? Why did it happen and what did this blood spill for? It was indeed a major crime against humanity, particularly those of both Iraq and Iran, that will take a long time to end its consequences because it has caused deep sorrow to both sides that have been in the hearts of both sides throughout history. The fighting lasted 2,888 days.

The attitude of the countries of the world toward the war

Iran was internationally closed, with only Syria, Libya and North Korea, and to some extent China cooperating with it, although Israel, with US consent, was selling parts of aircraft and tanks to Iran. Robert McPherlen, Ronald Reagan's security adviser, visited Iran in the mid-1980s and sent Reagan a letter to Khomeini, to some extent Iran was given weapons and Israel was given a quantity of aircraft reserves. The US and Western policy in general was that neither Iran nor Iraq would succeed in the war.

About Iraq

In the war, those who supported Iraq more were the United States, the West, the former Soviet Union, the Eastern Pole and the Arab countries, Libya and Syria.

In 1993, Shah Fahad told me, "We (Saudi Arabia and the Gulf countries) helped Iraq in the Iraq-Iran war for thirty-seven billion dollars, but Saddam gave us a reward by invading Kuwait and intended more."

Chemical weapons

Iraq, of course, used chemical weapons against Iran several times from 1983 until the end of the war, and benefited from it against the peshmerga forces. Ultimately, it engaged in chemical bombardment against Halabja and committed a big crime on 16th March 1988

Number of weapons and armed forces, held by both countries, prior to the Iraqi and Iran war.

Iran before the war.

390,000 Army personnel, 1375 tanks, 447 War planes, 744 Helicopters.

Iran after the war.

600,000 Army personnel, 1000 tanks, 50 War planes, 390 Helicopters.

Iraq before the war.

443,000 Army personnel, 2750 tanks, 399 War planes, 260 Helicopters.

Iraq after the war.

1,000,000 Army personnel, 4000 tanks, 600 War planes, 380 Helicopters.

Casualties and losses incurred by both sides.

Iran

730,000 deaths, 1,200,000 injured, POW 45,000, Displaced 2,000,000

Iraq

340,000 deaths, 700,000 injured, POW 70,000, Displaced 2,000,000

The infrastructure of both countries was destroyed, between the two sides with half a trillion dollars of losses being estimated. These numbers may not be very complete, but they are actually close.

After the war ended, I asked the Iranian officers, "Which Iraqi weapons were more effective on you and played a role in changing the balance on the battlefield?" "Iraqi tanks were very effective," they replied.

During the 1991 talks in Baghdad, I asked Iraqi officers the same question: "The Iranian artillery was very effective, and their motorcyclists were very fast, efficient, and active."

Negotiations between Iraq and Iran continued, and some points of the agreement were implemented, such as the exchange of captives, and a letter exchanged between Saddam and Rafsanjani.

On 13th May 1990, Mont Carlo's voice released further details of Saddam's letters to Rafsanjani, allegedly suggesting that they meet in Makkah and they appeared to be close to each other and the possibility of an agreement existed.

On 17th May 1990, Hani Hassan also sent Saddam's letter to Rafsanjani, saying:

- The Islamic world is in danger and is threatened by the United States and Israel, so both sides must unite.
- Saddam and Rafsanjani should meet and solve their problems without arbitrators.
- Makkah to be proposed by Iraq for a meeting between the two sides, because it is the home of God, not because of Saudi Arabia, or wherever it designates in Iran, Tehran, or Baghdad.

- Without US and Soviet arbitrators, they will solve their problems, so that no one will eat their blood products.
- Shatul Arab is a big problem and Iraq is ready, not the Algerian agreement. Iran's answer was as follows:
  - Agree to meetings.
  - Instead of Makkah , Pakistan was suggested.
  - The negotiations within the framework of the decision of the International Security Council number 598.
  - Implementing the Algerian agreement first.
  - Both foreign ministers will meet and prepare for the meeting of both presidents.

Iraq was not honest with its attitudes and intended to receive achievements and privileges, but Iran's response to Iraq's letter was somewhat balanced, as its non-response strengthened Iraq's stance.

According to the news, Italy sold and handed over eleven warships to Iraq; five more would then be handed over. Iran was concerned about the matter, and by Khamenei's decision for the Iranian military manoeuvre Sahand, in the Gulf, conducted to strike ships if they entered the waters of the Gulf. Hani Hassan also sent a letter that the Palestinian people were waiting for Iran's role to help. In the end, Saddam wrote a threatening letter to Iran, stating, "You know that Iraq is very strong, but because Islam is in danger, and he is threatened, so he has made this initiative."

On 3rd July 1990, for the first time since the cessation of fighting between the two sides, Iranian Foreign Minister Ali Akbar Velayati and Iraqi Foreign Minister Tariq Aziz met in Geneva. According to International Security Council Resolution 598, UN Secretary-General Khawir Perez Dekoyar attended the meeting.

On 16th July 1990, Iraq threatened Kuwait and the United Arab Emirates on the pretext of lowering oil prices and selling oil cheaply, and stealing Iraqi oil from the Ramela oil-well. On 21st July 1990, Iraq threatened Kuwait that they stole two billion, four hundred million dollars of Iraqi oil.

PDK's attitude towards Iraq-Iran war

After the fall of 1975, the Ba'athist regime systematically began to destroy Kurdistan and move a large number of Kurdistan's people from their homes to central and southern Iraq where they would reside in forced societies and most of the villages were destroyed.

When the war between Iraq and Iran began on 22nd September 1980, no one believed the war would last eight years, even though there were many clashes in the Khanaqin border before the start of the war.

During this period, the regime was not serious about a peaceful solution to the problems and did not take any steps in that direction. Although there has been a war between Hadka and Iran in eastern Kurdistan, there has been a good opportunity for Iran and Iraq to try to solve the problem.

The locals were given opportunities to do so, but it seemed that no one had taken the step.

According to every logic, when a state is at war, the first step is always to solve internal problems, in which the regime has demonstrated its readiness to negotiate and solve the problems through special forces and once through the Hadkawa. We welcomed the request and responded that we were ready to resolve the problems peacefully. We always kept the door to our discussions open.

We only acted to defend the rights and existence of our people and said that, if the government was serious about solving the problems:

- It should allow people in the community to return to their homes and places.
- It must end the policy of relocation, Arabization and the pursuit of the Kurdish citizens.
- The 11th March agreement should be made on the basis of negotiations.

The government did not care about the issue at all, and always reiterated that the country was at war and that it was not time to talk about such things, and that we should all agree and defend the country together, and then we would achieve more. Of course, we have bitter experiences with such promises. And if you do not believe, then know that Allah is all-mighty, All-Merciful.

The situation after the start of the war between the two countries was an important and golden opportunity for the regime to fundamentally resolve the Kurdish issue. For the Kurdish people, it was a good opportunity to strengthen their position and manage more activities, launching a big and more effective strike on the regime's bases and strongholds, and achieve more success on the ground and widen the liberated areas.

We may be complained of by many Arabs as to why we did not stop our wars and activities during the start of the Iraq-Iran war, nor did we agree with the government. In response, we said: it was the regime that didn't come before to solve the Kurdish problem peacefully, and on the way did not discuss or take any practical steps.

When the government continued its chauvinistic and racist policies against the Kurdish people, it was our right to defend our people and our homeland and avenge the blood of our innocent martyrs against the criminals, because thousands of citizens were expelled from their places. Civilians, Anfal and chemical weapons were carried out, thousands of villages were flattened, and a policy of racial and national cleansing was fully pursued aimed at eliminating Kurds and even their names. The regime was trying to complete that programme and policy.

In spite of all the crimes and anti-human behaviour committed against our people, we never closed the door to our negotiations and kept them open, but the regime was not ready, because it did not believe in a peaceful solution to the problems, always looking for ways to kill time and occupy us.

Even after the end of the war between Iraq and Iran, we tried to resolve the problems through peaceful dialogue, but just as the regime was not ready before the start of the war, it was not ready for negotiations and dialogue after the war. What the regime wanted, or was asking for, was a kind of surrender!

Many may ask, what was the PDK's stance on the Iran-Iraq war, or what it should have been like? It is true that the start of the war had opened up more opportunities for our people, and we tried to take advantage of the opportunities that came to us in the best way, without being part of it, or a party in the war, although there was a lot of demand and even sometimes there has been some kind of pressure on it.

Whomever asked us to be a part of the war, or sharing military attacks and activities, we refused in every way, because:

- Our struggle, and war was against Ba'athist regime, even before the start of the war between them, and the struggle and striving of our people had nothing to do with the war and the relations between them.
- The war between the two countries was much greater than our abilities, and the balance of power between the two sides was not discussed at all. Our total peshmerga might be attacked, or a war might occur between the two sides.
- Our goals were separate from the goals and interests of Iran and Iraq.

Therefore, we tried to take advantage of the war that existed on the border of Kurdistan to strengthen our position and expand our activities as partisans.

Although these wars were an opportunity on the one hand, the wars often caused great damage to us, our people, and our citizens in Kurdistan. The weight of the war between Iraq and Iran, in the south of the country, intensified 800 kilometres and continued fiercely, including on our borders.

Iran's intention in its attacks on Kurdistan was to put pressure on Iraq to reduce pressure on the central and southern fronts.

Several military actions took place on our borders, the most important of which were:

1- Haji Omaran Offensive:
Our policy towards the wars in Kurdistan was to continue the partisan war by taking advantage of any changes in the interests of the peshmerga.

In order to reduce pressure on the central and southern fronts, Iran has decided to open a new front in the Haji Omaran area under the title "Walfajri II", which is why it has planned to capture Haji Omarani Heights.

The purpose of this was to open the Qasre road to Nawdashte.

Sarhang Shirazi and Muhsin Razai visited the house to discuss their plan and asked for an interview with me. In part of the meeting, they asked for peshmerga's participation in the attack, and I explained that the peshmerga could not participate directly in the attack, because of the great forces, the necessary capabilities and experience.

We don't have a big military war; our war is a partisan war.

I said, "We are sending forces to the area of Nawdasht, so that you will be assured on the side of the war front, and for us a big door will be opened to the areas of Rwandese and Qaladze." On the western side, i.e. the Sidakans, we had forces, and any threats that came from these two paths would be confronted by the peshmerga, because they seemed to be in danger of being attacked on both sides, so they were very happy with my response. I also told them that the area of Nawdasht was very far logistically and it needed a lot of time to go to Qasre. It would be open ground, so I told the representatives that if they didn't help us transport injuries and deliver the necessary helicopters, it meant we would face disaster on that side.

For this purpose, we spoke to all the parties on the Jud council, and a meeting was held at the Party's political bureau, all of whom wanted the Jud force to enter the Nawdasht area. If the PUK prevented it, they would retaliate against the PUK, which had martyred dozens of captive peshmerga, for crimes committed against the peshmerga in the spring of 1983. In the meeting, it was decided that Mr Idris would oversee the attack by Jud.

The plan's details produced a dispute between us, a number of Iranian army officials and the Iranian army, who were unsuccessful and arrogant. One of them, Rabi'i, said, "It doesn't matter to you if a thousand guards are martyred, but you don't want a peshmerga to bleed." I answered strongly, and then they all criticized Rabi'i harshly. Participants in the meeting were: Sarhang Sattari, Jaish representative; Sarhang Jalali, representative of the Army of The Shet, The Fourth of Wrme; and Istika, the representative of the Pasdaran Army.

On 20th July 1983, Iran's attack on the northern, southern and western heights of Haji Omaran began. At first, they won hasty success in many places and held heights, but inside Haji Omaran itself and its street to Darband, Iraq defended fiercely. After a fierce battle, though, Haji Omaran was fully controlled by Iran. After the capture of the area, they soon changed the names of their places, which I was concerned about, and on 30th July 1983 in a meeting with Shirazi and Muhsin Razaei, I protested. I showed them strongly, and I asked them to give their forces instructions and advice to stop doing so, and they complied.

Iran had not been able to get further from The Rayat, and many people have fled the area because of this war. They made it to Iran.

The great battle then took place in Gardamandil, where the two sides did everything in their power to control the mountain, which was a very strategic place dominating the valleys. Attacks were reversed several times, and there were times during a day when both sides were seized.

Once, Iraq tried to land several helicopters in the Heights of Gardamandil, which was under Iranian control. The Iranian forces at the heights were defending the heights, and because before they went down, the area became one piece of hell under artillery fire.

More than ten helicopters were shot down from the sky, and about ten helicopters landed, but the passengers were killed and the helicopters burned. RPG7s proved vital in the battle. The casualties of Iraq and Iran in Gardmandil came to more than 5,000 people.

I asked Sarhang Sanjabi, a Kurdish officer from Kermanshah, "How was all the damage done?"

"90 per cent of our losses in Gardamandil were caused by 60mm mortars," he said.

From here, the offensive stalled. Iran did not reach Darbandi, not Galala and Qasre, and there was a lot of damage on both sides.

Iranian forces were commanded by Shirazi and Muhsin Razaei[3], and Iraqi forces were led by Lieutenant General Na'ima Hussein Faris al-Mahiawi, commander of the Fifth Legion. Saddam himself visited Diaana; in this battle chemical weapons were being used.

On the central side, where our forces had been attacked several times by Iraqi planes and helicopters, Iran had not helped us in any way. On 6th August our forces were heavily bombarded and two peshmerga were martyred and three injured.

It was during the PUK's agreement with Iraq, that Iraq provided all its needs in all aspects, particularly the Khanaqa Valley road, where everything was transported by car. But Jud's forces

---

[3] Sayyad Shirazi, commander of the Iranian army's ground forces, was a smart, intimidating and courageous officer, an artillery officer and commander of the Army Unit. Muhsin Razaei, commander of the Pasdaran army, which I felt the final decision was in Muhsin Razai's hand, and he was not arrogant and not successful.

would take two days by horseback, and they might not receive their belongings and needs.

Worst of all, Jud's forces were not united, so they were not unified, and there was no cooperation within the Party's own forces.

The failure of the Iranian attacks, according to the plan, was the main reason for judging forces to suffer major disasters in the war with the PUK.

After the war, relations between Saddam and the PUK were very good, and for a while they began to negotiate and many possibilities were given to the PUK. Although Saddam's defeat against Iran was not a major failure, he made it an excuse for his historical crime against the Barzani on 31st July 1983, when 8,000 Barzani from the ages of 12 to 90 years were subjected to genocide.

2- Penjwen Offensive (Walfajri IV):

In mid-October 1983, Iran launched another attack on Penjwen and Chwarta in Bana and Mariwan. Iran was able to advance on all fronts of the war and quickly captured the Area of Shleri. Iran's intention in this attack was to reduce pressure on the central and southern fronts, and the damage to both sides in this war was not great.

The offensive had no significant results.

3- Sidakan Offensive (Qadir Operations 1985):

This time, Iran decided to attack the Sidakan area in the Kelashin and Khrena area, and only the Iranian army attacked, and Krdi did not participate in this attack. Shirazi commanded the attack. The secret name of the attack was Qadir Gali Gadar, who continued from 15th July 1985 to 30th September 1985. Iran had both the 23rd and 64th armies and a special forces brigade was dedicated to the attack.

The Iranian attack began in the areas where all of our pesh-merga headquarters and our people were. According to their plan, at least, all the heights of the north of Sidakan were released and Iran reached them. Hassan Bag dominated the Rwandese Valley until Iran made the necessary preparations.

Iraq brought in a large number of forces to Rwandese and Sidakan, under the command of Lieutenant General Ziaadin Jamal, commander of the 5th Legion, and Major General Jayad al-Amara, commander of the 33rd Division, very well prepared for the operation.

"I tried hard to convince Shirazi not to attack, because it would displace a large number of locals, but he was sure he would achieve great success," he said.

To some extent, they were sure that one of the great command-ers of the Iranian army had come up with a plan and simply said, "We will go up Bradost and Korek mountains and we will take the Alibag valley."

He asked me, "What role can you play?"

I said to him, "When you have reached your Alibag valley, from there to Erbil, leave it to us!"

I ordered the peshmerga forces to stay at the back headquarters and deploy refugees to the east and west of the Sidakan area and to be ready for any possibility. Barzani forces were also warned to be present in the Mergasor area and to monitor the situation carefully on the plains and mount Qalaandar. Both Dr Saeed and Hali Dolmaer were supervising the task. Peshmerga in the Balaki area of branch two, led by Najmadin Goruni, were monitoring the fighting on the Halgurd, Hasarost and Horni Balaki fronts. We warned the people of the area that they should protect themselves and evacuate the villages that would become battlefields.

At the end of August, Iran's offensive began, like all other ones, first taking large positions and controlling strategic heights around the Sidakan, and then Iraq launched counterattacks.

In this way, the area was seized between the two sides for two months, and the artillery continued.

During the fighting, I was at the headquarters of our forces, and Lolan was in constant contact with our forces. Hamid Afandi and Lieutenant Younis were with me as helpers. Lieutenant Ali and Babakir Zebari fought in a field of honour on the front lines.

On 3rd September 1985, regime planes were shot down as they bombarded Lolan and Barzani's headquarters in Hayat. On 5th September regime planes again heavily attacked the slopes of Mount Shakew and around Lolan and they bombarded them.

On 7th September 1985, Mushir Gwani, who was in charge of monitoring and investigating the war front east of Sidakan, warned me that Iraq had heavily bombed the area and then launched ground attacks, encompassing the following areas: Mount Bole, Kunakoter, Gardekhat, Kanda and Kawbar, which meant Iran's failure on the eastern front.

On 9th September 1985, Iran attacked and captured The Sare Spendare Heights and won a major victory. Iranian forces advanced to the nearby Sidakan. But Iraq, advancing from Dolmarg, attacked Iran's forces and they were forced to withdraw. Consequently they lost their places.

On 20th and 21st September 1985, Iraq launched a major attack on the Ruby and Rual heights, and after a heavy and bloody battle, Iraqi forces were broken and 70 bodies were left behind, with some weapons and explosives seized, and a lieutenant colonel, a commander, and some soldiers captured.

On 30th September 1985, Iran launched a major attack on Barde Bafr and Sare Slpendare. I have rarely seen such heavy shelling in my life. These areas became one piece of fire, and Iraqi planes bombarded the area left and right. At the Headquarters of the Party's Treaty District Committee, as a result of the air strikes, Zikri Birokhi was seriously injured and transferred to Urmia Hospital. Unfortunately, because of the severity of his injuries, he was martyred on 1st October 1985.

On 30th September 1985, the Baghdad station announced that the Iraqi Air Force had launched 125 air strikes on the battlefield in the Sidakan area. The Iranian forces were in a state of confusion. Then it was revealed that the Abshnasan was injured and the news came that it was over and he had died.

After these unresolved battles, Shirazi asked us to meet. In the interview, he asked, "Why do you think the success we wanted was not achieved? Neither here, nor in the Haji Omaran war in 1983."

I told him: In my opinion, there were some reasons why it failed completely:

- Geographic nature and the hardship of the area.
- Lack of full coordination between Iran's forces.
- There was no air support for their forces.
- Because of the difficulty of the area, there were no opportunities to use tanks.
- The strong support of Iraqi aircraft in their forces and the heavy damage to Iran's forces.
- If there was no air and tank support, it was impossible for the military to fight.

- In the early years of the war, Iran had a large sacrificial force and scored a great success with their bravery and beliefs. Their numbers were now very small.

At the end of the meeting, he said, "We will stop Gadir's attack and leave an army in the area as a threat to Iraqi forces, and after setting up a line of defence, we will withdraw from other forces." Then the key question came. He said, "What are you doing?" I said, "Our forces will remain in place."

We were in the midst of a Hezbollah detachment with a Pasdaran detachment, under Rahman's command, who had visited the area and threatened the Communist Party to make them move their headquarters into the area. I ordered the peshmerga to warn them of their mercy and tell them, "This is our land. You cannot issue orders. "You can give the Communist Party headquarters orders inside Iran, but you don't have that right here." I sent a message to Hezbollah's crowd, if it behaved in that way, and we would drive them out of the area.

Attack on Kirkuk oil institutions

On 11th October 1986, an Iranian Revolutionary Guard force, in cooperation with the PUK peshmerga, launched a plan to hit Kirkuk's oil under the title of Fathi Ya.

For this purpose, an agreement was signed between the PUK and the Pasdaran army on the basis that:

- The PUK would make every facility for the Pasdaran force to reach its target.

- In the meantime, Iran would make every facility for the PUK and help them well.

According to the information published, the attack consisted of: 200 guards under the command of Friend Shafaq and several other commanders named Sadiq Mahsuli, Ghulam Pakruh, Friend Boyaqchi and Friend Naderi, in partnership with the PUK forces:

- Team twenty-one under the command of Sirwan
- Team 25 under the command of Mala Aras
- Koya team under the command of Mala Braim
- The 87th Qarachogh team under the command of Safin

For the operation, they gave the PUK forces the following weapons:

- 1,500 Kalashnikovs plus 30,000 bullets.
- 40 BKC with 1,000 bullets.
- 15 doves with 15,000 bullets.
- A Hawat 7 RPG with 50 rockets.
- Three 120mm mortars with 1500 shells.
- Two 81mm mortars with 1,000 shells.

The attack, called Fathi Ya, partially damaged Kirkuk's oil institutions but was not the way Tehran's station published it. Rafsanjani said the Pasdaran was not harmed, but his forces were. Mr Talabani suffered some damage.

CHAPTER 12

Establishing the Kurdistan Council

S INCE THE BEGINNING of the war, efforts had been made to take advantage of the Iran-Iraq war in order to launch more effective attacks on regime bases and strongholds and to widen areas under peshmerga control. To some extent, we succeeded in this goal, but at that stage and in that situation, the unity and harmony of all the parties of Kurdistan was a historical need, offset by a multitude of nationalist groups.

One of the decisions of the ninth PDK congress was to try and work to form a multi-party national Council that included all Kurdish parties and groups. The establishment of the Jud Council was an important step in this direction, and efforts continued to establish a Kurdistan council, which in fact began with Mr Idris's steps in public reconciliation and came to an end in 1988.

For this purpose, in order to prepare the project and draft of the Kurdistan Council, on 18th July 1987, with the presence of the PUK delegation and the Kurdistan Socialist Party, the Kurdistan Democratic People's Party and Pasok held a multi-party meeting, which consisted of Fuad Masum, Rasul Mamand, Sami Abdulrahman, Lieutenant Karim Paso, who discussed in detail the programmes, projects, work and duties of the meeting and finally decided to form a committee to prepare the final draft of the statement, so on 30th July 1987 the statement of the Kurdistan Council was published.

On 12th April 1988, Nawshirwan Mustafa, Rasul Mamand, Faraidun Abdulqadir and Qadir Jabari came to us; the Kurdistan Council was discussed in detail, and then in a special and bilateral meeting, Nawshirwan reiterated that the bilateral relations between PUK and PDK were a major task and a priority and they would like these relations to continue.

On the evening of 19th April 1988, we had a meeting with the Communist Party on the situation on the Kurdistan Council, whose delegation consisted of Karim Ahmed, Abu Hakmat and Rahim Ajina, known as Abu Shahab.

On 29th April 1988, the Meeting of the Kurdistan Council began its work and continued until 1st May 1988. Those present were:

PDK - Masoud Barzani, Ali Abdullah, Fazil Mirani, Falakadin Kakayi, Dr Jarjis Hasan, Lieutenant Younis Rozhbayani, Franso Hariri, Nechirvan Barzani and Muhsin Dzaie.

Hasha - Karim Ahmed, Rahim Ajina (Abu Shahab), Abu Hakmat.

PUK - Faraidun Abdulqadir.

Hask - Rasul Mamand, Qadir Jabari.

Gall Party - Sami Abdulrahman, Jamal

Pasok - Lieutenant Shwan, Abdullah.

The discussions were complicated and tense, and opinions were far apart. I tried so hard to get close and achieve resolution. Although the meetings continued again on 2nd May 1988, and the documents were completed, the local procedure took a long time, the discussions were tense again and I was forced to enter into discussions to help them resolve and consolidate. Thank God we agreed on this although there was a lot of tiredness.

From 10 am to twelve o'clock in the night, there were intense and long meetings, because I brought up the subject and did not think about our exhaustion. I was pleased that we had an agreement to be announced on 7th May 1988; this was a great victory for the Kurdish people. The parties we composed were:

1. Kurdistan Democratic Party. 2. Patriotic Union of Kurdistan. 3. The Communist Party of Iraq (Hasha- Kurdistan Region). 4. Kurdistan Socialist Party (Hask). 5- Kurdish Socialist Party (Pasok). 6. Kurdistan Democratic People's Party. 7. Kurdistan Workers' Party.

Gradually, politically, militarily, financially and socially, we published a newspaper called The Kurdistan Council. Gradually, it continued until the parliamentary elections and the establishment of the Kurdistan Regional Government. On 7th May 1988, Hasha called for a postponement of the Council's statement. Whoever is true, this was not the right decision , and we made many compromises for Hasha. We were doing what was going on the Kurdistan side.

At the end of May 1988, the Kurdistan Council sent a note to the summit meeting between Gorbachev and Reagan in Moscow.

The memorandum discussed the situation in the region in general, Iraq and the Kurdish people in particular, calling on both presidents to take serious steps to consider international agreements on human rights, peace, and stability. And the Iraqi government was asked to respect the rights of Kurds and the policy of relocation, changing the demographics of Kurdistan, and to stop the ethnic cleansing.

The meetings continued and on 4th June 1988, we held a brief meeting and recorded our opinions. The next day I went to the train and decided that Mr Ali Abdullah, Mr Fazil Mirani and Mr Falakadin Kakaei would go to the meeting of the Kurdistan Council which was hosted by Hasha and this was held in Khwakurk.

On 10th June 1988, friends Mr Ali Abdullah, Mr Fazil Mirani and Mr Falakadin Kakaei returned to the political leadership meeting and made a number of decisions.

Before the meeting of the Kurdistan Council, on 11th June, 1988 the political bureau met and friends of the central committee participated. We discussed the results of our commander's participation in the meeting of the political leadership of the Kurdistan Council; of course, on the 12th and 13th of June 1988, we met to discuss our visit to Kermanshah.

The general meeting of the Kurdistan Council's Executive Committee, held in Khwakurk on 20th June 1988, was attended by Mr Fazil Mirani and Falakadin Kakayi.

On 13th July 1988, Khairi came to us to discuss the following:

1. To know what would happen to the Kurdistan Council, because I had ordered him to ask for a meeting and announced that Mr Himat had become the commander of the army's ground forces and along with other changes which could be done and it was very positive.

2. A few days ago, Abdullah Islami and Muhsin Baqiri went to their homes and talked about meeting with me in

Kermanshah. Khairi also said they might take a stand. He said they wouldn't give in because they had fought for the last eight years and they would not give up on it now, or just give it away.

I think it is important and necessary that I record and write the history of the meetings carefully and precisely, because this was a new section in the history of the Kurdistan Liberation Movement and at the same time it was connected to subsequent changes in the region and Iraq.

Of course, after a long time and on 7th August 1988, the meeting of the Kurdistan Council started and these friends were present:

PDK - Masoud Barzani, Ali Abdullah, Dr Rozh Nuri Shawis, Fazil Mirani, Dr Jarjis Hassan and Falakadin Kakaei.
PUK - Fuad Masum and Jabbar Farman.
Hasha - Abu Faruq and Abu Hakmat.
Hask - Rasul Mamand, Qadir Jabari, Sheikh Mohammed Shakali and Teacher Saad Abdullah.
People's Party - Sami Abdulrahman.
Pasok - Lieutenant Karim.

After discussing the issues in detail, they made some decisions to create and negotiate politically, militarily, to defend, and then to fight partisan wars. The audience had their eyes on me and wanted to know what I was saying.

On 22nd August 1988, another meeting of the Kurdistan Council was held in Rajan to find out what issues to discuss during the last visit to Tehran in the extraordinary meeting of the Kurdistan side.

On 22ⁿᵈ August 1988, the Party's political delegation, the PUK, the People's Party, the Communist Party of Iraq, and the Kurdistan Socialist Party all participated. The meeting discussed in detail the general situation in the region and Kurdistan. Another part of the meeting was dedicated to evaluating its work and activities. At the end of the meeting, the importance of the need for unity and side work for the sake of harmony and high interests of the people of Kurdistan were emphasized.

On 1ˢᵗ September 1988, we received a single branch message, relating to the claim that all parties in the Kurdistan Council (Hasha, YNK, People's Party, Hask) had decided to come to Iran because it could not be defended.

A few days later, Dr Rozh came to us on the 13ᵗʰ and 14ᵗʰ September 1988, after a phone call with Mr Hoshyar Zebari about the meeting that took place in Damascus on 11ᵗʰ September 1988. In the meeting it was decided in Damascus:

- The centre would be moved abroad to Damascus and Jalal Talabani would be in charge of Damascus's office and have a seal.
- Inside Kurdistan, Mr Masoud Barzani should be in charge of the council.
- Jalal Talabani and Dr Mahmoud Osman were also responsible for Arab-Islamic relations.
- Karim Ahmed would be head of council relations in Eastern Europe.

The Kurdistan Council met on 19ᵗʰ September 1988, with the following people present:

PDK - Masoud Barzani, Fazil Mirani, Dr Rozh Nuri Shawais;
Hasha - Abu Hakmat; Patriotic Union of Kurdistan - Jabbar
Farman; Hask - Qadir Jabari were all present at it.

In order to follow up on previous decisions and set up a new
and appropriate program, the Political Leadership of the Kurdistan
Council began its work on 20th September 1988, in the presence of:

Party: Masoud Barzani, Dr Rozh Nuri Shawais, Fazil
Mirani, Farhanso Hiri
PUK - Nawshirwan Mustafa, D. Fuad Masum, Jabbar
Farman
Hasha - Abu Farouq, Abu Hakmat
Hask - Rasul Mamand, Qadir Jabari
Party Gall - Sami Abdulrahman
Pasok - Lieutenant Shwan.

Once again, on 22nd September 1988, they met and several
decisions were made, including the presentation of notes abroad.

On 21st October 1988, Rafat Mala and Hama-Tofiq came to us.
That same night, Jalal Talabani called me and talked about the
situation on the council and about the establishment of an Iraqi
council. He said that if it is was possible for it to be formed inside
Iraq, it will be easily done outside.

On 12th November 1988, another political leadership meeting
began with the presence of:

PDK - Masoud Barzani, Ali Abdullah, D. Rozh Nuri
Shawais, Fazil Mirani, Farhanso Hiri

PUK - Dr Fuad Masum, Jabbar Farman, Kosrat Rasul
Hasha - Abu Farouq, Abu Hakmat
Hask - Rasul Mamand, Teacher Saad Abdullah, Qadir Jabari
People's Party - Sami Abdulrahman
Pasok - Ahmed Hardi, Lieutenant Shwan

A detailed discussion took place on the Iraqi side and was agreed upon.

On 12th August 1990, the Kurdistan Council meeting in Rajan began its work. Although I was invited to a meeting in Kermanshah on 10th August 1990, I also attended with Nawshirwan Mustafa and Muhammad Shakali who were also invited to participate in the meeting. However, they didn't meet. Participants in the meeting were:

PDK - Masoud Barzani, Dr Jarjis Hassan, Masoud Salihi, Franso Hhiri
PUK - Abdullah, Hassan Kwestani
Hasha - Karim Ahmed, Mala Hassan, Rawand
Hask - Teacher Saad Abdullah, Teacher Amin
People's Party - Majid Rizgari, Pala, Hoshang.
Pasok participated but they didn't send an official representative.

The negotiations and discussions were detailed and even intensified, and the views of the Communist Party and the People's Party were strange, and they were tough on Saddam. Finally, it was decided by a total vote:

1. The executive committee's statement should be made within the framework of media policy.
2. Have softness if the regime shows softness.
3. Do not engage in military activity.
4. Outside, the committees will meet and the instructions of the council applied.

Between19th and 20th September 1990, at the official invitation of the French government, a delegation of the Kurdistan Council, including Jalal Talabani, Muhsin Dzaie, Sami Abdul-Rahman and Dr Mahmoud Osman, visited Paris, the capital, and met with senior French officials. This is the first time the French government had formally invited the Kurdish delegation. The invitation was after the French ambassador's home in Kuwait was raided It seems that France wanted to do this to show Iraq that it could take advantage of the Kurds to retaliate.

On 1st December 1990, an enemy force, consisting of the 507th Battalion of the 47 Brigade, attacked the Kurdistan Council forces in the Bole area. Thanks be to God, after a heavy battle, their attack was destroyed. As a result, nine soldiers were killed, seven wounded and eight captured by council forces. Some military equipment fell into the hands of the peshmerga.

The Kurdistan Council played a big and significant role in defending the Kurdish nation internally and at the same time in delivering the legitimate voice of the people.

Our nation did not hesitate with decision-making centres, the international community, foreign public opinion, and the strengthening of harmony and unity among the parties in Kurdistan and even Iraqis. If it had not been for the Kurdistan Council, the disaster of 1988 would have been bigger than that of 1975 by many orders of magnitude. It was bigger, but the existence of the Kurdistan Council, the unanimity of the parties within the council, and the protection of the unity of the Kurdish liberation movement, significantly reduced the effects of this disaster and made a great defence of the existence of our people, especially abroad.

CHAPTER 13

Khwakurk Battle

THE START OF the Iran-Iraq war opened up a great opportunity for the Kurdish people and the peshmerga forces, and much effort was made to take advantage of the opportunity and situation in terms of spreading bigger blows and widening the areas under the control of the revolution. We wanted to do this without being a part, or party to the war, and, to a large extent, we succeeded in this. Our people's struggle had nothing to do with it because before the Iraq-Iran war broke out, the struggle of the Kurdish People already existed. Peshmerga's activities merely continued. The start of the Gulan revolution and the launch of several activities against regime bases and strongholds in different parts of Kurdistan are evidence of this fact, and the epic of Khwakur is another living indicator of the fact that our people's struggle continued during and after the war and will continue until our people achieve their national rights.

Of course, in such a situation, it was necessary for us to show Iran, Iraq, and the whole world that our struggle was not related to the war between these two countries. This was despite the fact that the cessation of the war between the two sides had a major impact on the situation in the region in general, as Iraq was more involved in taking advantage of its forces and capabilities against the peshmerga.

After evaluating and considering the regime's attacks on our Party bases and headquarters and all the National Forces of Kurdistan and Iraq, particularly after the end of the war between Iraq and Iran, a decision was made to endure and resist at a meeting of our Central Committee on 20th July 1988. For this purpose, the decision of patience and struggle was made, and I visited the front line of war, the battles of Khwakurk and Khrena, and put in place a strong plan to defend the nation, and the national rights and goals of our people according to our abilities. Allah gave us a chance and a firm belief. Peshmerga Sherasa faced an attack by enemy forces and stood at the frontlines of defending the people and their legitimate rights. I have to say, unity and harmony between the people and peshmerga is an important factor that supported the impact of the peshmerga's defence and success.

The support of refugees from the peshmerga and the active participation of volunteers on the battlefield led to the recording of Khwakurk's historical epic. The peshmerga's sacrifice and selflessness reached a level where there was competition to participate in battles and attacks on the enemy. Khwakurk's epic in that respect was a record of independence and a historical epic in the struggle of the Kurdish people for their rights.

The epic of Khwakurk, one of the points of pride and sovereignties in the history of the Kurdish people, was a symbol of the defence and independence of the revolution and the struggle of our people.

Another reason for Khwakurk's patience, of course, was to defend a large number of our group that intended to reach the borders; and the Ba'athist regime tried to reach the border and prevent people from being rescued, so we decided to defend it in order to save the people. This also proved the fact that the struggle of our nation and the war between Iraq and Iran has nothing to do with one another.

In Khwakurk's epic, the loyalty, beliefs, and sacrifices of the peshmerga were the reason for the regime's massive and huge army's failure, because it wanted the peshmerga to participate in the attacks in a way, even occasionally. If they had not participated in the fighting, the peshmerga would have been worried.

The situation after the Iraq-Iran war was clear. Iraq survived the eight-year war and considered itself a success, but the economic, military, political, and social situation that followed the war in Iraq was showing signs of major changes. Iraq perceived to need to turn its face to another place and wage yet another war. At the time, Turkey was strong, Syria had an army, and the only place Iraq thought to have a weak spot was Kuwait. They did what they thought they had to do, so big changes took place with the invasion of Kuwait.

In Khwakurk, the peshmerga fulfilled their sacred duty and destroyed the myth of the regime's forces and armies, preventing regime forces from accessing the border triangle and averting the people from crossing the border; those who intended to reach Iran all escaped and were hit hard by regime forces. After that, the coming of the winter season made it difficult to stay at those heights, so we decided to end the war.

In light of the decision to meet the Central Committee, on 21st July 1988, we went to Shno, on the 22nd July 1988, to be closely aware of and monitor the frontlines of the war and to get closer to our brave peshmerga. We arrived at Khrena and Nazdardakh; Zaeem Ali was appointed as a commander for Khrena and Nazdardakh.

The regime's attacks on Khwakurk area, which is located in the north of Erbil governorate and consists of less than 150 square kilometers, began.

On 22nd July 1988, Hamrin's peshmerga attacked the regime forces that had descended by helicopter on Mount Shakew the previous day. After a heavy battle, the entire force was destroyed and three people were captured by our forces. A brave peshmerga named Hassan Samad was injured.

On 24th July 1988, we were in Shno providing supplies and preparations for the war fronts, and enemy movements continued on Mount Shakew and Sarsol. At 10:30 am on 27th July 1988, the enemy launched a major attack under the name of Tukukult Alialla, which took place on the side of the road, located at Shekhanok Heights. A bad incident occurred in the area, without anyone feeling the enemy was in the area, and a civilian named Mustafa Salih and his 12-year-old son, Omar, were arrested and taken away. The peshmerga then attacked the regime's forces and defeated the enemy, severely attacked them, and captured 24 people, four of whom were officers.

Unfortunately, Ibrahim Zahir and Fatah Osman Argoshi were martyred in the fighting in Musaka organization along with a pesh-merga in branch one. The enemy forces that came to the area consisted of the Third Regimental Force, the 2nd Brigade of the Special Iraqi Force and an independent regiment of the Third Division.

The previous day, Saeed Baqir Tabatabaei, commander of the Nasr-e-Ramazan headquarters, and several Hezbollah guards and gunmen visited Gali Rash to move their headquarters into Iranian territory. They had no information that the road had been blocked by Iraq, so when they left, they were ambushed by Iraqi forces. All were arrested and shot there. When the peshmerga destroyed the Iraqi forces and expelled them from the area, they brought back the bodies of the dead and handed them over to the headquarters.

According to peshmerga forces, more than 100 Mughirs had been killed in the aftermath of the war. Once again, on 29th July 1988, the enemy tried to advance, but after a heavy battle they were re-captured, and three soldiers were captured. One was Abdul Khaliq, named after the Iraqi Special Forces officer in the captives. Zaeem Ali was leading this attack.

It is worth mentioning that after its defeat, the regime used chemical weapons three times on 3rd August 1988, through a Pilates PC7 plane in Shno city, while several peshmerga bases and the headquarters in Gadar, Shno, and Khwakurk were bombed, injuring 60 peshmerga.

On 1st August 1988, Lieutenant Colonel Yaqub was chosen to be in charge of the force in order to organize and strengthen the refugee force. Then, two days later, Barzan's forces warned us via a communication that at 8 pm on August 3, 1988, the enemy had attacked their area.

The enemy's attack on the Khwakurk front continued until 7th August 1988, and the peshmerga resisted patiently, resulting in three Mughirs in the lower part of Mount Shakew being captured.

From the Gali Rash and Daryasor area there were successes for the regime, while Hezbollah guards and groups in Khwakurk detonated explosives and military equipment and fled, reinforcing the weight of the entire war on the peshmerga of the PDK and the

Communist Party. They remained with our forces, but all the other parties left the area and they didn't defend anything.

After taking the necessary measures in the Nazdarakh area, we knew that we should also visit the west of Khwakurk, for this purpose, at 4 pm on 8th August 1988, in the first step of the people we were on our way to the Bardi Sheka.

On 8th August 1988, the enemy launched a massive attack on Mosulok and the Shekhanok Front. After a fierce battle, the enemy reached Parawa and only one stage remained to reach Shekhanok, which would have allowed them to completely dominate Shekhan and Sipar. It was 9th August 1988, when Khanamir came to us through Dr Saeed and the Barzani forces to find out what to do with the families who remained in their homes and what their fate would be. It was clear that apart from their escape to Iran, they had no other way.

On the evening of 10th August 1988, I went and visited the forces there and spoke to them. They were happy with the connection. At 3pm of the same day, the enemy attacked the eastern front of the Melazard. Thanks be to God, the first lieutenant general, Hassan Abdullatif Sultan, commander of the 3rd Brigade of the 68th Special Forces, was wounded at the hands of the peshmerga, and later died of his injuries.[4] The peshmerga were safe and unharmed in the fighting. Rebaz organization and Jarjis Hussein had a role in this story of both vision and influence.

---

[4] After being wounded by the peshmerga, he was transferred to the back of the war for treatment by the peshmerga. He asked the peshmerga "What you are doing to me?" and they said "We would go to the doctor to treat the wound." He said, "No, kill me and kill anyone you have captured. You are satisfied with these mountains and this difficult life. You are still treating them, and kill me." from 5 pm to 11 pm He was alive and then died of severe injuries.

On the evening of 10ᵗʰ August 1988, a large commando force descended by ten helicopters from an area called Doltarshin, but the brave peshmerga forces did not give them a chance, and when the night came, they stalked them like hunters. In the battle, commando forces, numbering about 150 soldiers, were eliminated and none escaped. The one who was killed was captured by the peshmerga. By this, the enemy's forces were severely attacked, and the enemy's morale was destroyed, and the peshmerga's spirits were much higher and stronger and gave our forces more hope.

After this victory, Lieutenant Colonel Ya'qub was appointed commander of the Kurdistan Council, and Sergeant Darwesh and Hamid Argoshi were appointed assistants. On this occasion, I spoke to him and expressed his happiness in the decision.

On 11ᵗʰ August 1988, it was the second time I went up and spoke to all the forces. The status of the fronts was as follows:

Karokh and the September 11 organisation, led by Ahmed Malaswar, were in Brimshka and Seri Korawa, bravely confronted Kurdish traitors in a battle. In some places, Jash (Kurdish traitors) were forced to withdraw. Muhammed Chawshin was martyred in the Karokh organisation (his father was martyred in 1974), and three peshmerga were wounded, one of whom was Hussein Stoni. Fighting in all areas was fierce, leaving me proud and surprised by the patience and defence of the peshmerga.

On the evening of 11ᵗʰ August 1988, Jash again attacked the Bekas Front (Jarjis), despite the heavy bombardment of peshmerga bases, but the body of a Jash was badly destroyed. On 11ᵗʰ August 1988, Goraz and the 15ᵗʰ peshmerga organization with Rasul Faqe arrived at the battlefield to help the forces.

On 11th August 1988, I sent Haji Saeed Shirkan to the border to prepare and take necessary measures to meet with Turks.

On 12th August 1988, Sadiq and Salih returned, and fighting continued fiercely over Corawa. The Jashs could not be expelled. We had an intensive discussion with friends Dr Rozh Nuri Shawais, Mr Fazil Mirani and Dr Jarjis Hassan about Osman and Fatah's letters, which were specific to discussions with the regime. it was decided to respond positively, or we would send it, or send them and we suggested that direct contact be arranged immediately. On 12th August 1988, in order to go to war, about 80 national defence soldiers came to them.

No one went to the national defence force to ask for this, and it was a pleasure that they volunteered. Of course, the people and helped the frontlines well and had a significant impact.

On 12th August 1988, I saw Abu Faruq[5], confused and worried. During the conversation, I promised them that we would do what we could to help them, for however long it took.

There was a purpose:

1. Some of their friends were near us.
2. We would provide a place near us to stay and rest.
3. To cooperate when necessary and in the possibility of withdrawal.
4. In Qamishlo, they should be helped to come and go.
5. Qasmlu sent news to someone to be seen, but there was no chance of going, because the area was blocked.
6. The national interests were discussed in detail and stated that if there was even a chance, it was good enough.

---

[5] Abu Faruq (Omar Ali Sheikh) was a member of the Hasha political bureau.

At the same time as the heavy fighting that took place at 4 am on 13th August 1988, on the frontlines of the Seri Korawa, many of our people arrived in Zehir from Iraq. It was a great battle, and there was a battle in many places. Thank God, the Jash (Kurdish traitors) were defeated. Although we didn't get the details of Jash's damage, according to the news that came to us was a great loss to the enemy.

On 14th August 1988, when the forces of branches 3 and 4 arrived with Saeed Salih and Qadir Qadir, they had high morale and were strong. The arrival of these heroic peshmerga was promising, and the heroic commander Nasreddin Abed Hawrami, sparked feelings of excitement for a Kurdish victory, and was such that everyone began dancing including the commander, who led the people in their joyous response. That feeling came because, when the peshmerga faced battle spontaneously, despite their courage and patience, another force suddenly arrived to better defend and strengthen the barricades.

On 14th August 1988, the enemy attacked the Kani Rash, Kharwan and Siru at the Barzan Force Border, but were destroyed. In Khwakurk area, the enemy tried to win again, but with will and power from the arm of the peshmerga was badly destroyed.

This victories came one after the other, and it is indeed a matter of pride and appreciation. This patience and heroism of the peshmerga has shown throughout the history of the Kurdish liberation movement. In that regard, on 15th August 1988, the Halabja committee forces reached Khwakurk for the purpose of supporting their cooperation. We welcomed them warmly.

Throughout the offensive, the enemy often attacked the peshmerga continuously and tried to withdraw from the peshmerga, but fortunately, was destroyed. At 2 pm on 15th August 1988, the enemy unexpectedly bombarded all peshmerga points for two hours. The bombardment was so great that I expected a lot of casualties among the peshmerga forces. I was so eager for them and couldn't believe the excitement of their arrival. After the bombardment and at 4 pm, the enemy launched a ground attack.

The brave peshmerga came from all over and the enemy suffered a severe defeat. The bravery of the peshmerga was rare there, and this situation looked like a miracle. Using the field phone, I spoke to all the organizations, and they were courageous and hopeful. They did not care about the enemy, and they were heroes. Thank God that our forces had only a few wounded, in response to 46 bodies to Iraqi forces and Jash (Kurdish Traitors).

On 16th August 1988, fighting on the Khwakurk front was fierce, but the morale of our forces was high. The next day, Shekho Sheruki and Hamo Mawlawari of Barzan's forces were wounded by the artillery, and the fighting continued fiercely. We hoped that with the support of God, the shoulders and arms of the peshmerga, the enemy was going to be defeated.

Hamid Afandi and 40 other peshmerga arrived with us and marched to the front lines on 18th August 1988, along with Azad Qaradaghi and Dr Rozh, Lieutenant Younis and Lieutenant Colonel Ya'qub. On 19th August 1988, the fighting intensified, and some of our brave peshmerga were martyred. Qadir Saeed Mustafa of branch three, Babarasul of branch four, and Abdulkhaliq Ahmed Saeed Khalani of the national defence were also martyred. The bombardment was so loud that the world seemed to be destroyed, and the thunderstorm shook the area. But at once, bombs balls fell to the ground together, and the area became consumed by flames.

Although the Iraq-Iran war officially stopped, on 20th August 1988, a fierce battle continued between our forces and the enemy. On the evening of 20th August 1988, we spoke to the forces; the voices of Saeed Salih and Hamid Afandi were heard.

It seemed that they had a belt-breaking blow to announce; it was revealed that the 702 Brigade of the 45th Division of the First Legion had been destroyed and several officers had been killed, including Colonel Mohammed Sagra, the second commander, the first lieutenant, Walid Ismail Amrsriya, and others. The next day, after all the successive defeats of the enemy, the previous heat and violence had broken out, and a helicopter was shot down. On 22nd August 1988, two of our peshmerga were injured by the bombardment. As well as another plane, the helicopter was targeted and fell behind the village of Shekhanok.

On 23rd August 1988, I spoke to many officials of the refugee and Hamrin forces and the leadership's organisations. Younis and Yaqub were present. The peshmerga's morale was very high and strong, and the pictures were videotaped by Masrour Barzani. The enemy's movements were active throughout the region, especially within the borders of branch one, and an enemy force had been sent to Sherwan. I spoke to Omar Osman about this.

On the night of 24th to 25th August 1988, the enemy attacked the Korawa front, but thank God their force was subdued after a fierce battle.

According to experience, whenever the Ba'athist regime suffered successive failures, it engaged in inhumane acts and did not give up on anything. Chemical weapons, deadly arms, are prohibited, but after each loss, they were used as they wished. On 25th August 1988, it was the same weapon and at six o'clock in the morning chemicals were used, carried by ten fighter planes.

They gassed the entire border of branch one:

1. The villages of Bargine, Zarrawa, and Dargala in the Duhok area.
2. Swar and Spindaria in Shekhan area.
3. The villages of Ekamale, Warmel, Garago, and Babir in Amedi area.
4. Sare Koke in Nerwa area.
5. The border of L.N. Gulan.
6. The Gara front on the Akre border.
7. Toka in Zakho area.
8. Gali Zeuka, Shan, branch one headquarters, and Goharze village.

A large number of civilians were martyred and many injured by the unnecessary crime of using chemical weapons, as they were in the areas attacked by the fighter planes. The enemy had created such a tragic situation, and there was a lot of fear and anxiety among the public. It was published that many people were very worried and went to Turkey's borders.

On 27th August 1988, Sergeant Naziz Muhammad Tahir Nazir Nerwai and Mullah Bahri Shukri Majid Dari were martyred in Zahir's shrine.

On the evening of 28th August 1988, as a result of the bombardment at the Charchal organization headquarters, there were five martyrs: Hazim Muhammad Shali, Jawhar Ali Shali, Ismail Yassin Stoni, Abdullah Haji Stoni and Asaad Chicho Yahya Drey. Greetings to their pure souls.

On the night of 28th 1988, a force belonging to the degime's 66th Brigade attacked peshmerga headquarters and barricades in the

Korava area. We defeated the enemy after a fierce battle and they were forced to withdraw. The enemy suffered great damage in the battle. Unfortunately, some brave peshmerga, Wali Haji Arif and Rahman Majid, were martyred in branch four, and Anwar Haji Osman was wounded.

On 30th August 1988, there was a fierce battle in Corawa, which began at 5 am and lasted until 4 pm The four-branch force played an effective and major role in destroying the enemy's attack. A peshmerga named Kaifi Hassan Bradosti was martyred and five others were wounded. The evening of the same day, Barzani forces climbed to the top of Corawa and replaced the forces of the fourth branch.

Unfortunately, at 4 pm on 4th September 1988, Ali Salim Topchi and Zorab Ghazi Argoshi, head of the Musaka organization, and Ahmed Muhammad Ahmed (police) were martyred. Ali Salim's martyrdom was a deep pain in his heart when he left us.

Martyr Ali Salim Bajluri, the general head of the Revolutionary Artillery, was a brave, courageous and fearless peshmerga who played a major and important role in the Gulan revolution, particularly in the field of heavy weapons and artillery.

The September revolution also showed great sacrifice and heroism.

On 4th September 1988, Zmnako (branch four) launched a heroic attack on the enemy in the Chamcabi area, which caused great damage to them. The fighting lasted forty-eight hours, and according to reports, the enemy's killed, and wounded soldiers were about 1,000. In return, two brave peshmerga, Hama Khan Amin and Faraidun Abdullah, were martyred. The martyrdom of these peshmerga has had a major impact on the war.

On the night of 3rd September 1988, Barzan's group evacuated the head of Corava and withdrew. At 7 am on 5th September 1988, Chawshin Khano, head of the Piran Organization, was martyred due to the bombardment and he joined the immortal caravan.

After assessing the situation of our forces, on 5th September 1988, we announced the withdrawal decision to Lieutenant Younis and Lieutenant Ali, which was made for a variety of different reasons and factors. Cold food and equipment were one of the reasons because it was difficult to deliver food and supplies. Unfortunately, at 9 pm on 4th September 1988, the brave peshmerga Jabbar Osman Mardan, belonging to the third branch, was martyred. Considering the reason and analysis of the situation properly, the programme of withdrawal started. At 10pm Lieutenant Younis sent me the news that their withdrawal was over.

On 6th September 1988, all the forces arrived and had a regular and successful withdrawal, and on 7th September 1988, we welcomed the third and fourth branch forces and thanked them for their patience and resistance. In these days there was a lot of media pressure on the regime.

The continued heroic patience of our PDK peshmerga on the Khwakurk frontline has become a unique story in the history of our nation. Also, the patience and sacrifice of the destruction of all the branches of our Party while facing all the chauvinistic attacks of the Iraqi regime over twenty years and which wanted to leave Kurdistan with the people and change our national and historical reality have been recorded.

From July 19th to 5th September 1988, regime forces launched dozens of widespread attacks on peshmerga positions and headquarters. Regime forces used all kinds of weapons they had available, including air bombs, heavy bombardments, and even the use of chemical weapons, which are prohibited under international law.

The results of the war and activities are as follows:

First, our forces; these forces participated in the defences:

The forces of the revolutionary leadership headquarters, the forces of the second, third and fourth branches of our Party, the Barzan forces, the refugee and national defence forces, and a peshmerga detachment of the Communist Party of Iraq that allied us.

Second, the regime forces that participated were:

The First Legion of the Iraqi Army. The Fifth Legion of the Army. More than thirty regiments of traitors (light regiments). More than five field artillery units and a large number of mortars. Three tanks. A large number of fighter planes and helicopters. Chemical weapons, used in Zarwa village and other places in the north of Khwakurk so that 63 peshmerga were injured.

Third, enemy losses: the regime's military units that have suffered the most:

1. Division 33 of the Fifth Legion.
2. Division 45 of the First Legion.
3. Division 35.
4. Division 18.
5. The 60th Brigade of the Eighth Special Forces.
6. Sixty-six brigades of special forces.
7. An independent Regiment of Iraqi Special Forces in the 33rd Division.
8. The 702th Infantry Brigade.

9. The 422nd Infantry Brigade.
10. The 120th Brigade of Iraqi Special Forces.
11. The Second Brigade of The Iraqi Special Forces.

Enemy casualties:

According to the information, the number of killed and wounded in the regime reached about 1,000, and the identities of 350 fell into the hands of the brave peshmerga; among the dead were several regime ranks whose identities were known.

Their known names are:

1. Major Muhammad Sagar Slom, 2nd Brigade Commander 722.
2. First Lieutenant Walid Ismail, Amersriya in the same regiment.
3. Lieutenant Abdulkarim Jaber Muhammad.
4. Lieutenant Muhammad Tuama.
5. Lieutenant Aziz Atiya Alawi.
6. Lieutenant Abdulhalim Mardan.
7. First Lieutenant Hassan Abdullatif Sultan, 60th Brigade and Eighth Special Forces.
8. First Lieutenant Muhammad Yassin Ali, 2nd Division of the 60th Brigade and the Eighth Special Forces

Regime captives:

A large number of captives fell into the hands of our peshmerga in soldiers and ranks as follows:

1. Second Lieutenant Hafiz Jasim Hamadi, Amrfasil in the first tribe of the 1st Regiment of Iraqi Special Forces, 33rd Division.

2. Second Lieutenant Ramham Muhammad Fathi, AmrFasil in the same Syria. 3. Second Lieutenant Samir Abud Wahid, AmrFasil in the same unit.

3. Second Lieutenant Muhammad Naji, Amrfasil of the 3rd Regiment/ 2nd Brigade of Iraqi Special Forces.

4. Second Lieutenant Abdulkhaliq Hammood, in the third regiment of the Shet Brigade and eight special forces.

Four helicopters were shot down and several others were damaged.

Fourth, achievements:

The achievements of our forces were as follows: more than 400 pieces of light and medium weaponry were captured. They also captured 35 RPGs, 18 field telephones and military communication devices, along with a large quantity of military equipment and masks.

Fifth, the damage of our forces:

28 brave peshmerga gave their lives to the country's territory and victories in the struggle against the regime's brutal attacks and the use of all kinds of weapons and fighting equipment, and 140 peshmerga were injured, some of them wounded by chemical weapons. These patient and heroic peshmerga reached the convoy of the immortals:

1. Hamid Shivi, a refugee force, was martyred on July 21, 1988.
2. Ahmed Taha Ismail Warmeli was martyred in branch one on July 27, 1988.
3. Fatah Osman Argoshi of musaka organization was martyred on July 27, 1988.

4. Ibrahim Zahir Pendroi was martyred in Musaka organization on July 27, 1988

5. Mam Ali of the Communist Party of Iraq was martyred on July 27, 1988.

6. Jamal Muhammad Amin of Karokh Organization was martyred on July 27, 1988.

7. Muhammad Chawshin was martyred in Karokh organization on August 12, 1988.

8. Qadir Saeed Mustafa was martyred in branch three on August 19, 1988.

9. BabaRasul Sheikh Salih was martyred in branch four on August 19, 1988.

10. Abdulkhaliq Ahmed Saeed in students union and a democratic youth of Kurdistan was martyred on August 19, 1988.

11. Hassan Khidir Akrayi, a refugee force, was martyred on August 24, 1988.

12. Nazir Muhammad Tahir, a refugee force, was martyred on August 27, 1988.

13. Mahla Bahri Shukri Majid of the Kurdistan Islamic Scholars Union was martyred on August 27, 1988.

14. Wali Haji Arif was martyred in branch four on August 28, 1988.

15. Rahman Majid was martyred in branch four on August 28, 1988.

16. Hazim Muhammad Shali was martyred in Charchal organization on August 28, 1988.

17. Jawhar Ali Shali was martyred in Charchal organization on August 28, 1988.

18. Ismail Yassin Hamid was martyred in Charchal organization on August 28, 1988.

19. Abdullah Haji Stoni was martyred in Charchal organization on August 28, 1988.

20. Asaad Chicho Yahya Dri was martyred in Charchal organization on August 28, 1988.

21. Kaifi Ahmed Bradosti was martyred in branch four on August 30, 1988.

22. Arif Haris Chuchani, from the Penjwin district committee, was martyred on September 3, 1988.

23. Ali Salim Bajluri, B. Shorsh Artillery, was martyred on September 4, 1988.

24. Zorab Ghazi Argushi, B. Musaka Organization, was martyred on September 4, 1988.

25. Hama Khan Amin was martyred in branch four on September 4, 1988.

26. Faraidun Abdullah was martyred in branch four on September 4, 1988.

27. Ahmed Muhammad Ahmed was martyred at the Revolutionary Artillery on September 4, 1988.

28. Chawshin Khanu, head of the Piran Organization, was martyred on September 5, 1988.

29. Jabbar Osman Mardan was martyred in branch three on September 5, 1988.

More than 140 brave and struggling peshmerga were injured in Khwakurk's historical epic.

The struggling and strong people, with strong beliefs, were always determined in special and sensitive times but when difficult situations appear they showed a positive and courageous attitude.

One of the great fighters was Qadir Saeed's brother, when Qadir Saeed, his brother, was martyred. He returned behind the line of war and handed the body to his friends and said to them, "He was my brother so far, but from now on he is your brother. Hurry to give me the bullets that I can deliver to my brothers in the front lines of the war, a stance that will forever be in history, I will not forget and will remain alive in my memories."

In Khwakurk's historical epic, friends Dr Rozh Nuri Shawis, Fazil Mirani, D. Jarjis Hassan, Lieutenant Ali, Lieutenant Babakir, Hamid Afandi, Said Salih, Qadir Qadir, Nasradin Abed, Lieutenant Younis Rozhbayani, Azad Qaradaghi, Dr Saeed Ahmed Nadir, Omar Osman and Lieutenant Colonel Yaqub participated in the attacks and activities against the Ba'athist revolutionary forces and played a significant role in supervising the frontlines. They fought and recorded the victories.

At the end of Khwakurk's historical epic and prosperity, such as appreciation and respect for the bravery, fearlessness, and bravery of the peshmerga, I presented a speech that read:

Brave peshmergas

After the end of the Iraq-Iran war, the regime put all its weight on Kurdistan and the peshmerga forces, and the regime's main goal was to seize and control the main traffic route of the branch one with the leadership and other areas, in order to completely cut off branch one and traffic was no longer on the route, so it began shelling the area very heavily, and then with artillery, they set the area on fire was bombarded, causing a difficult situation. The peshmerga were forced to do so. Rescuing the citizens who were trapped in the area, so we did our best in order to defeat the Ba'athist plan.

Of course, our war had nothing to do with the Iraq-Iran war, because our war was there even before the changes that took place in Iran and Iraq. The regime's situation was at its most weak, in a way that its forces were running away from responsibility and putting the responsibility on the other side. In order to avoid responsibility and war fronts, bribery and deception are visible among the regime's forces, it had developed.

Politically, Ba'athist dominance and prestige have been broken, which is more important to us than anything else, and it has been proved to the world that the PDK has its own independent decision.

Any nation in the world that has a peshmerga situation and against a force like the Ba'athist forces, not ten days, will not be defended even for two days as you have done, so we thank you and thank all the other friends in the organizations, in other forces, refugee forces, and all the brave peshmerga.

Our struggle is a legitimate struggle because the rights of our people have been violated by a dictatorial regime that does not believe in any principles or principles. Not only does he not believe in the rights of the Kurdish people, but they do not believe in human rights. All its goals are to prevent and destroy the Kurdish people and their country, so even though the regime's pressures are greater and our capabilities and capabilities are

*low, we will carry out our duties properly with that faith, and
we believe if we face the enemy, and I'm sure we'll succeed.*

*But we need to know the truth, that we must rely on ourselves
and our people. The great danger is when we face a political setback because it will be difficult to get up. Thank God I can say
that we are politically strong, whether internationally or internally, and we have a very strong stance, and this patience has
strengthened this stance tenfold. Therefore, we will rely on God
to not suffer and fail anymore, but there are certainly so many
loyal, brave and courageous peshmerga who feel responsible and
know what duties and responsibilities they have today. What's
true today is the day that we say: "Kurdistan, or we die".*

*The situation is hopeful, there is no danger, and the decision is
that we will defend and rely on God. Even if we die in patience
and defence, it is much prouder to be humiliated and wan-
dering in the streets of Europe, or in that city, this city, and
on the other side. The only way in front of us is to achieve our
goals, whether by force, or by negotiation, and the only way
is for our policy to be true. We will defend and not surrender
to the oppression of our enemies. We will achieve our goal.*

*Of course, it is impossible for a war to end easily after eight
years of nearly one million deaths, injuries, and missing
persons. Stopping the Iraq-Iran war does not mean the collapse and destruction of the PDK peshmerga forces. The
PDK's policy is a clear policy towards all the hardships,
and now that this agreement has been reached, the results*

216

and consequences are not clear, as I mentioned, it is not easy for a war to escape after eight years and the loss of one million people easily. I am sure that after a short time, many more things will become clear, the events that are happening, the changes that are taking place, or the situation in general, the internal situation in Iraq and the changes that are expected to happen, or if this patience and defence continue, the enemy will be forced to think about their situation.

In any case, our goals are clear, and we will not give up on them, and whatever is done to this holy land is incomplete. The struggle will certainly not be without martyrdom. The sanctity of this land is that thousands of people have been martyred for it, otherwise it would not have been so.

We claim to be lawyers for Barzani's path, holding the Flag of Barzani and PDK, of course when we raise these slogans

We must accept all hardships and be patient.
Thank God for being a good and proud defence.
God Bless you all and never give up.

In these wars, these regime's military units were destroyed and disappeared permanently:

The 2nd Iraqi Special Forces Brigade, the Sixty-Eight Special Forces Brigade, and the forces, which will not be reorganized for a long time, have been severely damaged: the 2nd Iraqi

Special Forces Regiment, the Independent Regiment of Iraqi Special Forces, the 421st Brigade and the 121st Brigade.

According to local information, the number of regime casualties in the fighting reached 1,000.

We would like our problem to be resolved peacefully, and a statement has been issued, and all sides have agreed on the steps that need to be taken, but this situation has been proven, and the fact that the PDK is in all parties played a role more in patience and defence.

A few days ago, a political leadership meeting was held and a memorandum was sent to the UNITED NATIONS and all organisations and countries.

The regime has reached zero point in terms of the internal situation, and internationally it is under enormous pressure, it is about to develop a kind of hysteria, so we have a strong political stance and there is success.

A statement was issued today on Baghdad Radio, which, of course, is a sign of the regime's weakness, not its strength, and we are doing our research.

Whatever happens, it is necessary for us to give thanks to Allah day and night. To be thankful to God, is more import-ant than anything else, and for he has given us strength, faith, and patience. Believe me, women are braver and more

*competitive than men. I don't know how much they are aware
of the sacrifice and selfishness of our nation. Today a saw a
woman who only had a thousand Tomen (Iranian currency),
and I will offer this to the war front to buy a pair of shoes for a
peshmerga, and the mother of a martyr came to help her. She
presented her martyrs pension to the Pershmega's war front.*

*Once again, I welcome you warmly, and I wish you vic-
tory. Indeed, my heart has brightened with your sight
and my eyes have become clear. I am very pleased to meet
you all, and wish you all have victory and to be safe.*

And do not give up, and rely on God, the victory is always Holy.

On this occasion, the PDK political office bureau published a statement, below:

Dear citizens,

*During this great war, the regime has launched a massive
attack on the areas of Duhok and Mosul provinces with the
participation of nearly 100,000 soldiers, tanks, artillery,
various planes, helicopters, and the use of weapons Chemical
scattered, the regime carried out genocide in these attacks,
destroying and destroying villages that have displaced more
than 100,000 people to the Borders of Turkey and Iran. All
of them were unable to break the will to defend the People
of Kurdistan, inside Kurdistan and on the frontlines of
the war, the regime has tried to be a nationless country.*

The brave peshmerga challenged this policy of the regime that targeted the annihilation of our nation and its liberation movement, our patient peshmerga have made Kurdistan the hell of the enemies, and in the near future the regime will face a group of internal hardships and the Iraqi people will become the fuel of war and its wrong policies Ba'athist regime.

Dear Regime soldiers,

We will not oppose you, and we will only defend our existence and our people and protect our land against the genocide and destruction that you see as the regime has fought in Kurdistan. This is a good opportunity to change our minds about the events of the past years because they are killing your brothers, Iraqi's being killed by Iraqis. The regime has imposed a special situation on us that continues to kill, terrorize and intimidate all Iraqi peoples, Arabs, Kurds, different components, and the genocide of thousands of war survivors and the opposition has been troubled by the Iraqi people.

Soldiers and officers! We call on you to join the ranks of the Iraqi revolutionaries in order to overthrow the regime, freedom, democracy, peace in Iraq, and autonomy in Kurdistan, and to restore the climate of brotherhood and love to our country, instead of war, killing, and intimidation, the disaster that has caused the ongoing civil war.

Dear people of Iraq! Liberals and Democrats in Arab countries...

The policy of bloodshed and anti-humanity of the regime will harm the historical brotherhood of Kurds and Arabs, this stage needs unification and there is a great duty of salvation and nationalism to confront imperialism, racism and old-fashioned ideals.

O brave people of Kurdistan, on the 27th anniversary of the National Revolution,

In 1961, under the leadership of the leader of our nation's liberation movement, immortal Barzani, we defend the epic of Khwakurk in the spirit of patience and struggle among our people and are ready to give more sacrifices until victory.

We will continue to endure and strive in new ways in this new situation, and we still have great duties and goals ahead of us to achieve them. Our war is a just and legitimate war, that requires patience, continuity, and patience, and continued endurance will lead to our people's trust in its legitimacy and just problems, and will increase the world's political and media importance. Violence does not solve the Kurdish issue, but complicates it, as stated in the statement of the previous meeting of our Central Committee on July 20. For the first time, a peaceful and stable climate has emerged between the Iraqi opposition in order to unify the abilities and expand the activities against the dictatorship regime and its oppression war in Kurdistan and welcome this right and national direction for the purpose of the diversity of the Iraqi Kurdistan Front in all fields.

We wish immortality and pride for the martyrs of
Khwakurk epic and the hope of safety for the wounded.

The immortality and pride of the martyrs of the regime's
attacks on Badinan salute our people, tens of thousands of
refugees who have taken refuge in Turkey and Iran in the
past weeks died and disgraced for the attacks of the rac-
ist chauvinist regime long live our party led by Mr Masoud
Barzani greetings from the Iraqi Kurdistan side.

Of course, success is for the struggle of the Iraqi people for
democracy, freedom, and peace for a free Iraq in which it
will provide real autonomy for Kurdistan and cultural and
administrative rights for national and religious structures.

September 5, 1988 Political Bureau
Kurdistan Democratic Party – Iraq[6]

During the Khwakurk war, some PKK militants were in the area, but they disappeared shortly afterward. It was not known what happened to them and where, why and how they went, or where they hid.

The Khwakurk war had a significant resonance in the international media, with London radio reporting on Masoud Barzani's speech: "The war is still in Erbil province, in northern Iraq, among the fighters. The Kurdistan Democratic Party and the Iraqi army are continuing."

---

[6] See Document number 6

The Associated Press agency also said: Iraqi forces, after they fought with Iran, returned their military movements to the Kurdish areas and fired chemical weapons, poisonous gas used in the war against the Kurdish people.

On 10th August 1988, the Tehran-based newspaper Resalat published an article about the Khwakurk war: Kurds in northern Iraq are struggling to rescue refugees and wounded from the brutal regime attacks. The Kurdistan Democratic Party , in the north of the country; challenged the regime's aggression swells.

On 10th August 1988, Voice of America radio described the Khwakurk war as follows: "There was a war between our forces and regime forces in north-eastern Iraq," said Massoud Barzani. "Gulf affairs investigators say the Kurds may be able to continue their struggle even though the Iraq-Iran war has stopped."

The story of Khwakurk, the neglected and forgotten position of the Kurds in general, and the Kurdistan Democratic Party in particular, has been brought back to the field after eight years of war, genocide, chemical weapons, and Anfal. This resurgence came at a time when, after eight years of bloody and destructive war, the Kurdish national issue could be marginalized once and for all, and after Khwakurk, which was intended to cleanse and cleanse, the issue between the enemies Iran and Iraq will not only remain trapped but will be destroyed.

On August 14th 1988, from Khwakurk in a forgotten and distant triangle, I wanted to reach the ears of the world, Iran and Iraq, which were two sides of an eight-year war against each other: We, the Kurds, are in struggle and success, meaning we are alive, we are here, on the land of our ancestors.

Khwakurk, 1988 during Khwakurk battle

Khwakurk , branch four 1988, during Khwakurk battle

Khwakurk, 1988 during Khwakurk battle

Khwakurk, 1988 during Khwakurk battle

Khwakurk, 1988 during Khwakurk battle

1988 during Khwakurk battle

During the excellent news of significant suppression of Peshmarga, 1988 Khwakurk battle

1988 during Khwakurk battle

1988 during Khwakurk battle

1988 during Khwakurk battle – Branch three

1988 during Khwakurk battle – Branch three

September 1988, the family of the martyrs of the Khwakurk battle

1988- Khwakurk battle, a few captured soldiers of the Iraqi regime

1988- Khwakurk battle, some identifications of the dead soldiers of the regime

CHAPTER FOURTEEN

The organized crimes of The Iraqi governments against the Kurdish people

The policy of relocation and Arabization of Kurdistan

THROUGHOUT THE IRAQI state's life, the policy of genocide, relocation and changing Kurdistan's demographics. These efforts, to dismantle the Kurdish people, have become a stable and unchanging basis in Baghdad's successive government programmes outside all human rights laws, regulations and documents. All these policies and procedures go to the international crime cell against humanity, genocide, and dissolving nations.

International laws, regulations and documents on human rights have clearly defined crimes committed against ethnic groups and different peoples by the ruling nation. In the definition of a contract to prevent genocide and punish this crime, genocide is described as follows:

> *The intentional annihilation of a people, ethnic group,*
> *racial or religious group. This destruction is a complete*
> *extermination, of a part of people related to a group, or*
> *a nation, or a severe blow to safety and health. the body,*
> *or soul of this nation, as well as a separation for the pur-*
> *pose of dissolving, or cleansing a generation, emigration*
> *and relocation of the children of this group, or its people.*

In article 2 of this treaty, the forms of this genocide are discussed as follows:

- Killing members of the group.
- Issuing a severe blow to health and safety the group.
- Imposing a situation, or a deliberate quality to this group
  for physical destruction, to cause complete destruction, or
  to destroy part of the group.
- Imposing a status and taking specific measures to prevent
  the coherence of the group.
- Forced migration and forced transfer of children from this
  group to another group.

According to this document, the groups that can be subject to
genocide are:

National groups: a minority living under the control of an
independent state, which differs from most of their surrounding
society, to protect its existence, such as national, religious and
language feelings. The national group consists of people who
share national origins, but may have chosen another country to

live in. That is why the nation is a sign of political power and the right to individuals.

Ethnic groups: a people, or ethnicity, is a human group that has common biographical, social, linguistic, historical, and cultural elements. Of course, separating an ethnic group is not an easy task. That's why some of the organizers of the articles and the resolutions don't see a difference between these two words, and some of them say that functionally, an ethnicity can be a national group, or a small group of national groups and its nationality.

Ancestry groups: small groups of humans who have common physical characteristics and opportunities for psychological development. The word ancestry, or race, means its biography and the purpose of this word is to categorise the various physical characteristics and images among humans that are descendants of ancestors and who have inherited their genes.

Religious group: This being a group of people who follow a common spiritual belief and ideology. Religious followers who have a set of special actions showing unity of opinion and belief between them but are easily separated from the followers of other religions and will be recognised as such.

Sectarian and religious groups are also those people who are members of this sect, religion, or form of worship in the same way and have common beliefs and ideologies. Article 3 of the treaty states that the following actions deserve some form of punishment:

- Genocide
- Plotting for genocide but not instigating this directly
- Giving direction and publicity to the genocide
- The beginning of genocide
- Direct participation in or deputising others to commit genocide.

The official documents about Arabization in Kurdistan show that Iraq's policy worked in two directions: the first by importing Arabs by distributing land to them, and the other by transferring and expelling the Kurdish population in consideration of the regime's decisions to change demographics and reduce the number of Kurds in Kurdistan Region.

Point 100 of the UN document, the Report of the Human Rights Committee in 103, says: "The most dangerous misbehaviour against the Kurdish people was that in an orderly and systematic manner, but Kurdish families were executed due to their involvement in disputes and civil unrest, and chaos in public."

Kurdistan's Arabization policy was implemented in four main stages:

First stage: 1869 to 1914

This phase began before the establishment of the Iraqi state, since Madhat, King of Baghdad's governor, intended to carry out a number of reforms, one of which was the resettlement of Iraqi Arab tribes. The Arab tribes of Iraq were searching for grazing areas, fertile land, and pasture, and so crossed the border as defined during the Ottoman period after the invasion of Kurdistan and Iraq making

Arabs the border of Sharazur state. The natural border between Arab tribes and Kurdish tribes, was Mount Hamrin.

Second stage: 1925 to 1958

This stage includes the whole of the King of Iraq's reign. At this stage, several areas such as Hawija, Jalawla, Mandali and Badra, and part of Mosul and Qaraj were Arabized.

Between 1933 and 1934, to quell the Barzan uprising, Iraqi and British forces were attacked and destroyed, only in the areas of Barozh, Mzori, Sherwan, 79 villages were destroyed. Out of a total of 2,382 houses, 136 houses were burned and destroyed, resulting in 6% being obliterated.

Third stage: 1958 to 1963

Although only a short time period elapsed, some areas between Zummar and Shingal and the Iraq-Syria border were Arabized.

Fourth stage: 1963 to 1987

This was the most dangerous stage for the Kurdish people, because this policy was implemented extensively and swiftly and many military and financial capabilities were allocated and implemented in many stages and periods. In the summer of 1961, Abdul-Karim Qasim's regime attacked Kurdistan and more than half of the Iraqi army was engaged in an attack on the people of Kurdistan, killing nearly 3,000 people, most of them civilians, over a year and a half. More than 100,000 refugees fled into the mountains, and a 150 villages and cities were destroyed.

In 1963, after the February coup, the Ba'athist regime immediately began Arabizing the Debs area, and on June 9, 1963, declared a general decree against the Kurdish people and subsequently destroyed hundreds of villages.

In 1974, the Iraqi army's attack on the Kurdish people began, and the regime began to fire on and destroy Kurdistan, killing thousands of people in Kurdish cities and villages. In 1975, after the collapse of the Kurdish movement, the relocation of the Kurdish people to the bottom of Iraq had begun.

20,000 Kurds were moved in Zil military vehicles and trucks. In November 1975, the German-Guttingen Support Group, along with the Human Rights Group in the Netherlands, said: "The number of deportees has reached 200,000, 160 villages have been destroyed, and 25,000 Yezidi Kurds had been annihilated. They were transferred from Shingal."

In 1976, regime institutions began to confiscate and burn books on Kurdish history, and there was a prohibition of Kurdish history in schools, while relocation and Arabization continued until the end of 1976. Nearly 300,000 people were forcibly deported to southern Iraq, reaching 700,000 by 1979. The relocation and attacks included 1,222 villages in Diyala, Sulaymaniyah, Erbil, Kirkuk, Duhok and Mosul, which were evacuated. In addition, the border villages Iraq and Iran were destroyed.

In Khanaqin district, from 1975 to 1976, approximately 154 villages and 9,340 families, were relocated to the central district of Khanaqin, Maidan district, Qoratu district, Jalawla district.

Barzani, like other Kurdistan citizens, had a bitter and long experience with forced relocation and emigration. Barzan was subject to burning and destruction more than 16 times, and more than eight or nine times the whole area was destroyed, and became living evidence of the attempts of the government to cleanse and wipe out all Barzani citizens.

The dissolution of the Barzani has a long historical background, for example:

- Nafirhami, father of Al-Ali's Istanbuli against Sheikh Abdul-Salam Barzani in 1907, after his national meeting and the attack on Mohammed Fazil Daghestani.
- In the early 1920s, Barzani and Barzan areas were heavily and severely attacked by British joint forces and the Baghdad authorities at the time. As a result, nearly 400 Barzani families were forced to leave their homes and homeland, during a very difficult winter, and relocate to Turkey.
- In 1945, a significant number of Barzani were forced to go to eastern Kurdistan as a result of fierce attacks in their area and reside in the cities and villages of that part of Kurdistan. About 1,500 Barzani died due to the lack of health services, the poor environment and the lack of a suitable place to live and rest. Most of them were children, elderly men and women.
- After their return to southern Kurdistan, they settled in the town of Diana and were surrounded by military razor wire. After a while, they were transferred to different parts of Iraq.
- Even the behaviour of the Soviet authorities, at the time, with the Barzani can be counted as a way of trying to destroy them collectively, because 500 people were divided in a vast country where they were deprived of the needs of life.

8th November, 1975, was a dangerous day in Kurdistan, as the Ba'athist authorities began to carry out one of their most dangerous plans during the policy of relocation, destruction and Arabization of Kurdistan's territory. The plan was to kill or permanently remove the Barzani in Iraq (in their opinion), to initiate the relocation and emigration of Barzani to southern Iraq and consequently to reside in the plains and the dusty deserts of the south, which were as follows:

- On Saturday, 8th November 1975, a large Ba'athist regime force arrived in Barzan village to relocate Barzani, the first village to be relocated after the 1975 collapse.
- On Sunday, 9th November 1975, people and residents of the villages of Barzan, Hasna, Hasnaka, Hanfandaka, Bana, Hamdla, Razian, Alayan, Baze, Balanda and a part of the population of Bele were transferred to southern Iraq and to the Nafar community no. 2 in Qadisiya province (Diwaniya).
- On Monday, 10th November 1975, residents of the villages of Bele, Rezan and Asta were organized into southern Iraq and settled in the same forced community.
- On Tuesday, 11th November 1975, people from the villages of Pirasal, Shanadar, Saku, Shakafeta and Soranke were moved to the southern plains and made to reside in Jahish district, Community No. 3.
- On 14th November 1975, the other part of the inhabitants of the villages of Barzan, Resha and Hustan were transferred south.
- On Friday, 14th November 1975, residents of the villages of Nizar (Safte, Sarkafar, Zorakvan, Shre, Darbutke, Zewa, Isomaran, Alka, Irwan, Saka and Kolaka) were first transferred to Mosul and from there by train to the south, and on 17th November 1975 they were sent to Marajuj District, Community No. 4.

- On Wednesday 19th and Thursday 20th, November 1975, the residents of the country region (Tel, Shangal, Hazan, Babsefa, etc.) were first transported by military helicopter to the towns of Ble, Barzan, Baze, and then to the south of Iraq, and were resettled in Jahish and Marajuj.
- On Sunday, 25th June 1978, residents of the villages of Sherwan Great, Mzuri and Gardi were deported and resettled in the forced communities of Diana, Harir and Bahrka camps.
- The destroyed villages of Sherwan were: Lere, Sherwan Great, Sardari, Bardari, Kaniyata, Chame, Kani But, Bee, Tatki, Zrara, Koran, Kakala, Kanialnj, Bersif Maran, Masane, Benbia, Kurke, Bidarun, Dore, Kaniader, Bedial, a Christian village, Herebir, Sar-e-Kerry, Khairuzuk, Sarkani, Kolaka, Babake, Mergasor and Sheikh Sida, Mamisk, Waji.
- The destroyed villages of Mzuri were: Glana, Mawata, Ikika, Argush, Banan, Shiffe, Some, Selor, Ravin, Tuwee, Bose, Bizhyan, Barkale, Merooz, Koran, Palana, Sina, Moka, Dezo, Spindari, Pendro, Banawe, Nawkurka, Selke, Stope, Goze, Edlib.
- Some of the villages of Gardi were destroyed: Hupa and Zit.
- After all the disasters, relocation and destruction of their villages and their resettlement in forced communities, the early eighties of the last century were a tragic beginning for the Barzani, as they had faced one of the most dangerous incidents against humanity and international law in this decade, which had been planned and staged. They faced genocide and extermination attempts.
- On Monday, 21st February 1980, part of the Barzani was transferred from the south to Kurdistan and resettled in

the Qushtapa district of Erbil province and in the forced community of Quds.

- On Thursday, 24th April 1980, the other part of the Barzani were brought from the south to Erbil province and integrated in the forced camp of Qadisiya.

1983 was the year of tragedy for the Barzani, because in that year their attempts to purge and commit genocide went into practical action that resulted in the disappearance of a number of personalities of the Barzan family and Barzani's Sheik in both Baghdad and Erbil provinces. It began on30[th] July:

- On the morning of 31st July 1983, a large army of regimes besieged the camps and forced societies of Quds and Qadisiyah, whilst detaining all Barzani men between the ages of 7 to 90. They were arrested and taken to the desert of southern Iraq were bordered by Saudi Arabia.
- On 10th August 1983, the regime's army carried out another phase of the annihilation of the Barzani, and the civil Barzani of the camps (Harir, Diana, Bahrka, Goretu) were taken south.
- On 1st October 1983, Barzani's houses were buried in camps in order to arrest and detain Barzani who survived the expulsion to the south and the pit of death.
- The number of Barzani arrested at these stages reached 8,000, of whom 315 were children.
- On 10th May 1983, we received news of our Barzani's arrest in Qushtapa. All the Barzani, who were arrested and detained, were civilians, workers, employees and ordinary people, and after being taken to southern Iraq, contrary to

all international laws and regulations, they were buried in mass graves in the deserts of Bosa as part of the regimes policy of genocide.

- On 10th December 1989, residents of Dolamar were transferred to Sardawa and Mazne.
- People from the villages of Harki Benaje (Herke, Bedav, Dre, Stone, Sate and Kie), were transferred to southern Iraq on 18th November 1975 and brought back on 7th April 1977, to Qourato, before being taken to another camp at Shaholan on 1st June 1990.

As a result of the relocation, expulsion and changing living environments, a large number of Barzani died in different places, most of them children and the elderly, such as:

- In the first six months of 1946, more than 1,500 Barzani died at the White Mosque in Mahabad.
- The death of 20 immortal Barzani friends in the former Soviet Union.
- The deaths of more than 400 civilian Barzani in the camps 1, 2 Marajuj.

This shows the fact that Barzani people had always been victims of genocide and they had become used to the fact that this happened.

According to the regime's own evidence, 250 villages had been evacuated and destroyed in Barzan area, and their people taken to the south, into forced camps and the deserts of southern Iraq.

In 1976, in the context of changing demographics and distorting the national structures of Kurdistan, the regime attacked

Chamchamal and Kalar districts in Sulaymaniyah province and put Kifri district on Diyala province and then put Duzkhurmatu district, on Salahaddin province (Tikrit).

The first relocation of the villages of Pshdar border in Qandil by the regime began on 7th July 1977. In 1979, a 10-kilometre-wide plan to evacuate its borders was intensively implemented. This destroyed all the villages on the Qaladze-Iran border and relocated its people into the forced communities of Pemalk, Bastin, Zharawa and Tuwasoran. Also, some of the residents of Pshdar villages, on the Rania district border, were moved to the Erbil governorate border.

Another important stage in the minds of the Iraqi authorities was to prevent crossing the Iranian border in either direction, so in June 1975, it signed a border agreement with Iran on the issue. According to the agreement, strict measures were to be put in place to prevent crossings. Even Saddam admitted that those Kurds, who returned from Iran, would be transferred back to central and southern Iraq.

Then in June 1976, a border agreement with Turkey was signed and three other border agreements agreed with Turkey in 1978, 1979 and 1984. One of the results of these agreements was the creation of a security belt along 10 to 20 km on the northern border of Iraq and the transference of the residents of the villages to the depth of the Kurdish areas and even to southern Iraq.

In February 1976, the government began separating the administrative areas of Kirkuk province, cutting off the majority Kurdish areas and putting them in Sulaymaniyah province, and keeping Kirkuk and the oil rich Hawija district in a small administrative unit. Kirkuk's name was also changed to "Tamym" as a sign of the localization of oil and the area, thus depriving Kurds of their land and identity. Khanaqin's name has been changed to Arob, and Haji Omaran's name has been changed to Nasr.

Another Ba'athist step was to ban the use of the name Kurdistan and to replace this with the word "northern region", or "autonomy zone". The words "Kurds" and "Kurdistan" were removed from schoolbooks and the titles of vocational groups. A Ba'athist activist responded in this way about how to remove the Kurdish name from the Kurdish Women's Union. "We will not use this word again".

Further steps were taken to ban Kurdish language education in schools outside autonomous areas, ending the activities of the Women's Union and the Teachers' Syndicate, the Academy of Sciences and Arts. Kurds were being dissolved, many obstacles put in front of the University of Sulaymaniyah to limit Kurdish national activities, teachers at the University of Sulaymaniyah have been transferred to other universities, the number of colleges had been reduced and Arab students were added.

In 1981, the government moved the University of Sulaymaniyah to Erbil to dominate its activities, and later closed three Iraqi-backed Kurdish newspapers.

During a visit to northern Iraq in March 1979, Saddam Hussein said: "There is no conflict between Kurds and members of the Ba'athist party, and there is no contradiction between Kurds and part of the Arab nation."

Between 1975 and 1988, more than 341 villages were relocated, 43% in the Shangal district and 31% in Shekhan. It means during this period the following were relocated: in the border of Shingal district, 146 villages (43%), Shekhan 106 villages (31%), Talafar 39 villages (11%), Tlkef 15 villages (5%), Akre 35 villages (10%).

According to a letter from the Revolutionary Leadership Council (No. 134 on 21st January 1978), about 7,800 houses, including 81 residential camps in Nineveh, Tamim and Diyala provinces, were registered without comparison as belonging to Arabs.

In addition to this, according to a message from the Interior Ministry (no. 163 on 11th April 1977), Kurds were separated from the residents of Kirkuk, Diyala and Mosul provinces to return to their districts and their accommodation was extended (in the central and southern provinces of Iraq), or transferred to the autonomous border provinces.

The Third Baath Party congress in 1979 defended the point that "nations with special languages and culture, living in the Arab nation are part of the Arab nation".

One of the most important steps taken by the Iraqi authorities in the early 1980s was to implement the second phase of the expulsion of Faili Kurds from Iraq to Iran, most of which are sources suggest, the number of Faili Kurds was about 200,000 people.

The population of Mosul province, in different censuses, was as follows:

In 1957 Arabs 56.1% Kurds 30.7%
In 1965 Arabs 58.7% Kurds 25.1%
1977 Arabs 85.1% Kurds 13.4%

The Arabization policy in Kirkuk province was quickly implemented, particularly wehn Hawija became a district in 1962 and the population of the district rapidly increased to 5.5%, up from 2.8% percent in Hawija in 1965, to 17.5% in 1977.

Between 1965 and 1989, the population of more than 779 villages was displaced, which was 37,726 families, and 198,640 people. As a result of the policy of relocation and exclusion, the number of villages in Kirkuk province was 1,372 in 1957 but this reduced to 519 villages in 1987.

The following table shows the number of Kurdish residents in Kirkuk:

Kurds: In the British statement 48.9% in the Iraqi declaration 42.5% in the Turkish statement 52.7%

Turkmen: In the British statement 38.0% in the Statement of Iraq 23.4% in the Statement of Turkey 37.5%

Arabs: In the British declaration 10.9% in the Statement of Iraq 31.9% in the Statement of Turkey 4.4%

Other nations: in The British Declaration 2.2% in the Statement of Iraq 2.2% in the Declaration of Turkey 5.4%

Kirkuk's population structure nationally (1957-1977):

Kurds: In 1957 48.3% in 1965 36.1% in 1977 37.6%
Arabs: In 1957 28.2% in 1965 39.9% in 1977 44.4%
Turkmen: In 1957 21.4% in 1965 19.5% in 1977 16.3%

During the war, the Iraqi government, in retaliation for Kurdish revolutionary attacks, executed several Kurdish civilians. In 1987, thousands of Kurds were deported from towns and villages and resettled in forced communities. According to reports, Iraq had more than 1,200 villages of the Kurds destroyed.

In steps taken by the Iraqi regime to further implement genocidal policies, in 1984-1985, it closed 776 schools in Duhok. In Erbil, the director-general of education was removed from his position and issued an order to close 200 schools in the villages of Erbil province. In Sulaymaniyah and Kirkuk, 340 schools were closed by regime orders, and dozens of schools were closed in Akre and Shekhan.

The crime of bombarding Zewa

Throughout the Ba'athist regime's eight-year war against Iran, there had been no result, except for the waste and destruction of the country's economic infrastructure and wealth, and the killing of a large number of citizens of both countries. During the eight years of the war, the Ba'athist government committed numerous crimes against civilians in different places, through the use of chemical weapons, Anfal, executions and mass murders. One of the major and most disgusting crimes committed by the Ba'athists, was the bombing of the Zewa camp, which killed and injured civilians, most of them children, women and the elderly.

During the eight years of war, the Ba'athist regime bombarded Zewa on 24th September 1980, 6th October 1980, 9th June 1985, 1st July 1985, and 6th April 1988, but there was a major disaster on 9th 1985. This was a black day in the history of our people and a day which will never be forgotten.

On this day, the Ba'athist regime bombarded Zewa with a brutal attacks and committed one of the biggest crimes against humanity, which was contrary to all international laws and regulations. The

Zewa disaster is another black point in the history of Baathist criminals. At 9:15 am, several fascist Ba'athist planes targeted the Zewa camp and within minutes dozens of children, women, the elderly and the disabled were covered in blood.

Document (1)

June 9, 1985, during an Iraqi airstrike in the Zewa Camp

June 9, 1985, during an Iraqi airstrike in the Zewa Camp

June 9, 1985, during an Iraqi airstrike in the Zewa Camp

When I heard the news, I immediately visited Zewa. Death engulfed the camp, and few were able to see and endure the tragedy. All the halls were destroyed. Dozens of women, children, the elderly and the disabled were martyred, and their heads, hands and feet were mixed. I went to the cemetery and in a funeral lasting until 7 pm 89 people were buried.

According to the information, 160 people were sent to Urmia hospitals for treatment. The statistics for the martyrs reached 124 people, 368 injured. Although it was a terrible disaster, our people's patience and faith were greater and stronger than the disaster. Indeed, given the level of patience and sacrifice of these people, the expression 'brave' is not sufficient.

Dozens of voices were heard at the site of the disaster, shouting, "Be your sacrifice. Let us all die and we are ready to die. We're not afraid of dying." This strong revolutionary endurance and voice shook and excites human souls more, but Amina Khan's heroism and patience were something different that would never be forgotten and will live forever in my memory, and therefore it will remain alive.

The strong woman had gathered pieces of two of her boys and one grandchild in a bag. When I met her, I couldn't help but become emotional, but she came to me and hugged me and said, "I don't want to see you crying, all of them are to be your sacrifice, and I have two sons left, and they can be sacrificed for Kurdistan."[7]

In this way, until the end of the 1980s, a wide and visible area of Kurdistan's territory was under the influence of Arabization, Baathism, with relocation, and a large number of southern residents. Kurdistan was also home to forced communities.

---

[7] Amina Khan was the wife of the martyr Naji Bag Berokhi and the mother of four martyrs and the sister of three brothers of the martyr.

For example:

By 1987, of the 86,000 square kilometres in southern Kurdistan, 42,488 square kilometres, 49.47% had been subject to transportation policy.

More than 2,000 villages were destroyed between 1987 and 1988, reflecting Ali Kimai's absolute authority in Kurdistan, which he received on 29th April 1987.

According to letter number 2883 of 9th September 1990, the mayor of Shingal district for Mosul governorate asked for the urgent implementation of the decisions on the relocation in Shingal and Talafar districts and he asked that the poor be punished.

Until 1991, when the glorious uprising of the Kurdish people and the removal of Ba'athist dictatorial institutions, 51% of the territory of southern Kurdistan was invaded by the Ba'athist sectarian policy, meaning: relocation, Arabization, Baathism and emigration had also fallen.

Chemical bombardment and burned land policy.

The appointment of Ali Hassan al-Majid as the ruler of Kurdistan, 29th March 1987, in order to protect and support security, system, and stability, was a major turning point in the regime's attacks on the Kurdish people and their territory. Its policy of annihilation, and efforts to dismantle the Kurdish people went to a more dangerous and rapid stage.

Ali Hassan al-Majid was given full authority over all civil, security and military institutions. Baghdad's strongman declared the situation unusual and sudden, after his decision was issued. The purpose was to destroy the Kurdish revolution once and for all.

According to a letter from the Leadership of the Northern Organizing Office, no. 4008/28, on 20th June 1987, for the leadership of Legion 1, 2 and 5, signed by Ali Hassan al-Majid, and the official communication "The Leadership of the North Organization", signed by the Revolutionary Leadership Council- The Northern Affairs Committee, must gather all villages in Kurdistan where their lives would be banned by 21st June 1987, and on 22nd June 1987. The orders were as follows:

- All villages would be forbidden areas.
- Humans and animals are also forbidden in the area.
- Shooting was permitted. The army could use all kinds of weapons.
- All types of traffic were prohibited in these areas.
- No agriculture or animal husbandry could be done in these areas.
- The army was free, day and night, to capture and kill any human and animals in those areas.
- Anyone who, aged 15 to over 70, was found in these areas would be arrested, and would be hanged.
- The Servants (Jash – Kurdish traitors) would plunder any loot for themselves, except for heavy weapons.

Ali Hassan al-Majid, appointed by Saddam Hussein as the ruler of Kurdistan, was given every authority to suppress the Kurdish people in general. In a statement issued on 14th June 1987, he announced to his military units: "The work of the military forces is that any human being and creature seen in these areas, would be destroyed immediately."

In another statement directed at the military commanders, he said:

> *Anyone who stands against the expulsion order from*
> *his homeland and violates it, will be subject to our*
> *use of artillery, helicopters, tanks or airplanes and*
> *will be detained and executed, and destroy agricul-*
> *tural land and trees, poisoning anything edible.*

In 1987, the regime declared a restricted area. It moved the people of the villages, but many of the people were not ready to go under Ba'athist control and went to the liberated areas and re-established villages in those areas through the rebuilding of a new village.

The area was divided into two areas of revolution and government. The revolutionary area was often gassed, but people believed strongly in the cause and were ready to remain there even when under chemical attack.

Ali Hassan al-Majid added a new style to the old principles of partisan annihilation, namely the use of chemical weapons to kill and intimidate the villagers of Kurdistan, so the Kurds named him Ali Kimawi (Chemical Ali).

According to documents obtained, the regime obtained chemical weapons in November 1983, but did not use them for unknown reasons in the war. They were used only once on the northern side of Haji Omaran against Iran, but then the regime used all kinds of chemical weapons against the Kurds through warplanes, missiles, large bombs, long-range shells, truck mounted multiple rocket launchers and more.

During the Ba'athist regime in general and the reign of Ali Hassan al-Majid in particular, Kurdistan and the Kurdish people faced chemical attacks several times, killing thousands of civilians, with many suffering from chronic diseases.

The first major attack began on 15th April 1987 in Sulaymaniyah province, with the chemical attack on the villages of Haladan, Chalawa, Tu, Sargalu, Bargalu, Awaj, Sirwan, Nulchka, Chenarne and Chakhi Gojar.

Dozens of people were hit by them.

Residents of the Kani Ashqan neighbourhood of Halabja protested against the government's behaviour but these were strongly rejected at the request of Ali Hassan al-Majid, commander of the first Legion.

He ordered the shooting of civilians, and the Kani Asheqan neighbourhood was completely destroyed, while the police, army and security forces were given full authority to destroy any buildings and houses they were in that they using to shoot or using as a shelter.

Tanks and military vehicles were used.

However, the brave and stoic Kurdish attitude of the people of the villages in the Margwear of eastern Kurdistan cannot be forgotten, because from the first moment of the bombardment, they poured into the camp at once and did not hesitate to provide them with any kind of help and assistance. They opened their doors to the disadvantaged people, who took refuge, and provided them with a resting place. That's why we do not forget the sympathy and love of our brothers and sisters in death in that bloody day. It is impossible to thank them in a few words.

Some officials from Wrme province came to us to convey their condolences. On that bloody day, I announced that we reaffirmed our sympathy and promised to avenge the blood of these martyrs and innocents from Baghdad's anti-humane regime and to continue our struggle until the liberation of our people. On 18th June 1985, a delegation from the Islamic Labour Organization visited us and brought 100,000 Tumans as aid to the families of the martyrs, who in themselves were aided by Mr Said Muhammad Taqi Mudarresi in order to convey their condolences for the bombing of the Zewa camp.

The organization's stance has always been open and positive.

Once again, on 1st July 1985, five Ba'athist regime planes bombed the Zewa camp, martyring Haval Dasko Ahmed Isqaeli, a member of the Zewa district committee, and injuring nine. civilians.

The bombardment was much more intense than before, but fortunately the camp was empty, so the damage was less. They bombed the camp approximately 70 times, and thanks be to God, many of the bombs did not explode.

On 10th November 1985, in the Amedi area of the regime's planes dropped children's dolls (containing bombs) which exploded in children's hands resulting in the death of two children. During the Ba'athist era, by the end of 1986, more than 1,895 villages and cities had been relocated, making the number of displaced 1,476 villages and 84,877 families.

Between 1985 and 1986, all villages in Duhok province were deprived of education and schools, so the school revolution in the liberated areas took over, bringing the number of schools to about 24 and the number of students reaching 1,100. Later, a large number of students and teachers were injured by the chemical attack on the area and revolutionary health centres helped the victims.

After the regime's attack on Kurdistan began, particularly in Duhok province. Residents of a large number of villages were besieged by regime forces for two weeks, and according to some data, they reached 221 villages with the purpose of killing, exterminating and destroying the people. In order to annihilate the people of Kurdistan, the regime employed different methods and tools such as:

1. Chemical weapons. Apart from genocide, torture and relocation of residents, the use of chemical weapons was one of the tools to annihilate the Kurdish people.
2. Destroying villages, arresting, and expelling them to southern and central Iraq.
3. Air bombardment, artillery, missiles, and all forms of destruction.
4. Killing prisoners. The Ba'athist regime executed a large number of civilians who surrendered to the regime after the attacks.
5. Burning and destroying villages, districts, cities, and towns, destroying agriculture, farmers' products, and animal husbandry.

According to a secret letter from Erbil governorate, no. 6493, on 2nd October 1986, the Real Estate Registration Office was notified that these places would be evacuated to create forced camps: Benaslawa, Baghamra, Konagurk, Daratu, Diana, Taqtaq and Dibaga, along with all the land belonging to these villages. Seven camps were to be constructed with each consisting of 16,000 houses.

As partisan fighting escalated with the PDK and PUK, Communist Party, Dawa party and other groups, the government felt in serious danger, so the Iraqi president's office in mid-1986 ordered Ba'ath issuance officials and military commanders in autonomy areas to place further economic blockades on villages and areas evacuated by security. One of the other steps of Ba'ath was arming and organizing Kurds.

They were named after the light regiments, and after a while they were renamed the National Defence Regiments. The regiments were helped a lot by the Ba'athists, reaching 250,000 armed men in the partisan war and they helped the Iraqi army in the mountains.

According to confirmed information, during 1987 and 1988, the Ba'athist regime destroyed 799 villages, 493 schools, 598 mosques and 40 health centres. More than 37,726 Kurdish farmers were also deported from their homeland, whilst the Kurds in Kirkuk, Dabs, Kifri, and Chamchamal districts during 1987-1988 were relocated, reaching 136,008.

During the destruction of Kurdistan, the regime destroyed 488 villages, with a population of approximately 12,000 families, between 25th August and 15th September 1988.

It was as follows:

The number of destroyed villages was Shekhan – 19 (275 families); Duhok – 62 (1720 families); Amedi - 2326 (180 families); Zakho – 100 (3,350 families); Akre- 35 (560 families).

The Iraqi authorities in general and the Ba'athist regime, under different pretexts, separately tried to annihilate and purge the Iraqi people, who were among the most severely hit by the Barzani. This can be summarized in a number of points:

First: Security and political reasons: Khanaqin, Mandali, Badra, Shekhan, Tlkef, Talafar, Shingal, Zakho and Semel districts were allegedly security and strategic places, because of Iran, Turkey and Syria, so they need to be evacuated, resulting in the evacuation of 930 villages and the relocation of 22,529 families.

Second: The existence of oil and natural resources in Kirkuk, Dabs and Koya. Because of the existence of natural wealth, a large part of their villages was evacuated and people were moved.

Third: Border factors. From the Ba'athist point of view, the districts of Halabja, Penjwen, Sharbazher, Dukan, Choman, Rwandese, Amedi, Zakho and Qaladze were border areas and the civilian population had to be evacuated. Consequently, 29 communities in Sulaymaniyah province, 16 in Erbil province and 14 in Duhok were forced to leave and people were settled there.

Fourth: The reason and excuse of Iran-Iraq war. The other part of Penjwen district, Biara district and the centre of Choman district were evacuated under the pretext of the area being near the front lines of the war, which left 660 villages empty as they were evacuated and 18,000 families were moved.

Fifth: Relocation because of the Kurdistan Revolution. The Ba'athist regime destroyed the areas under the pretext that some districts and villages of Kurdistan had become a place of rest and shelter for the peshmerga so these were displaced.

Sixth: Relocation for other reasons, for example, in order to create military camps and barracks, a large area of relocation and exodus. For example, 4,500 acres of land, meaning $18.2s \text{ km}^2$ was evacuated between Kirkuk and Erbil to create a military base containing 14 villages.

Seventh: Because of the uprising, a number of villages and areas were evacuated.

Eighth: Under the pretext of building the Mosul and Bekhma dams: 8 villages and 205 families in Mosul, including 10 villages and 200 families, were hit by the Bekhma Dam.

Using chemical weapons against Kurdish people

1. On the morning of 15th April 1987, for the first time, the regime used Sukhoi 22 aircraft, chemical weapons in the Bargalu area and the villages of Kani Tu, Sekani, Sharstein, Marga and Jaffayati Valley.

2. On 16th April 1987, in Erbil governorate, the villages of Balisan, Sheikh Wasanan, Kani Bard, Darshir Mountain Series, Zini Balukan and Sausukan area in Qaradagh were bombed by 12 planes. They launched chemical warfare. The areas were liberated, but about 280 civilians were martyred, and 320 were victims of chemical weapons - 190 people were martyred during the bombing, but the number of martyrs increased later.

   The wounded went to Erbil, Shaqlawa and Rania for treatment, but most were arrested, killed and buried by the regime so that they could not be revealed, especially those who went to Erbil hospitals. Men were separated from women and imprisoned at Rashkin barracks, and after a few days the women were released, and their men buried alive. After the uprising, the bodies of six people at the barracks were found.

3. On 17th April 1987, in Sulaymaniyah province, the villages of Qezeler, Birke, Sangar and Miwlaka were gassed. Only a

few people were affected by the imminent attack and were hiding, so the number of victims was low.

4. On 18th April 1987, in Sulaymaniyah province, mountains and villages (Qaiwan, Korang, Khaja Lazok, Qawal, Qulajakh, Chokhmakh and Kolardi) were bombarded with chemical weapons, and 50 civilians killed.

5. On 5th April 1987, in Sulaymaniyah province, the villages of Mawat Qaiwan and Piramagrun were bombarded with chemical weapons, and dozens of people killed.

6. On 20th April 1987, the areas attacked on the previous days were chemically bombarded again.

7. On 21st April 1987, in Sulaymaniyah province, the villages of Qaradagh district, the surrounding villages and Garmian were chemically bombed, killing and injuring a number of civilians and burning the land, the agriculture and their products.

8. On 8th April 1987, the Balisan Valley was gassed in Erbil province.

9. On 1st May 1987, Zewa village was gassed in Duhok province, martyring several peshmerga.

10. On 22nd 1987, villages in Erbil province (Malakan, Gorsher, Kandok, Ble and Bardoun) were chemically attacked.

11. On 22nd May 1987, in Kirkuk province, villages (Tomar, Gurgan and Qamar) were chemically bombarded.

12. On 27th May 1987, villages (Malakan, Blay-e Sofla, Tarina, Kandok, Gorsher, Nazanin and Smaquli Valley) were gassed, resulting in eight martyrs and 23 casualties, and according to reports on that day, 20 chemical attacks were carried out by warplanes.

13. 5th June1987, in Duhok Province, villages the district of Amedi was chemically bombed, causing one martyr immediately and 100 people to be injured. The headquarters of branch one was also gassed.

14. On 27th June 1987, in Sulaymaniyah province, the village of Zewe was gassed at the foot of Piramagrun mountain, killing 35 people.

15. On 28th June 1987, the eastern Kurdish city of Sardasht was gassed, killing 130 civilians and injuring 825.

16. On 3rd September 1987, in Sulaymaniyah province, villages (Bargalu and Yakhsamar) were bombed with chemical weapons, martyring 14 peshmerga and killing several civilians.

17. On 14th September 1987, the Mergapan area of Sulaymaniyah province was chemically bombed and several people were killed. After a campaign in the Blassan Valley on 16th September 1987, 286 of the wounded went to Erbil to be treated, but all were arrested by the Iraqi army, and they were immediately martyred.

18. On 24th November 1987, the Ba'athist regime poisoned the food of a peshmerga family with Salum gas through a hired worker who arrived in the village of Marga, resulting in the martyrdom of the peshmerga and the death of a 20-year-old girl and injuring four others.

19. On 25th February 1988, in Sulaymaniyah province, villages (Sargalu, Yakhsamar, Haladan and Guzila) were gassed and several people were hit.

20. 26th February 1988 in Sulaymaniyah province, Sargalu villages, Yakhsamar, Haladan and Guzila were gassed, killing eight people and injuring 201.

Omar Khawar, a Kurdish father, holds his baby in his arms in
Halabja, the city in Kurdistan of Iraq, on March 16, 1988

Halabja, on March 16, 1988

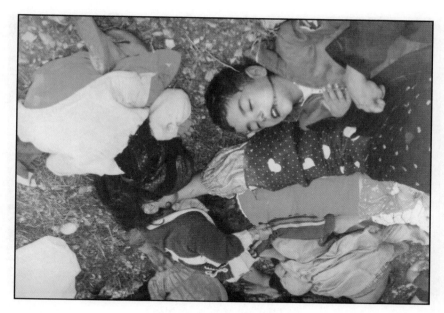

Halabja, on March 16, 1988

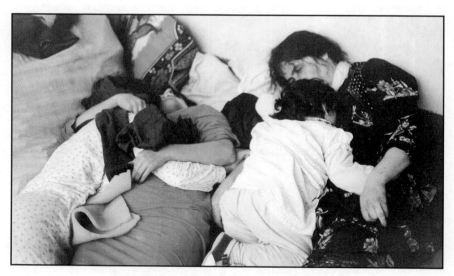

Halabja, on March 16, 1988

Halabja, on March 16, 1988

Halabja, on March 16, 1988

21. On 28th February 1988, in Sulaymaniyah Province, the villages of Takia, dozens of peshmerga were wounded in the Qaradagh area of Balakjar, Balkha and Gomata.

22. On 9th March 1988, Sina, Mariwan and Qalaji villages were gassed with mustard gas, 30 were martyred and 30 were wounded.

23. Halabja was a historical city with a prominent place in the cultural, political and economic life of Kurdistan, with a population of about 70,000. On 16th and 17th March 1988, the Iraqi regime committed a brutal crime against Halabja and its surrounding areas, poisoning them with chemical weapons. Most sources say the number of martyrs in Halabja was 5,000. They estimate that the number of wounded and injured is 10,000. The gases used against Halabja civilians were:

Phosgene gas, a colourless gas with the smell of grass and new vegetables. This quickly affects the body with symptoms of coughing, inducing vomiting, sneezing, shortness of breath and burning of the respiratory system.

Blood gas (cyanide, edrogen, chlorid, cyanogen). These smell of bitter wind, and its symptoms include weakness, dizziness, difficulty breathing, rapid heartbeats, lips and cheeks become bright red.

The scallop (mustard, arsonists, gases), a dry gas with the smell of garlic, and long-term influence, reddens the skin of the body after two hours, and after two days, peels the surface of the skin which will not heal.

Nerve Gas (Sarin, Suman), is a boiling gas that smells of fruit and has a long-term influence which loses its smell. The symptoms include the nose and mouth being affected, eyes burn and vision becomes poor, with muscles twitching, general weakness, confusion, headache and difficulty breathing.

"We cannot distinguish between insurgents and others, because they all wear Kurdish clothes, except for some people, have weapons in their hands," said Iraqi Defence Minister Adnan Khairullah Tulfah.

While Halabja was gassed with banned weapons and bloodshed, thousands of civilians were martyred and wounded and became victims of Baathist racist policies, Tariq Ramadan, the pilot who gassed Halabja, was quickly released and forgiven for his crime.

24. On 17th March 1988, chemical bombing was carried out in Kermanshah province, Hawraman, Nodsha town, killing 140 people and injuring 700 others. And again, on 24th March and on 2nd April the bombardment was reopened.

25. 17th March 1988, in Sina governorate and Mariwan city, the villages Daranakh, Zakaria, the road between Dzli and Bikara border crossing which was the road for the traffic of displaced people from Halabja, Hawraman and other areas, was gassed. Several people were killed and one was martyred.

26. On 22nd March 1988, chemical weapons (Sarin and Tabun) were used to gas Sulaymaniyah province, Qaradagh area and Sewsenan village.

27. 23rd March 1988, in Sulaymaniyah Province, villages in the area Qaradagh (Dukan, Dukaro, Walian and Jafaran) were attacked and dozens of people were killed.

28. On 23rd March 1988, in Sulaymaniyah province, the village of Shanakhse in the Sharbazher area was gassed, 22 peshmerga were martyred, and 720 civilians were killed.

29. On 24th March 1988, in Sulaymaniyah province, Balakjar village in Qaradagh district was gassed with nerve gas.

30. On 3rd May 1988, villages (Goptapa, Askar, Chami Rezan, Shunka, Mahila, Sadi, Chenar, Shekhan, Glasher, Haji Zirabar, Kochbalakh, Zarzi and Church) were chemically bombarded in Sulaymaniyah province.

31. On 15th May 1988, in Erbil province, hundreds of people were bombed in the villages of Kamusak, Spindari, Aliawa, Barka, Kawazian, Harir, Smaquli and Maluk.

32. On 15th and 18th May 1988, in Sulaymaniyah province, the villages of Rania (Were, Gulan and Bote) were gassed. These three villages were under the regime's control.

33. On 20th June 1988, in Erbil province, villages (Sarwchawa, Smaquli, Ganaw, Sharsten, Khatta, Darash, Balisan, Nazanin and Garawan) were gassed. Because the villages had previously been evacuated it was therefore less effective.

34. On 31st June 1988, in Erbil province, villages (Smaquli, Balisan, Hiran and Garawan) were gassed, killing five people and injuring several others.

35. On 2nd August 1988, in Erbil province, the villages of Ari, Siru, Zarwa, Haden, Kakala, Kherazuka, Kharwan and Bele were gassed, six peshmerga were martyred and 117 people were affected.

36. 22nd August 1988, in Kermanshah province, in Dalaho district, the village of Zarda was gassed, resulting in 300 martyrs and nearly 1,000 affected.

37. 23rd and 24th August 1988, the regime bombarded the village of Korime with airplanes and artillery, shooting down soldiers by helicopter around the village. However, the villagers did not think about the risk of chemical warfare, even though they had previously been gassed around the village. On 25th and 26th August 1988, people in Kurime and Chalk were conscious of the danger of chemical weapons, so they tried to go to Turkey's borders.

38. On 24th August 1988, in Duhok province, Gara mountain and Zewshkan village were chemically bombed and ten peshmerga were martyred.

39. On 25th August 1988, in Duhok province, at the beginning of the eighth phase of Anfal, the regime began chemical bombardment of the area, including the areas and villages: Barwari Bala, the villages of Warmele, Babire. Grago, Hise, Ekmala, Asahe, Baze, Miska, Toshmbek, Mergachia, Kani Balaf, Brigini, Tuika, Zewa, Siri, Penyinsh and Revala, resulting in five peshmerga being martyred and 75 people affected.

40. On 25th August 1988, in Duhok province, Amedi district, Sare Gara, villages (Ekamala, Kiri, Balite, Bawaka, Barkafre, Grka, Kuvlink, Redina, Sarke, Zeuka, Sherana, Bilejane, Bane, Amedi, Barwari, Spindari and Savari) were gassed and two people martyred and 40 people were affected.

41. On 25th August 1988, Mirstak village was gassed between Amedi and Kani, injuring more than 100 people and

according to some, in subsequent, reports, the number of injuries later reached about 200.

42. On 25th August 1988, in Duhok province, Amedi district, villages (Kanika, Baska, Avoke and Bemenansh) were hit by chemical attacks, within minutes. The regime fired nearly 80 chemical missiles at the Zeweskan area of Amedi district and was later gassed by several missiles, killing three peshmerga and injuring several others. Between 25th and 29th August 1988, regime forces were constantly armed with chemical weapons in the Zewashan area.

43. On 25th August 1988, in Duhok province, in Akre district, villages (Presse, Jazgira, Chamchamali, Cham Shrta, Cham Rabatke, Miruki and Belmbas) were bombed and many people were killed.

44. On 25th August 1988, in Duhok province, in Zakho district, the villages of Tuika, Bilijan and Zhrawa were gassed, killing 14 people and injuring 15. The first martyr of the chemical attack in Zakho area was the commander of the area (Ismail Tabir) and 11 peshmerga who were subject to poisonous gas were martyred.

45. On 25th August 1988, in Duhok province, villages (Brijini, DargalaSheka, Zinava and Dbanki) were attacked and several people were killed.

46. On 25th and 29th August 1988, Iraqi regime planes gassed the Duhok area. During the regime's attacks in Badinan, 430 families took refuge in the caves and hid in the Baze valley, 2,470 of them children and women. In the morning of 29th August 1988, six planes of the Iraqi regime bombed the Baze valley with chemical weapons. In a few minutes,

six other planes attacked the Baze valley again, killing 2,980 people.

47. On 25th August 1988, chemical weapons attacks were carried out in the Mergasor district, the high estuaries, but there were few casualties due to the mountains' difficulty.

48. On 25th August 1988, chemical bombardments were carried out in Erbil province, Shaqlawa and the villages of Hiran and Nazanin, but the damage was unknown.

49. On 25th August 1988, in Erbil province, Rwandese and the villages of Khati and Warte were finally gassed, but the damage was unknown.

50. On 26th August 1988, in Duhok province and Amedi district, villages (Sari Amedi, Sper, Sina, Nerwa, Kharakul, Kujrzka, Kharab, Zewa, Barchi, Kani, Diri, Dargani, Siri, Sari, Sargali, Firstak and Chiarashk) were chemically bombarded, but there is no Information available about the victims.

51. On 27th August 1988, in Erbil province, the Muzri Bala and the Zei Shin area were gassed the result being the killing and injuring of several people.

52. On 28th August 1988, in Duhok province, in Nerwa-Rekan area, villages (Shivi, Hetot, Kania Pink, Bashi, Serni, Kara, Karu, Bawanki, Zewa and Gali Kutke) were attacked by chemical attacks, but the number of victims is unknown.

53. On 27th and 28th August 1988, 27 people from the village of Kureme were on their way to the Turkish borders and were forced to return to their village, where they were shot. 18 of them were from Kureme and seven were from Chalki village. Six survived the atrocity.

54. 29th On August 1988, in Duhok governorate, there was a chemical bombardment of Banke village. Many were martyred, and many others were injured.

55. On 14th September 1988, the Voice of Iraqi Kurdistan Station reported: "We express our deep sorrow and sadness that another humanitarian disaster has occurred in Zamdar Kurdistan, and nearly 2,980 people, including children, women and men, from the Baze valley, were martyred on 29th August 1988 through the use of poison gas." According to a report by the US House of Representatives Foreign Relations Committee on 21st September 1988, the Iraqi army was charged with using chemical weapons against Iraqi Kurds and harmed thousands of people at the beginning of 25th August 1988. It arrived and acknowledged that it was a violation of international law.

According to a 1988 tape, Ali Hassan al-Majid, under the pretext of destroying Kurdish villages in the forbidden area, which was half the area of the entire England area, said, "If we don't, our insurgent activities will not be stopped for another one million years." "I don't want their wheat," said Ali Hassan al-Majid, referring to the damage to agriculture. "We have been importing wheat for the last 20 years. Let's get five more. We will increase it for another five more years."

In a speech to several his aides in early 1988, Hassan al-Majid said, "Why should I have made them prosperous? No, they should have been in my pit with bulldozers." During his speech, he said, "What should I have done about all this? Over various provinces. I divided them, and I had to push them into position by bulldozer."

Journalist Goin Roberts[8] played a major role, as a major reason for the discovery of the use of chemical weapons in Kurdistan. On his return, he took some equipment with him for chemical weapons tests and presentations, after arriving in Europe and checking and testing, he found out that chemical weapons had been used in Kurdistan and against the Kurdish people.

This can be counted as the beginning of the disclosure of the use of chemical weapons in Kurdistan. It should also be said that all parts of Kurdistan had been subjected to the use of chemical weapons by the Ba'athist regime, but the chemical attack on Halabja expressed the magnitude of the disaster, the martyrdom and injury of a large number of innocent people in a short time and became the symbol of the victims of the chemical attack.

Genocide of Failis

In the standards of the Convention on the Prevention and Punishment of Genocide, published on 9th December 1948 by the General Assembly of the United Nations as resolution no. 260, the actions committed by Iraqi governments in general and the Ba'athists in particular against the Kurdish people can be considered crimes. They constitute genocide, such as the Anfal, Barzani genocide, Halabja chemical attack, Genocide and Relocation of Failis, Relocation of Pshdar and its surroundings, Qaladze bombing, Relocation of Said Sadiq, Makhmur, Kirkuk and its surroundings, the bombardment of the Zewa camp, the genocide of Dakan cave and Soria village.

Genocide and ethnic and national genocide were the first steps in the Anfal process, which began by the Ba'athist regime and Baghdad authorities chasing and arresting Failis and Barzani.

---

[8] Journalist Goin Roberts, in honour of his role in conveying the voice of the Kurdish people to the foreign public, received the Barzani Medal.

Faili Kurds, who live in many cities and towns in central and southern Iraq, who religiously follow Shia sects, were subjected to genocide in every way since 1963 by the Baathist-ruled Iraqi state. References and statistics identify this and confirm that tens of thousands of people in this Kurdish class were killed.

Both Saadun Shakir and Barzan Tikriti directly supervised the genocide and the destruction of the Failis, and then, for this purpose, in 1980, the Interior Minister ordered the expulsion of Faili Kurds.

"Iranians who are in the country and do not have Iraqi nationality, as well as those who have dealt and have not decided on it, will be expelled," the interior minister's order said. His decision was reinforced by the Iraqi government who further included:

"Faili Kurdish youths between the ages of 18 and 28 will be arrested and detained in provincial prisons for an indefinite period of time." As the decision of the Interior Minister of the Iraqi government reiterated: "Anyone who is being deported to Iran, if they try to return, shoot them. This means kill them!"

On 26th February 1981, Saddam Hussein, in the Iraqi government's linguistic newspaper Tawara, said of the Faili Kurds, "Eradicate this class in Iraq, so that they do not pollute Iraq's land and air, and when their blood is mixed with Iraqi blood through women and marriage, we don't want to dirty the blood of Iraqis."

The attention and scrutiny of Saddam's remarks, the former president of Iraq, is enough to understand the extent to which chauvinism and racism of the Ba'athist party, its president, leaders and government in Iraq had been trying to destroy those who differed from him.

According to available information, before 2003, more than 200,000 Iraqis were displaced or chased to Iran, 65 per cent of whom were Faili Kurds, many of whom remain in the country.

During the Ba'athist party authority thousands of Faili Kurds were imprisoned and they were executed and massacred.

There are many other references and statistics that count the number of Faili Kurds expelled from Iraq, subjected to imprisonment, murder, confiscation of their wealth and disappearance, at 500,000. They faced genocide and the effects of it remain for many and they will stay for decades.

The Genocide of the Barzanis.

After the Algerian agreement in the mid-1970s, the Ba'athist regime, in a planned manner, began the Barzani genocide campaign, and the preliminary steps of the genocide began in this way. At first, the Barzani faced displacement and fell on the other side of Iran, with Persian cities scattered or divided.

The beginning of this action and the outbreak of the genocide of the Barzanis was carried out in several stages, under the direct supervision and supervision of Fazil Rak and republican guards:

- The first phase was the arrest of prominent Barzani figures on 29th to 30th July 1983.
- The second phase, on 31st July 1983, was the mass capture of all Barzani, males of the Quds and Qadisiya camps.
- The third phase, on 10th August 1983, was the mass capture of all Barzani, the males of the forced camps of Harir, Bahrka and Diana.
- The fourth phase was the mass pursuit and capture of Barzani who had survived the raids anyway.

As we mentioned earlier, 8,000 Barzani males, young and old, were killed or subject to genocide by the Baathist state in Iraq.

Saddam Hussein later confessed to genocide and the martyrdom of the Barzani at a multi-party meeting. (Video of those confessions released)

On 12th September 1983, in front of a large crowd, dictator Saddam accused us of allegedly participating in the attack on Haji Omaran with Iranian forces and said that a number of us had helped them there, so they were punished, but the dictator's remarks were baseless and untrue. The only purpose was to cover up his failures and expel his hatreds, because he was very sensitive to the Barzani's name existing.

So on 15th September 1983, Ali Abdullah, through Abdul-Muhammedin, asked me to visit Mohammed Khalid and his relatives for comfort and partnership in the great grief. On 16th September I left Konalajan for Silvana, and on 17th September 1983, I left Silvana for Karaj. We were all saddened by the great crimes committed by the Ba'athists against civilians, because the Barzani's arrest and genocide was a major crime against humanity committed on a baseless and far-fetched accusation, assuming that we participated in the war, and these Barzani were civilians and under his rule.

Following the genocide of the Barzanis, regime agents committed two other despicable and anti-human crimes against two Barzani figures:

First, the assassination and martyrdom of Sherwan Nazir Barzani who was 20 years old and a sophomore, on 26th October 1988.

The College of Justice was the translation department of the University of Mosul, which had nothing to do with the armed forces or peshmerga. The reason for his martyrdom was only that he was Barzani. Sherwan was killed in Mosul and in front of the school centre by the Ba'athist security forces.

Second, the assassination attempt on Barzan Luqman Barzani on 23rd September 1987 in Erbil, who was severely wounded. This was another crime of the Ba'athist dictators and their officials against civilians in general, but Barzani in particular.

Between 1980 and 1981, two Party commanders were martyred, Dara Tofiq and Salih Yousefi. Also, friends Abdul of Soran, Sadiq Amin (Sadiq Afandi) and Ali Hazhar the members of the leadership Party was martyred.

The stages of the Anfal process

Anfal crime manifesto

20th June 1987   Decision: 4008 Number:8004/28

*In the leadership of the office of the
north organization secretariat*

*To Commander of The First Legion, Commander of
the Second Legion , Commander of the Fifth Legion*

Since the official period for collecting these villages ended on 21st June 1987, we decided to start work on 22nd June 1987 as follows:

*1. All villages will be considered restricted areas in
terms of security, as they are still home to Iranians
and supporters of the Iranian regime, destroy-
ers, traitors, examples and the traitors of Iraq.
2. It is completely forbidden for people and animals to
remain in these areas which are considered restricted areas
and shooting orders are free without conditions, unless
other instructions are issued by our headquarters.
3. Travelling traffic, or agriculture, seeding, indus-
try and animal husbandry are prohibited, and on
the related agencies, each of them should have a serious investigation according to their characteristics.
4. Prepare the presidency of the special strike legions,
occasionally working artillery, airplanes, and helicopters at night and day to kill the largest number
of people in the forbidden places and notify us.
5. The imprisonment and detention of all those arrested in the
villages, who are over the age of 15 to 70 within these areas,
will be sentenced to death by the security agencies, after taking advantage of the information they have. Notify us.
6. The relevant agencies are investigating those who surrender to governmental and party institutions for a period
of one to three days, and we must be notified of these cases,
if the period needs to be extended, by phone, or by letter.
Haval Tahir al-Aniye, get our approval.
7. All the goods and equipment, albeit heavy weapons,
medium weapons or light weapons obtained by the National
Defence Regiments and their fighters must be for themselves. They must warn us of such weapons and register*

277

*only their numbers. The Commander of the Jahafels must
be active, to inform all the advisers, the Commander of
Syria and their detachments, and in detail notify us of
the activities of the National Defence Regiments.*

*Presidency of the Legislative Council, Presidency of the
Executive Council, Information Agency, Army Chief
of Staff, Governors, Head of the Security Committees of
Nineveh, Diyala, Salahaddin, Sulaymaniyah, Erbil, Duhok,
Dean of the branches of the provinces mentioned above.*

*The general military effort, the general director-
ate of security, the security director of the Zaati
district, the security director of Nineveh provinces,
Tamim, Diyala, Salahaddin, Sulaymaniyah, Erbil
and Duhok provinces. Please view and apply*

Each person according to their property. Warn us.

Signature
*Ali Hassan Majid, a member of the regional leadership
The leadership of the Northern Organizing Office*

Although Ali Hassan al-Majid was the first, direct and
full-fledged official, Lieutenant General Adnan Khairullah, Nizar
Khazraji and Lieutenant General Sultan Hashim, Lieutenant
General Kamel Sajid al-Janabi, Lieutenant General Ayad Khalil
Zaki and Lieutenant General Barq (Barq Abdulhaj Hantah) were

all involved in the Anfal process and the disappearance of thousands of women, men, children and citizens of Kurdistan.

The Anfal crime is one of the major and dangerous crimes committed by the Ba'athist regime, which was carried out in eight consecutive stages in 1988, according to a strongly formed plan. After the fall of the Ba'athist regime, the Anfal was recognised by the Iraqi Supreme Criminal Court as one of the crimes committed against the Kurdish people and Kurdistan.

From here, we will identify and present each stage, as stated in the Documents of the Supreme Criminal Court, although outside the documents of the Supreme Criminal Court of Iraq, there may be different opinions on the date and time, there will be a place for the stages of the crime and its execution, as are some of the opinions that have been proven and confirmed by the court.

The Process of Anfal and Genocide and the attempt to purge the Kurdish people by the Ba'athist regime were carried out in eight stages as follows:

Stage One:

The Jaffayati Valley attack began on 9th to 23rd February 1988, and was located in the area of Sargalu, Bargalu, and also located in the border town of Surdash in Dukan district. This stage started under the command of Sultan Hashim and included about 150 villages. Several military units of the regime participated in it as:

1. The 38th Infantry Division, known as the Force (Omer's son of Abdulaziz), consisted of the 18th, 447th and 130th Infantry Brigades, the Baba Battalion and the Maghavir Regiment.

2. The 5th Ali Brigade, known as the Muhammad al-Qasim Force, consisted of the 15th Ali Infantry Brigade, the 200th Ali Brigade, and the 2nd Maghavir Brigade.

3. The 8th Infantry Division, known as the Musanna Force, consisted of the 22nd, 48th and 44th Infantry Brigades.

4. Infantry Division 2, commanded by Khalid son of Walid, consisted of 4th, 2nd and 36th Infantry Brigades.

5. Three Brigades of Haras Jamhuri with all the advanced military needs.

6. Badr Force.

7. 4th Infantry Division known as Qa'qa'a.

8. Division 33.

9. Mu'tasem force.

10. Several other units participated, including
   - Chemical units.
   - Military aircraft.
   - Air Force
   - The Fifth Legion
   - Engineering units to destroy villages
   - Majud Harbi who was the civil office of Reuban, to open roads and establish a travel bridge
   - Military Intelligence Units.

It is worth mentioning here the defence and wars of The Patriotic Union of Kurdistan forces in the area, because they did not hesitate according to their ability, fought and defended well in the area and they faced the enemy with a strong front.

Stage Two:

Anfal II began on 22nd March to 1st April 1988, in the Qaradagh area, under the direct supervision of Major General Ayad Khalil Zaki. These units and forces participated:

- 15th Infantry Division in the name of Faruq Force which consisted of the following units:
- 436th Infantry Brigade
- 14th Infantry Brigade
- 76th Infantry Brigade.
- Nahrawan Tanks

1. The 34th Infantry Division, known as the Al-Haris Force, consisted of the
   - 502nd Infantry Brigade
   - 504th Infantry Brigade
   - 90th Infantry Brigade
   - Tanks

2. The 3rd Brigade, known as the Salahaddin Force, consisted of:
   - The Infantry Brigade of Ali.
   - 12th Major General
   - 6th Brigade of Medarea
   - Special Force Brigade

3. Division 50 under the command of Colonel Zuher Younis Ali.
4. The commander of the first light regiment, meaning the Jashs (Kurdish traitors), under the command of Brigadier General Saad Shamsaddin.

5. Command of Force One.
6. The Commander of the light regiment.
7. Qaradagh Sector Command.
8. The full force of Sulaymaniyah.
9. Mixed regiment.
    - Chemical
    - Soupa plane
    - Air Force a class of tools to destroy villages in Chaufle Bulldozer
    - Majud al-Harbi, specializing in opening the roads
    - Military Intelligence Units.

Stage Three:

Garmian Anfal: The Garmian Anfal was the third phase of a genocide process aimed at annihilating the Kurdish people, which began on 7th April 1988, and ended on 20th April 1988, which bordered Kirkuk to the south of the city, meaning the cities of Khurmatu, Kifri, Kalar, south of Darbandikhan and Chamchamal. These forces participated in this Anfal phase:

1. The 2nd Legion Force under the supervision of Kamel Sajid, which consisted of these military units:

    - Infantry Division 15.
    - Infantry Division 34.
    - Ali Medarea Division 3

2. The First Legion, led by the criminal, Sultan Hashim, consisted of these military units:

- The Light Regiment forces are led by Saad Shamsaddin
- The 10th Armored Division, led by the criminal, Khalid Dlemi
- The oil guard force, led by Barq Abdullah
- The Commander of the First Legion, led by Munzir Ibrahim.

3. Al-Jahad al-Daneshi for destroying villages.
4. The Staff of the Intelligence Forces belongs to the Legions and Divisions.
5. Chemical class.
6. Soupa planes.
7. Air Force.
8. Security units in Kirkuk and Sulaymaniyah provinces.

On 21st April 1988, for the Northern Organizing Office in Kirkuk, the army achieved all its goals and led the people of the area to an uncertain fate, according to a letter from the 2nd Legion Intelligence No. 11386 to the Northern Organizing Office in Kirkuk. They were sent and the villages were destroyed. According to statistics from the campaign, 34,770 women, children, young people and the elderly were missing.

Stage Four:

The fourth phase of Anfal began on 3rd May 3 to 8th May, 1988, and covered a large geographical area around the small area of Shwan, Sheikh Bezani, Qala-e Seuk, Taqtaq, Koya and Khalakan. Sultan Hashim direct supervision. He did the fourth Anfal and it consisted of these military units:

1. The commander of the First Legion, which consisted of the following units:
   - The Infantry Division of Ali 8
   - Division 38
   - 8th Infantry Division Infantry Division 2

2. Nasr forces under the command of Brigadier General Khalid Ahmed Ibrahim.
3. Force 46 under the command of Brigadier General Ali Ahmed Muhammad.
4. The oil protection force under the command of Brigadier General Barq Abdullah.
5. The first legion was commanded by Brigadier General Alla and Muhammad Taha.
6. The security detachments of Sulaymaniyah and Kirkuk.
7. Engineering units to destroy villages.
8. The intelligence staff of the Legions and Brigades.
9. Chemical class.
10. Military planes.
11. Air Force.
12. Military intelligence.

28,550 people were missing in the fourth Anfal campaign, killed and buried in mass graves.

Stages 5, 6 and 7:

These Anfal campaigns were a series of crimes carried out on 5th May to 26th May 1988, under the command of Colonel Rukn Younis Mohammed al-Zarb, commander of the Five Legions.

This campaign attacked the villages of Koya and Koya districts, Degala district, and some villages around Erbil, Shaqlawa, Choman, and Qandil mountain, Rania, Chuaqurna, Hezop, Bawaji mountain range, and many other places. This stage began in Anfal on 15th May 1988, which was the first day of Eid al-Fitr, while the people themselves were for Eid al-Fitr.

The military units that participated in the attack were:

1. The Fifth Legion of al-Amouriyeh, under the command of Brigadier General Younis Muhammad al-Zarb, consisted of the following units:

    - 16th Infantry Division (Zulfaqar Force)
    - 4th Infantry Division (Qa'aqa Force)
    - Infantry Division One 1 (Abu-Obedia Force)
    - 7th Infantry Division (Mansur Force).

2. Units of the First Legion.
3. The engineering groups including bulldozers, and instruments for opening roads and flattening villages and religious and holy places.
4. Military planes.
5. Air Force.
6. Chemical equipment.
7. The use of special explosives means chemical weapons.
8. Army Intelligence Units.

Stage Eight:

The Anfal phase in Badinan started on 25th August 1988 and continued to the end of September. The eighth phase of Anfal was different from the other seven stages, because in the seven stages of Anfal, the regime was engaged in war with Iran, but after the end of the war, it devoted all its power and forces to implementing this phase of Anfal and an opportunity for more in front of the regime to carry out his plans.

At this stage, chemical weapons were used in several locations, such as the villages of Nahel area in the Deraluk district, and on 23rd August 1988, 54 people were killed in the villages of Sherana, Yekmala, Sarke and Bibe and the regime-held Kani community. On 24th August 1988, regime planes used chemical weapons in most areas of Badinan, as preparations for ground attacks that began in the morning of 25th August 1988

Regime forces remained under the supervision of military intelligence in the area to completely flatten all villages (numbering 633), as well as destroying any food and all sources of life, and to plant mines so that no one could enter the area. The forces involved in the Eighth Anfal were:

The Fifth Legion, led by the first Lieutenant General Younis al-Zarb, consisted of the following units:

1. The 16th Infantry Division of the Zulfaqar Force consisted of:
   - The 1st Infantry Brigade
   - 505th Infantry Brigade
   - 606th Infantry Brigade

2. 4th Infantry Division, Qa'aqa Force, consisting of:
   - 29th Infantry Brigade
   - 69th Infantry Brigade
   - 5th Infantry Brigade

3. Infantry Division 1 (Abu Bayda Force) consisted of:
   - Ali 1 infantry brigade
   - Infantry Brigade Ali 27
   - Ali 34th Infantry Brigade

4. Infantry Division 7 (Mansur Force) consisted of:
   - 38th Infantry Brigade
   - 39th Infantry Brigade
   - 116th Infantry Brigade

Several other units were brought in, and the total number of units and brigades that participated in the Anfal reached 38 infantry brigades, 2 brigades, 3 Madfai brigades and several others.

5. Engineering material, which consisted of several shovel loader tractors, bulldozers and other materials.
6. Military pilots.
7. Air Force.
8. Chemical classes.
9. Special war effort for opening mountain roads.
10. 1Military intelligence units.

Several Light Regiments of Jash (Kurdish traitors) and all governmental and civil institutions were under the control of the 8th Anfal Command.

The bitterest and worst days of my life were when the Anfal process was carried out in Kurdistan, with many people leaving their places. While the Ba'athist regime was behind them, Turkey had closed its borders to the deprived people who tried to reach

Turkey in order to escape the regime's pursuit. Although some of them reached Turkish borders, many were trapped in Gara mountain slopes and were besieged by regime forces. The situation of these people shook people's souls, it was difficult for them to deliver help, we couldn't save them, and a tragic scene was created.

I sent a message to branch one and asked the people to be notified so that women and children could surrender to the regime, because the regime had blocked the public streets and they had no chance of being rescued. In response, branch one said the public had told women and children that they were all ready to die here but would not surrender to the regime. The truth is, I have not cried as much as this event in my whole life and for any other event.

Although it took a long time for Turkey to open its borders to those who could be rescued from regime forces and had reached the border, it was not ready to shelter refugees who were planning to cross. Although opening the borders to citizens was unexpected, we did not expect Turkey to open the borders at all, however, opening the borders and crossing citizens into Turkish territory allowed for the rescue of a large number of women, men, children and disabled people from death, so opening the borders to refugees was a good thing, even though they suffered a lot.

During the Anfal process, 90% of Kurdistan's villages and more than 20 cities and towns were removed from the map. The rural areas were mined with fifteen million road mines. About 1.5 million Kurds had been transferred from their villages to camps and forced communities. About 10% of southern Kurds were destroyed. By this, about 23,270km were affected by the regime's Anfal campaign.

On 27th August 1988, families across branch one tried to cross to get closer to Turkey's borders, and Turkey closed its borders, and even the wounded and families were not allowed to enter their territory. It is a situation, disaster, tragedy, and clearly defined. It is impossible to imagine and shakes the hearts of human beings.

According to news on 28th August 1988, the situation in branch one, due to the chemical attack, was very complicated and unpleasant, and there were no solutions left. The Turks had the opportunity to escape and pass. They did not return, and the wounded remained untreated, and there was a plan between Turkey and Iraq to hide and cover up Iraq's crimes against the Kurdish people. The forces withdrew as there was no significant fighting or defence.

On 28th August 1988, we were completely busy with the situation in the branch, which suffered a semi-collapse, due to the situation of families and homes; the crime of the Turks was no less than that of the Ba'athists.

On this day, Ali Abdullah and Muhsin Dizayee went to Tehran to attend a meeting scheduled for Tehran. The peshmerga of Gulan district committee attacked their enemy's advances in Balanda. They stopped, seized many captives and belongings in the hands of the peshmerga.

On 28th August 1988, Qaraqul Sarasive refused to negotiate with branch one and announced that they had nothing to say to them. On 29th August 1988, the situation with the families of the branch was deteriorating. The Turkish stance remained the same and no one was allowed to enter Turkish territory.

On 29th August 1988, branch one answered the letter, the text of which is below:

To/MB

Number / 20 29ᵗʰ August, 1988 in / branch one Communication
No . (6929)

Majid Bag sent us a letter saying that if they had any requests
from us, they should be sent via a letter. If we liked, we would
set a meeting time, and if we didn't like it, there would be no
meetings. A man of Majid Behg said that Majid Beg said that
any request sought by Turkey should be handed over and that I
would hand him over to his destination. In this stance, it became
clear how hostile and cruel Turkey was and how much it partic-
ipated in the Ba'athist regime's crimes. What were they saying
a while ago and how much they were forging and breaking
themselves, but now they were so arrogant and untrustworthy.

The loyal people who helped us well on those dark and difficult days were Haji Nayef Shaf Razani, Agid Bechuhi, Muhammad Rashid Bayi, Muhammad Qayum Bayi (because of Ahmed Haji Abdulhadi), Salih Nabi (because of Ali Shabowa), Haji Muhammad Salih Samad (because of Ahmed Haji Abdulhadi).

On 30ᵗʰ August 1988, Turkey showed readiness to take families and allow them to enter Turkish territory.

On 2ⁿᵈ September 1988, we spoke to Fouad Mirani and told him that his people should protect themselves and stay in their places, and eventually he agreed to stay in L.N. Golan. After unparalleled defence and patience, on 2ⁿᵈ September 1988, the enemy's attack on Khwakurk was defeated. Fouad gave a message that read:

To / MB no . 27 on 3ʳᵈ September 1988 in Fouad Mirani

Letter number (30, 31, 34).

Mr Mohammed Qasim, Haji Muhammed Salih and Haji arrived at us last night and received their secrets and quantities. On your behalf, we have nominated Mohammed Al-Qasim for the purpose of protecting objects with all trusts. We warned him to keep secrets and information safe on your behalf.

The situation after the Anfal process and the reactions

For information.On 4th September 1988, many families from the Areas of Muzuri, Barzan, Harki area on Halane Road arrived in Zewa on their way out of Turkey.

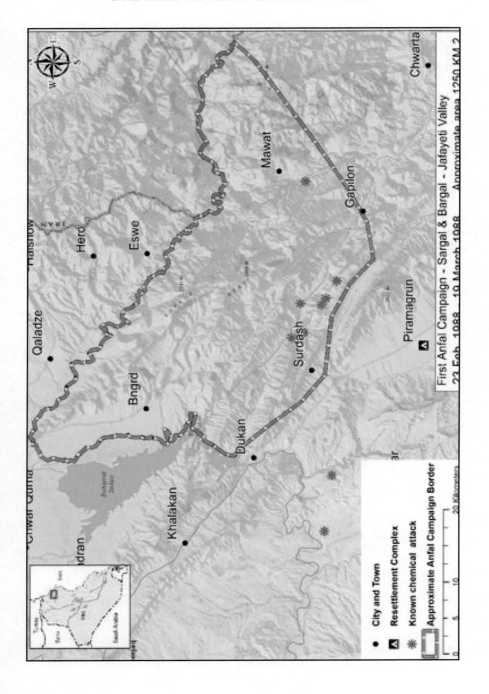

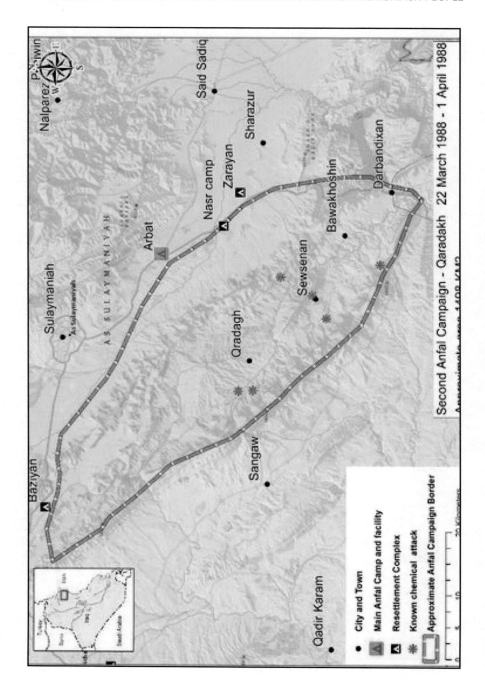

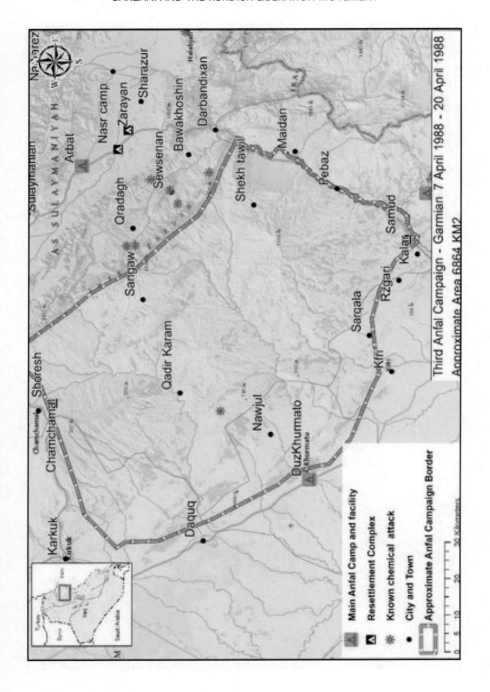

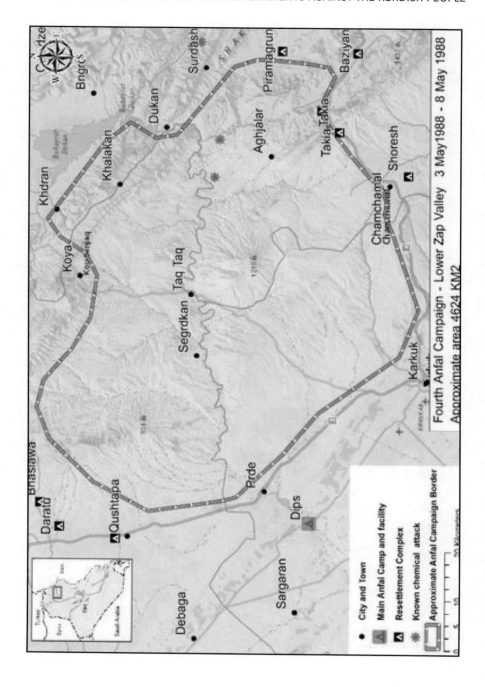

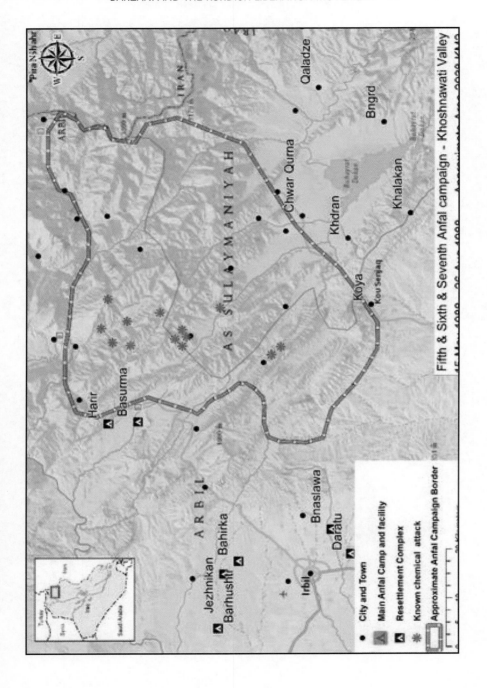

Fifth & Sixth & Seventh Anfal campaign - Khoshnawati Valley

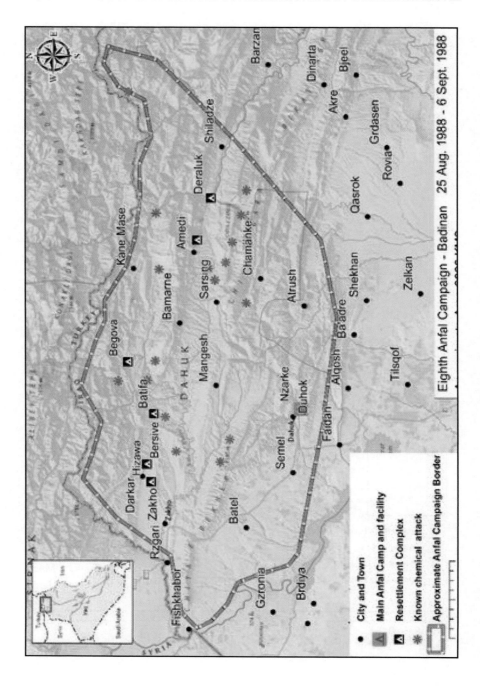

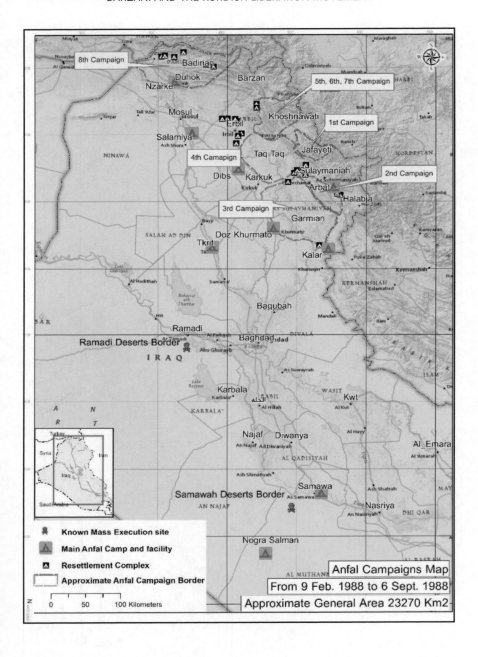

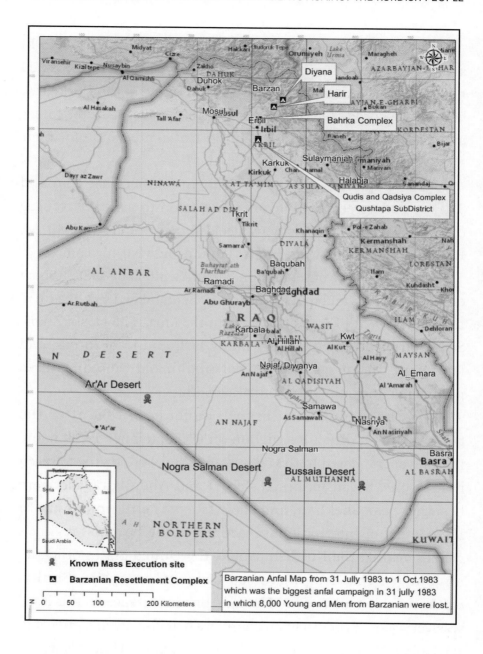

Barzanian Anfal Map from 31 Jully 1983 to 1 Oct.1983
which was the biggest anfal campaign in 31 jully 1983
in which 8,000 Young and Men from Barzanian were lost.

☠ Known Mass Execution site

◣ Barzanian Resettlement Complex

On 7th September 1988, I received a letter from Saado Korki and Sarbast Bamarni discussing the situation, and we received news of Fatah, Qadir and their friends arriving in the Doski area beyond the border. On 8th September 1988, I met with the forces and leadership organizations, and we had appreciation for their struggle and defence of the homeland.

On 8th September 1988, Mr Muhsin told me that Iran and Turkey had agreed to allow our delegation to visit the refugee camp in Turkey. That's why we decided that friends Muhsin, M. Babakir, and Shukri would go to Turkey and visit the camps.

After a few days of separation, on 8th September 1988, branch one contacted us and told us that on 5th September 1988, the force that had left with Fatah and Qadir in the area. The Doski Zhori, Shet Younis attacked, killing many Jash and Iraqi forces, and martyring peshmerga Fendi Avdal Sindhi, and wounding three peshmerga, including Mr Qadir Kachakh.

The Shekhan district branch announced that after the blockade and a difficult situation on 6th September 1988, many families surrendered to the regime and they were trying to reach branch one, because Shimal Zebari and Abdullah Qado were besieged near Shekhan, and their fate was still unknown. In the context of international reactions to the Ba'athist regime's crimes against the Kurdish people, the United States officially announced that Iraq had used chemical weapons. Shultz, spoke harshly with Saadun Hamadi. Britain's stance on this issue was very good. Scandinavian countries had also given a project to the United Nations, and Dekoyar, secretary of the United Nations, said, "I am very sad about the Kurdish situation and I hope I have the power to help them."

Shortly after the Anfal process, a peshmerga detachment returned to Kurdistan, including friends Mohammed Muhsin, Sheikh Alo, Tamer Kochar, Zaeem Ali, Shukri Nerwai, Mohammed Khalid Bosali and a number of peshmerga. After preparations in eastern Kurdistan, they reached the Khomar and Haqi Bag areas. Locals helped them a lot and brought them to the village of Baye, where immortal Barzani and his friends had gone to Russia. I'm sorry to say that the brave peshmerga, Sherko, was martyred by a road mine. One of the tragic events that followed the Badinan Anfal in the Turkish camps was the martyrdom of the old and loyal peshmerga Mehoagawda, who was kidnapped and handed over to Iraq between 1988 and 1989 by Ba'athists in the Diyarbakir camp and martyred by Iraq.

In 1991, during the Kurdistan Council negotiations with Baghdad, Ali Hassan al-Majid told some friends about the Anfal, saying the numbers were exaggerated, 180,000 killed, rather than 2,000,000.

The next day, at a meeting we were at the Situation Normalization Committee, I discussed the matter with him and said, "Let's not be 100,000, let there be 50,000 people. What is the fate of those 50,000 people?"

According to the documents obtained, the number of disappearances of Majid's time in power is estimated at 60,000 to 100,000.

According to Amnesty International's predictions in Kurdistan and all of Iraq, it was hundreds of thousands of people in the 1980s, except for the period when Ali Hassan al-Majid lost power and they estimated that more than 100,000 people had been executed without a trial and they sacrificed themselves for Kurdistan.

A UN report also found that Saddam Hussein's brutality against the Kurds was so deadly and it engulfed so many people that it had been unimaginable since World War II.

Other nations, such as Chaldeans, Assyrians and Yazidi Kurds in Kurdistan, had been pressured to consider themselves Arabs and belong to the Baath Party.

A letter from Kirkuk's secret relations department no. 11/8231431 on 13th July 1998, directed to the leadership of the Kirkuk branch of the Ba'athist party describes the relocation of 545 families in the neighbourhoods of Shorija, Askari, Baghdad Road, Azadi, Iskan, Middle, Hairan, Musalla, Imam Qasim, Military Number One and Kask).

According to Amnesty International, nearly 200 Kurds were hanged in the 18 months after the Algerian agreement.

Iraqi media ministers and Tariq Aziz, in a misguided attempt, announced that the transfer of Kurds from small communities, consisting of five to 100 families, to the villages of Arabs, would then be able to understand their Arab brothers, and that, when the process of understanding and their enlightenment was over, they could travel throughout Iraq.

Regarding PDK and peshmerga activists, Tariq Aziz said they would participate in seminars held by Ba'athist cadres in the camps on the Patriotic Union and Autonomous Region.

The regime's army, with the help of Saeed Asaad al-Shal, entered the Dolmari area and besieged the village of Shekhan, asking the residents of the village to hand over their weapons, then set fire to their houses and expelled the residents of the village. According to the information, the health situation of two people was not good.

Within the framework of the policy of changing Kurdistan's demographics and in light of the policy of correcting the national situation, according to the instructions of the Northern Affairs Committee, written instruction no. 1142 on 23rd February 1989, the national situation of the Yezidi Kurds was changed from Kurdish to Arab nationality. In this context, in the 1977 census, about 96% of the Yezidi population of Mosul province and 97.5% of Kurd Yezidis in Duhok were considered Arabs.

French journalist Reina Morris explained that from 1965 to 1966, the Iraqi regime used poison gas in Kurdistan.

In a special report, no. 23 of 1989, on the rights of minorities around the world, the London International Association for the Defence of Minorities in the World recorded many factors of genocide, particularly in southern Kurdistan, where the regime destroyed 40,000 homes out of 700 villages in 1960-1970. The number of displaced people reached 300,000, with 60,000 killed and wounded.

The same report explained that, in 1988, many people were killed and displaced from Turkey and Iran as a result of the use of chemical weapons.

On 14th March 1989, Amnesty International in London announced that in Sulaymaniyah between September and October 1985, the Iraqi regime had executed 300 Kurdish children between the ages of 17 to 23 years old.

According to the latest census of the Kurdistan-Iraq Front, which the political leadership handed over to the UN Human Rights Committee on 24th February 1989, 55,000 to 60,000 square kilometres had been evacuated and destroyed, with more than half a million Kurds displaced and emigrated to Europe, more than one million Kurds having been displaced from their homes.

In a secret document issued on 23rd June 1989, it was stated that the relocation of the residents of Qaladze had come to an end, and the equipment of the 24th Division began to destroy houses.

In order to solve the problems of our refugees in the Diyarbakir camp, on 20th March 1990, I spoke by phone for more than two hours with each of my friends Saado Korkai, Akram Mai, Said Nayef, Nayef Musa, Saeed Kestai, Salih Haji Hussein, Hussein Chalki and Osman Qasim, because the election of the committees had problems, and we tried to make decisions for them, but they refused, and then they promised to agree internally and each of Akram Mai And Saado Korkai and Salih Haji Hussein was to temporarily supervise the camp, and then officials would make a final decision at a meeting in which they would notify us of the result. In the call, Akram stated that:

- The human rights movement in Turkey would be strengthened.
- On the anniversary of the Halabja disaster, demonstrations were held in major cities such as Istanbul, Ankara, Azmir and Adana and all provinces of northern Kurdistan, particularly Diyarbakir, where many people are from cities Diyarbakir, Jazire, Slopi and Nussebin were arrested.

On 2nd April 1990, the Baghdad station published a statement saying that we had weapons and that if Israel attacked us, we would destroy half of its territory. This statement was made because of the need to stand up to public and international opinion against Iraq.

According to Mosul governorate letter no. 1741 on 10th April 1990, in light of the instructions of the presidency of the republic in writing no. (Q9611) on 3rd April 1990, it was decided by the regime to form a committee to destroy all the houses of the moved networks, distribute their property and lands, and transfer their personal status record (population) out of the province.

On the night of 3rd to 4th May 1990, Israeli and Monte Carlo stations reported that the Washington Post stated in a Pentagon report that Iran had bombarded Halabja with cyanide gas, arguing that Iraq doesn't have this gas.

We thought there was a suspicious purpose behind this announcement, why this secret would be revealed after two years, apparently aimed at hiding and whitewashing Iraq's crimes.

After the chemical attacks on Kurdistan and the implementation of the Anfal process, which killed tens of thousands of Kurdistan citizens, commanders of the PDK's foreign relations bureau played an important and significant role in alerting and conveying the voice and disaster of our people to the international decision-making and public opinion centres. For this purpose, they visited capitals, forums, associations, international organisations, and international civil and legal institutions to cover up and show the truth about Ba'athist racist and anti-humanist policies against our people. Their work, activities, and visits were good reasons for attracting the sympathy and interest of the international community and foreign public opinion for their problems and the disasters that had occurred our nation and foreign aid to the People of Kurdistan.

CHAPTER FIFTEEN

10th Congress

Holding the tenth congress

ACCORDING TO OUR party's internal rules, the congress was to be held in 1983 or 1984, and this issue was discussed at most of the central committee's meetings. Of course, certain things were taken into consideration which would impact on the congress taking place, such as:

- The situation in the region in general and Kurdistan in particular,
- The Kurdish people enduring a sensitive and dangerous stage,
- An outbreak of the war between Iraq and Iran,
- The notorious Anfal process by the Ba'athist regime,
- Development of Arabization, relocation, change in the demographics of Kurdistan,
- Chemical attacks on Kurdistan,

- Cessation of the Iraq-Iran war,
- Emergence of a group of political issues,
- Both military and economic problems within the region.

As a consequence of these events, the decision was taken to postpone the congress.

After considering the interests of our Party, and for the sake of reviewing the affairs of the Party, the Committee met and a new policy was adopted and an advanced and modern programme established that was compatible with the new conditions of Kurdistan, the region, and the international community.

The 10th PDK congress, which was held between November 15 and 16, 1988, was scheduled take place and the necessary measures initiated. For this purpose, a preparatory committee was formed, which of them are not members of the PDK leadership:

1. Nechirvan Barzani, head of the committee.
2. Abdulaziz Taib, member.
3. Qadir Qadir, member.
4. Haji Deloi, member.
5. Mahmoud Muhammad, member.

Shortly afterwards, the committee began its work and elections were held within the refugee organisations in Iran and among the peshmerga. In the elections, a representative for every 150 members was elected; for branch six, five representatives and two for the seventh branch were selected. In October 1989, the election of the congress's representatives ended, but for some external reasons, the congress was delayed. After the preparations and situation were completed, our tenth Party congress was held between 2nd and 12th December, 1989 in the village of Heshmawa. 332 representatives participated.

During the congress, several articles and reports were read, including:

The central committee prepared a general and extensive report approved at the central committee meeting and read by Haval Ali Abdullah.

In the report, the shortcomings were identified in all areas, referring to problems and procedures for solving them were presented.

The departments of organization, finance and military in the political bureau, each according to their expertise, presented their reports and these were read in the congress. We also gave a detailed speech in which we welcomed the guests and participants of the congress and expressed our wish that the congress be successful.

At the congress, a delegation of parties from both inside and outside the Kurdistan Front, a representative of the Islamic Republic of Iran, attended the opening session of the congress and the representative of the Islamic Republic delivered a speech. A speech of the Patriotic Union of Kurdistan was also read.

Members of congress then began their work and several special committees were formed internally to discuss issues related to the congress, taking into account and reading the situation in the world in general, the region and Kurdistan in particular. It was necessary to review the Party's procedures and programmes in a way that would be compatible with the new situation, any developments and the new phase of our nation's struggle. Therefore, at the tenth congress, a fundamental change was made in Article 5 of the PDK programme, as references to it being Marxist-Leninist were removed, and this article was generally edited.

The important issue was that these changes preceded the collapse of the former Soviet Union and the Communist Party's authority in the country, which showed the Party's rightful reading and prediction of new changes and developments.

Also, changes were made to the authority of the president of the PDK, because previously the authority of the president was split according to the rules and a secretary was appointed, but the post of secretary was no longer held at the congress, and the Vice President was elected as secretary, whose powers would be determined by the president. The changes proposed by the previous central committee were presented to the congress and were approved.

According to the modern situation and struggle, a number of changes in the programme were made to enable compatibility with the new phase of the struggle of the Kurdish people, the region and the world. Due to the congress being held in a situation where the region, Kurdistan and the Kurdish people were enduring a sensitive and dangerous phase; the Anfal disaster had happened to the Kurdish people; and a large number of Kurdistan citizens had been displaced to Iran, Turkey and abroad, and the war that occurred had ended.

Two new figures entered the leadership, Mr Nechirvan Barzani and Jawhar Namiq Salim, who returned to the party for good.

Former PDK leadership members such as Muhammad Mala Qadir, Rashid Arif, Khurshid Shera, Nadir Hawrami, Sergeant Hamid and Dr Saeed Ahmed Barzani did not nominate themselves, each for their own special reasons.

At the end of the congress, I was elected president of the Kurdistan Democratic Party (PDK) through the vote of all the participants in the congress appointed Ali Abdullah as Vice President of the PDK Party.

At the end of the congress, and through a democratic process, the friends of the central committee were elected:

Nechirvan Barzani, Falakadin Kakayi, Dr Rozh Nuri Shawis, Fazil Mirani, Jawhar Namiq Salim, Hoshyar Zebari, Dr Jarjis Hassan, Abdul Muhaiman Barzani, Hamid Afandi, Masoud Salihi, Rebwar Yalda, Izzadin Barwari, Azad Qaradaghi, Zaeem Ali, Dr Pirot Ahmed, Qadir Qadir, Qadir Abdulaziz (Qachakh), Dr Ali Baba Shawis,[9] Dr Muhammad Salih Jumaa, Omar Osman Mergasori, Kamal Kirkuki.

Later, at the meeting of the central committee, the members of the political bureau were elected, including:

1. Nechirvan Barzani
2. Fazil Mirani.
3. Dr Rozh Nuri Shawisi
4. Dr Jarjis Hassan
5. Jawhar Namiq Salim
6. Hoshyar Zebari
7. Zaeem Ali

Because Mr Idris's death had created a great gap, we tried to give Nechirvan more attention and importance as a gesture of loyalty to Mr Idris Barzani and fill the role, putting him in charge early, so he had the opportunity at the tenth congress and allowed to take responsibility.

---

[9] At eleven o'clock at night of 6th/7th December 1990. Ali Baba Shawais, who died of heart disease in Mariwan, was elected as a member of the Central Committee at the 10th Congress of our Party. The person named is the son of Ismail Haqi Shawais who was a loyal and honest human being.

After the end of the congress and at the meeting of the central committee, the way of party work and the structure of the branches were reviewed with new structures and staff being appointed, as well as a detailed review of the military structure and the peshmerga were reorganized and in a modern way, in line with new situations and developments.

Although the peshmerga platoon remained in Kurdistan, with Haval Simko Amedi and other friends being martyred in the border of branch one, it was not an easy task, and it was decided that the other peshmerga platoon would be sent to internalize the country.

At the end of the congress, several important and necessary decisions were made on different subjects and fields, and essential and appropriate recommendations were made:

First, in the interior of Kurdistan

1. The decision to commemorate the great and immortal patriotic president, Mustafa Barzani.
2. The decision to commemorate Mr Idris Barzani.
3. A decision would be made regarding the continuation of the struggle and the diversity of the forms of struggle.
4. The decision about the cease fire of the Iraq-Iran war.
5. A Decision on chemical weapons.
6. The decision on the divided Kurdish nation.
7. Decisions on missing persons.
8. Decisions on political prisoners.
9. A decision on the pursuit of war deniers.

Decision on refugees

1. Decision on refugees in general.
2. The decision on refugees in Iran.
3. The decision on refugees in Turkey.
4. Decisions on our refugees in Pakistan.
5. The decision on the Kurdish movement in other countries

Decision on council work

1. The national issue.
2. Unification.
3. Decisions about publishing democracy in the liberation movement Kurd.

Decision on Kurdish organizations

1. Decision on the Union of Islamic Scholars of Kurdistan.
2. Decisions on Kurdish writers, writers, and artists.
3. Decisions on the mass and professional organizations of Kurdistan.

In the international sphere

1. The decision on the death of Imam Khomeini.
2. The decision to send congratulatory letters to countries that have supported our Nation's problems.

On the Arab level

A letter of support for the Palestinian liberation revolution and the parties and our allies were sent.

Decision on sending these greetings

1. Greetings to Immortal Barzani's friends.
2. Greetings to the families of the martyrs of Kurdistan and Iraq.
3. Greetings to the brave peshmerga and the national defence and appreciating their sacrifices, heroism, and patience.
4. Greetings to the members and supporters of the Party's patience.
5. Greetings to the displaced and the masses of the forced camps.
6. Greetings to all the Kurdish parties, brothers and the Iraqi Kurdistan Council.
7. Greetings to the Iraqi national parties.
8. Greetings to the people of Iraq, whether in Kurdistan, Baghdad, the middle or the south of the country, for their struggle for democracy for Iraq and real autonomy for Kurdistan.
9. A letter of gratitude and respect to all parties, organizations, social, political and cultural individuals who have sent their greetings to the congress.
10. A special greeting to Gorbachev regarding the new policy that served the issue of peace and freedom in the world.

Decision on the situation of international countries

The decision to respect the countries that have come to the aid of the Kurdish people, as well as the importance of cooperation, support and sympathy with the world's liberation movements.

These topics were decided at the congress

Cooperating with the problems of global liberation

During the conduct and after the end of the tenth congress of our party, many letters and messages of congratulations and support from the organization, political parties, intellectual and social personalities were sent to the president, our party and the tenth congress:

Kurdistan Liberation Party (Rizgari), Philippine Democratic Union of America, People's General Congress in America, People's Movement Against War in America, African Democratic Socialist Organization in Virginia, Philippine People's Support Center in America, Information Movement. Chicago - John Stoke, editor-in-chief of the magazine called Research and Information of the Middle East.

Al-Awsat), Kurdistan Socialist Party, Kurdistan Students' Association in Europe, Kurdistan Workers' Party -Iraq, Kurdistan People's Democratic Party, Islamic Movement of Iraqi Kurdistan, Federation of Kurdish Groups in Sweden, Iraqi Kurdistan Front, Patriotic Union of Kurdistan, Flag of Revolution, (Islamic Reaction Organization in Iraq, Islamic Dawa Party, Central Committee of the Kurdish People's Union Party in Syria), Pasok, Mr Muhammadi, representative of the Islamic President of Iran, Secretariat of the Parliamentary Fraction of the Labor Party Holland, speech by the Iranian Islamic Revolutionary Guard Corps, friends of the Tunisian Communist Party in Damascus, (Al-Qaeda of the Syrian Democratic Union, The Islamic Assembly of Lakrad al-Filin, Foreign Organization, Union Al-Dimaqratin al-Iraqi al-Fara al-Third, Staff writers of Barbang magazine,

Egyptian Communal Party, Iraqi Democratic Assembly, Swedish Democratic Party, Communist Party Iraq, Al-Issar al-Communist Party in Sweden, Kurdistan Central Committee, Kurdistan Socialist Party of Turkey, Federation of Kurdistan Workers' Associations (Komkar), General Committee of Kurdistan Liberation Movement (Tavgar), (Al-Shaabia Organization in Jordan, Salim Fakhri, Al-Ba'ath Al-Arabi Party (Qatar Al-Iraq Command), Hans Dingils Al-Skrtir al-Dawli for the Democratic Community Party in Western Germany, Saad Saleh Al-Jaber Of The New Ummah Party, Volkmar Ruhrsh School of Foreign Affairs in the International Committee For the solidarity with the Kurdish branches, Maria Lisner of the Swedish branch, member of the Swedish Branch, the Iraqi-Iraqi Coalition, the Iraqi Religious Community, the Iraqi Democratic Party, the Book and Journalists' Association, The Kurdish Democratic Party in Syria (Barti), the Kurdish Progressive Democratic Party in Syria, the General Alliance in the Iraqi Republic, the Patriotic Union of Iraq for the Al-Nafizi School, the Turkish Communist Party (Middle East Organization), the Communist Left Party (VPK), the Party The Syrian Communist Party, the French Communist Party, the Norwegian Socialist Left Party, the Social Democratic Party (SPD), the Green Party of the Netherlands, the Syrian Communist Party (al-Qaeda organizations), the Iraqi Democratic Union in the United States and Canada, the Al-Shaabi Front in Bahrain, al-Bahrain The Central Committee for the Communist Party of Palestine, the Al-Shaabia Al-Tahrir al-Palestine (Political Circle), the Palestine Tahrir Al-Tahrir Al-Jabhat, the Communist Party in Lebanon, the Al-Communist Party in Saudi Arabia, the Damascus School's Al-Tahrir Front, the Egyptian National Assembly in

The Outside, The Front Al-Tahrir al-Watani- Bahrain, Lebanese Communist Party, Iraqi Community Party, Kurdistan Ulema and Islamic Union, Dutch Workers' Party, Second Congress- Lahi, Kurdish Party in Syria, Students and Youth of Kurdistan/Iraq Democracy, Jürgen M Air (Germany), Mohammad Bahr al-Ulum, Al-Moqadam Munzer al-Musalla, Jamal Bakhtiar (Kurdistan Artists Association), Dr Vera Biodin Saeedpur (Kurdish Program) New York, Goin Roberts, Partik Boadon, Hussein Ardem, Dr Peter Pilts, Austrian Parliamentarian, Chris Kochera, Hassan al-Mala (Chol), M. Amin Boz Arsalan, Singer Shvan Parwar, Professor Roland Mush, head of the Scientific Council of the Colleges of Bremen University in Germany, Karl Smola, Austrian parliamentarian Hassan Mustafa Naqib, Paul Shafi, norwegian parliamentarian from the leftsocialist faction, A Libs, left of the Dutch green, Til Izmat Sharif Wanli, Muhammad Baqir Hakim, Ayatollah Saeed Muhammad Taqi Mudarresi, Mrs. Mirama Aziz Tablisi, Hasan Al in Germany, Dr Rahman Garmiani, teacher Hazhar Mukryani, Nadir Nadirov Academy, Professor Samir Nofa, Kurdnas at the Oriental Institute in Leningrad, and Dr Karim Ayubi, Professor Shakoye Khdo, head of the Modern Kurdish Problems Chamber at The Orientalist Institute Soviet Union Scientific Academy, Dr Sharaf Asherian, cooperation of Kurdistan political organizations in the Soviet Union, Union of Students of Arab Countries organizations in the Soviet Union, Muhammad Suleiman Babaeev, chairman of the Founding Committee of the Republic of Soviet And Socialist Kurdistan Autonomy, Hussein Ardam, secretary-general of the Kurdish Writers' Organization outside, Tosani Rashid, chemical doctor and Kurds writers in the Soviet Union.

Political report of the central committee of the tenth congress 1989/12/12

Dear President of our Party, Mr Masoud Barzani, the struggling friends of the central committee of the holy revolution of May 26, brothers and sisters, the struggling representatives of the tenth congress, and dear guests,

Let me present the report of your central committee to a revolutionary and warm brotherly greeting.

We welcome you very much, we hope that your participation in this congress will be our best motivation for the success of our congress by evaluating the reality and the situation of the past ten years so that the Kurdish liberation movement in Iraq will be at the highest level of its true and realistic slogan that has developed the struggle for democracy for Iraq and real autonomy for Kurdistan.

On this historical occasion, we renew our covenant with the martyrs of Kurdistan, Iraq, immortal Barzani, and Mr Idris, who, in the best and newest form of struggle, will continue on the path of PDK and Barzani, so that our nation will be saved from this moment in which such a monument has not been seen or even heard in the history of our nation. Here we ask you to stop for a minute to respect them and commemorate their immortality.

New world and Kurds

Dear brothers,

Today's world is a new world, requiring new world political thinking towards new world peace (Al-Anfattah al-Doli) and becoming more stable day by day. Both socialist and capitalist camps, particularly the Soviet Union and the United States of America, have reached the conclusion that another war, or World War III, would involve atomic weapons that would not only be dispatched by this side, or the other, but would result in the extinction of all sides and all humanity. That is why they have come to the decision that the policy of peaceful coexistence (Taish Salmi) would establish, deepen, carry and destroy nuclear, chemical and biological weapons, and the reduction or destruction of traditional weapons would be considered. Democratic, political, and economic changes in eastern European countries and the strengthening of the democratic movement and human rights opened the door for the whole of Europe (east and west) to be united in the service of world peace and progress.

The changes that will happen to the relations between the countries will direct the Kurdish people and their movement. The countries of the Eastern region, and the new political idea, wants to establish the relations between the countries and nations based on democracy, humanity, human rights, freedom, and the rights of the nations which is in the interest of our people.

That's why the socialist camp and capitalist countries are considering rapprochement with each other to a good extent, instead of war (political, ideological, economic and social opposition), it will be stronger, so human rights and nations will take greater consideration, the need for global and regional stability to be established.

We can proudly say that Article 8 of our PDK programme is on the cusp of implementation in terms of protection, global peace and slowing down the tensions within countries and will follow the UNITED NATIONS Convention, promoting the beginning of peaceful coexistence and the solving of state problems through dialogue, prohibition of weapons, atomic and test elimination.

In socialist countries in general, and in the Soviet Union in particular, the Perestroika programme, meaning the return of the foundation, has made the strongest political, economic and social changes, and is being followed with the utmost courage. Its sole purpose being to serve socialism, global peace, and democracy, and this has gained great hope for humanity, and the world is moving towards the destruction of the dictatorial, racist and fascist regimes, or forcing them to do so with a new or adapted policy.

Directing and understanding for solutions for Palestinian, Lebanese, Afghanistan, Cambodia and the South African issue and deciding on Namibia's independence, are the best evidence for humanity between the East and the West to resolve regional disputes under the auspices of the State Board and by The State Conference

This is both a summary and explanation of the global situation, new ideas and policies, and the relationship between the two world camps. The Kurdish nation in general but the Kurdish nation in Iraqi Kurdistan in particular, which has made sacrifices for years to achieve uncountable goals, must be considered and in the light of political thinking.

The new world will adapt its liberation movement to this new reality, hoping it will no longer lose the opportunities available and reach its goals as soon as possible with the least sacrifices.

Kurdish liberation movement in general and in Iraq especially

Of course, the Kurdish nation in general, all the humiliations and evils of the ummah have been realized and developed according to the science of politics, so it has the right to establish its own mass, like every other nation in the world, and we believe in this right. "Our Party supports the struggle of the Kurdish nation, which is forcibly divided, in all parts of Kurdistan, in order to achieve their own destiny, as do all other nations in the world," as stated in article 10 of our PDK program. As a result of the logical division of global colonial influence in general, and in the Near and Middle East in particular, after World War I, the Kurdish and Kurdistan nations were divided, according to the Sykes-Pico 1916 Agreement, without considering the rights of the Kurdish nation, which is the fourth nation, if not third in the region, however, Alanin acknowledged according to Articles 62-63-64 against the subordinate nations of the Ottoman Empire (1920-1920) according to Wilson's principles and allied declarations against the subordinate nations of the Ottoman Empire. The near and distant rights of the Kurdish nation in general, and the Kurdistan of Turkey and Iraq in particular, should have mattered, but what is true is that the conflict between colonial countries to divide their territory has caused the political situation of the Liberation Movement to be severely inappropriate and greedy. The Kurdish people in general, unfortunately, have been largely behind the internal and intellectual situation of our movements in terms of thought, politics, organization, and ignorance of the changes in the global and regional political equations, particularly at that time.

Therefore, the Treaty of Sevres - 1920 could not be implemented and established, even the Treaty of Lausanne -1923 included the establishment of colonial policies in the region, the rights of the Kurdish nation by colonial countries and the resilient entities of the region. They were violated and remained deprived, divided and suppressed, although as a result of the policy of global imperialism and the region's hardship, the Kurdish nation in Kurdistan has waged many revolutions to achieve their national and human rights and has given thousands of martyrs. Even the majority of their lives, which now exceed 25 million in their own country, and left behind for decades.

In Turkey, after Ataturk's victory, a policy of violence was pursued, even denying its existence in the country, which has been used in Iraq by Baghdad's chauvinist dictatorship, the most brutal war of genocide since 1975. In Iran, the Kurdish issue was not yet been resolved in a peaceful and friendly way which would be the basis for a solution, so we called on the Islamic Republic of Iran to provide them with their national rights within the framework of their common entity, which by this policy, was not only for local Kurds, but also the friendship of the Kurdish nation in general and in the interest of all Iranian peoples and the area.

We also called on the Republic of Syria to provide them with administrative and cultural rights, giving identity to the Kurdish brothers who have been removed from them, but at this point they were without ethnicity, and to remove the Arabic belt, which is the programme of the old governments. We hoped that in the Soviet Union, the Perestroika programme would be included. to achieve their national rights.

The Lebanese Kurds needed to achieve their social and national rights, and we called on all patriotic, progressive, Islamic forces and Lebanese officials to support their legitimate demands regarding Lebanese nationality. This meant, the Kurdish issue in general in the Near and Middle East, if not the being the paramount priority was certainly the second, after the Palestinian issue, so resolving it in agreement with the progressive, national and Islamic forces in the common political entities they lived in was very necessary. This was providing that a realistic and reasonable view of solutions would strengthen and ensure their progress for all nations living in the common country, in a way that reflected the will of the Kurdish people, meaning that we have always offered a peaceful and democratic solution, and we would be able to solve the Kurdish problem, especially in Iraq, if it is the most honest and right direction.

In order to prove to all the world's liberal nations that we, the PDK in Iraqi Kurdistan, carried weapons against the Dictatorship of Baghdad, because over the years every other way to achieve our rights had been blocked, and we were obliged to defend the legitimate rights of our nation, destroying our current rights and placing us at more at risk of extinction than ever before.

Establishing an Iraqi political entity in 1921 and not solving the problem of authority and Kurdish problems

Of course, the history of the Iraqi political entity has witnessed, since 1921, two main Arab and Kurdish nations, along with national minorities, which unfortunately had not yet been established.

This was because neither the problem of a democratic government had been solved by a free democratic style in Iraq for the benefit of the Iraqi people, nor had the Kurdish problem, which was the biggest problem in Iraq, in the interests of the Iraqi coalition political entity, and the interests of both nations. The main problem had been solved, so both issues would be resolved with a free and democratic style, and with the consent of the Iraqi people and the Kurdish nation, and day by day in terms of politics, economy, social, and culture administration, to move forward, to avoid obstacles to the development and evaluation of their shared political entity, meaning political power and democratic governance, by both main nations, are in the best way in the structure of the regime's organization. In their new future, they would show themselves and make both nations feel that this political entity was common, and that the collaborations, taking into account and providing the legitimate rights of national minorities well, in accordance to the beginnings of solving the problems of nations. This exists in many developed countries of the world, meaning that under the wing of a just peace, they could live with happiness, freedom, democracy, and detail, and the historical and Islamic brotherhood, the common struggle of Kurds and Arabs would be stronger, and their shared struggle would be better. A democratic and free Iraq in general, with the real autonomy of Kurdistan in particular, would become a stronghold of their lives against imperialism, Zionism, and the region's reality, which would put the best flag in the series. The struggle of liberal and progressive nations on the ground and humanity, for the sake of maintaining and better establishing world peace and solving regional dignity through peaceful dialogue, in the light of new world political thinking.

The fascist regime of Baghdad and the opposition forces of Kurdistan and Iraqis

The period after the dictatorship, which began in 1968 with the support of colonialism, was brought to power, was characterised by fire and iron, even with chemical weapons, biology, mustard, phosgene, and cyanide in the movement. Kurdish liberation, Iraqi democracy, National, Arab Democracy, and the Islamic Movement were attacked in the region and could not raise their heads for their rightful rights, because they would be slaughtered through the dictatorial and chauvinist regimes. The fascist regime of Baghdad, over the ensuing 21 years, would not be able to reach the right solution to the problem of Kurdish rule in Iraq. The force of Kurdistan's activists had been created but could not be dealt with by Baghdad's fascist regime, even shamelessly regarded by Baghdad's fascist regime and Arab Raja'i as foreign servants and generals. Iraqi Arab, democratic and Islamic nationalities had not reached an understanding of the rule of law. Why did they not yet want to end the instigation, to hold a free and democratic election directly, to establish and enforce the permanent constitution? Whatever political parties had to be dissolved, why had democratic freedoms not been granted and not given to include freedom of the party organization, independence, Niqabat's organization's independence, and election freedom?

The human rights of Iraq in general and those of Kurds in particular had been violated, which was underestimated and unheard in human history.

It should have been known that the forces of the Kurdistan and Iraqi opposition were involved in a deep conflict, because of the chauvinistic and fascist practices of this regime and why they were brought, meaning that the conflict between the Iraqi peoples and their advancing forces and the fascist regime. It would be difficult to resolve it, so it was necessary to settle our internal problems one by one, in a way that was in the interest of the Iraqi and Kurdistan people, thereby strengthening the Iraqi Kurdistan council in the right way. These were all aspects that became the foundation stone for creating a wider Iraqi front in all four groups of Iraq's opposition forces: national-Arab, national-Kurdish, democratic, and the Islamic movement, including representatives of national minorities, would be more complete and stable, with many of the ties between us, enabling a stronger stance against

Baghdad's fascist regime. We hoped that all of us would feel our historical responsibility at a high level.

Why Kurds and Kurdistan in Iraq are under the war of Annihilation

Baghdad's dictatorship, used the rule of fire, iron and execution, Arabization, Tabis, Tahjir, and the destruction of more than 4,000 villages in Kurdistan. This included a large number of districts and sub-districts of Kirkuk, Sulaymaniyah, Erbil, Duhok and Mousl in July 1989, the villages of Khanaqin, Shingal and Zummar districts, which were the expulsion of the people of Qaladza district and Sangasar district. They ended the villages in the Dulamer area of Mergasor district, which they had buried in the Sardaw camp, with the utmost disrespect. Like all other forced camps they were not officially counted, because they were seen as second class citizens, meaning that according to the latest census, a small number of villages in Kurdistan remained, which were near and on the edge of the main roads between the provinces of Kurdistan, according to the latest census of the Iraqi Kurdistan Front.

Politically, on February 24, 1989, a report given to the UN Human Rights Committee shows that 55,000 to 60,000 square kilometres were evacuated, leaving more than half a million Kurds homeless and more than one million becoming refugees in countries around the world. Half of the Kurdish citizens had been transferred from their villages, districts, properties and homes, and even water springs and resources had been filled with cement and destroyed, so that there would be no life in Kurdistan and that the people and peshmerga would be unable to live there. It was observed, that Iraqi forces and Jash military bases, along with military cars on the roads, were designed to meet their needs, and this policy began after 1975. In 1976, the Turkish borders of Iran and Iraq were extended 800 kilometres wide and 15 to 20 kilometres deep, and no one was allowed to enter it on pain of death. The fascist regime in Baghdad did not confess its crimes until later, but then they showed their dishonest face to the whole world. Their inhumanity had been revealed, through their embassy in London, using it to announce that the Border Strip of Iraq with Turkey and Iran would be evacuated along 1,200 kilometres and a width of 30 kilometres; it was alleged that this decision was not only for the areas of Kurdistan, but also for the Arab areas and it was in the interest of the people, with the idea that the fascist regime intended to serve them more and save them from the backwardness they lived in. Of course, the demagogues, shamelessness, and lies of the fascist regime would not allow escape from the Kurdish nation, but even the Iraqi ethnic and the world of humanity had come to terms with the fascist regime's despicable plan, knowing that they intended to slaughter Kurds and Kurdistan, and to include and capture the most beautiful and blessed region of Iraqi Kurdistan.

If there was a danger to the Border Strip of Iraq and Iran in the future, why did the destruction include the border of Iraq and Turkey, where relations between the fascist regime of Baghdad and the racist regime of Turkey were very good, even according to their bilateral agreement of 1978, stating that Turkish and Iraqi forces had the right to enter each other's territory 10-15 kilometres in order to strike and destroy the Kurdish peshmerga. If they are honest, why was Faw, which is called Medina al-Fada and Bwaba al-Nasr al-Azim, and Basra (Medina al-Madan) and the small cities bordering Iraq and Iran being rebuilt, with allegedly peaceful intentions, as soon as possible.in the middle and south, and Saddam was proud of this.

If the Kurdish nation in Iraq achieved its rights with the fascist dictatorship and the autonomy zone, why didn't they believe in the Kurdish people and why had all the Iraqi forces and Jash crossed their borders? Why did they impose a genocidal war on the Kurdish people? He worshiped them with brutality, crime and execution in Baghdad's fascist dictatorship regime, in Halabja Ranjaru, Balisan, Jaffayati valley, Sargalu, Bargalu, Qaradagh, Garmian, Shwan, Qalasuka, Koya plains, Smaquli and other areas of Khoshnawati in general, and with the last enemy attack from August 25, 1988 to August 29, 1988. In the last year, the areas of the heroic branch in Duhok and Mosul provinces, which are wet and dry, were hit with chemical and biological weapons, and the Jaish and Jash forces, brutally evacuated all villages within the land, and more than 100,000 people, including women, children, old people, and Jawan forced their way to Turkey and Iran and became refugees.

More than 30,000 people were prevented from doing so and forced to surrender to the fascist regime, which led to them suffering in the Bahrka camp and other Ba'athist camps and suffering from the worst living conditions and suppression. It was acknowledged that a large number were unaccounted for due to the use of chemical and biological weapons in the villages, Gali and the valleys of Zakho, Amedi, Akre, and Shekhan. This was especially true of the Baze people as their escape roads had been hardened and dried up. Even birds and the savages of the mountains do not approach them, because their bodies have all been desecrated. This was the enormity of the disaster of the Kurdish nation under the fascist regime of Baghdad, the most disgraceful regime, which separated the men and women of Iraqi Kurdish citizenship, and tortured thousands of children in front of their parents in order for them to confess their loyalty to Kurdistan.

Because of the fascist regime, Baghdad did not take a peaceful and democratic path to resolve the Kurdish issue in Iraq, so it could not end the annihilation war against the Kurdish people in Iraq, even for all Arab countries and the Arab nation in general and for both camps around the world. It was shown that the Kurdish liberation movement in Iraq was strong and was rooted in the masses even as it attacked it with both traditional weapons and the new technology of war by Iraqi forces and soldiers, as well as thousands of planes, artillery and tanks. They could not defeat Kurdistan's peshmerga and Kurdish nation in the liberated areas, without chemical and biological weapons.

The partisan struggle in Kurdistan would not be silenced, which is the best evidence of the strength of the Kurdistan Revolution to continue the defence and patience of the Iraqi Kurdistan Front forces, so if Baghdad's fascists were able to strike the peshmerga forces and our PDK militarily, but politically it was viewed as extremely dishonest in the world, and it had become clear to the major forces that peace and stability in Iraq and the region would not be achievable until the problem of power in Iraq and the Kurdish issue were resolved.

Of course, Kurdistan, which is the stronghold of all the opposition forces of Kurdistan and Iraqis for democracy for Iraq and true autonomy for Kurdistan, is therefore the enemy of the fascist regime of Baghdad. By their own account, they would continue the war of Kurdish and Kurdistan's annihilation, but Saddam and his regime had lost their imagination, and the Kurds will not die as this is written in blood. We would continue our tireless struggle until we reached our goals.

The war of Kurdish and Kurdistan genocide

The role of the United Nations against this war

Unfortunately, the United Nations in general and neutral countries in particular had not, so far, been unable to prevent Baghdad's fascist regime from committing crimes. The Kurdish nation in general and specifically the Kurdish nation in Iraq, were waiting to hear the open condemnation of humanity, socialist camps, and Arab countries, but we regret that their role was not visible, and this attitude harmed our people and themselves.

Of course, the use of chemical weapons internationally was prohibited under the Geneva 1925 Agreement. Member states of the United Nations could reach a joint resolution on this issue regarding Iraq, but for the benefit of the majority, particularly the five permanent countries of the Security Council, they ignored the issue and hoped for the world of humanity to prevail. This greatly diminished the future of humanity, which would be the biggest threat to themselves.

Our endless thanks are given to those Iraqi, Arab and international organizations, political and scientific figures from the West and East and countries who strongly condemned the crimes committed by the Ba'athist regime and brought the regime's dark character to the world. This is especially the case with their evil intentions, exhibited during the Halabja disaster of Ranjaro, which on 16 and 17 March 1988, involved 5,000 children, women, old and young people, who were subjected to cyanide gas and who fell like autumn leaves. This event also injured more than 10,000. It was not only humans who suffered, but even the animals left in the region succumbed to the gas. Many humanitarian organizations around the world endorsed making March 16 the day of the global prohibition of chemical weapons; we hoped that the United Nations would decide to support this movement. To make it a global day and the role of Amnesty International, and most human rights organizations in western countries, in the United Nations, and the sympathetic committee with the Kurdish nation, consisting of the political and human personality of seventeen countries. The country and other sympathetic committees, and the International Social Democratic Congress in Stockholm, in which the delegation of the Iraqi Kurdistan Front led by the president of the Party participated, Mr Walid Junbalat, the leader of the Socialist Party, participated in the congress.

The advanced Lebanese helped the Kurdistan council delegation to a great extent, and they played a very prolific and beneficial role. The Iraqi Kurdistan people and even the loyal Iraqi people always looked at PDK with all their respect and hope, and now they were completely leading the movement. They know who Kurdistan's liberators are. Of course, our Party delegation defined the problem of Kurds in general and Iraq's crimes in particular, showing the congress, especially the war of the Aflaqi Ba'athist regime and the bloodthirsty Saddam.

This was supported to a great extent by most of the eighty delegations of social democratic parties and their guests, which we thank. We needed to strengthen our relationship with all the parties, organizations, political, scientific, and humanitarian personalities and to follow up on their achievements. More recently, on October 14 and 15, 1989, the Paris congress, under the supervision of Madame Mitran and the Kurdish Institute in Paris, focused on human rights and the identity of the Kurdish people.

They played an excellent role, so that three hundred global figures from the West and East, parties and organizations from all parts of Kurdistan participated, and gave good speeches about the violated rights and freedoms of the Kurdish nation, as a nation of twenty five million people. As a result, the congress reached some very good decisions in the interest of the Kurdish liberation movement, most importantly to call on the United Nations. It accepted and formally introduced a Kurdish delegation with representatives from of all parts of Kurdistan to observe, monitor and protect the human and national rights of the Kurdish nation.

This meant that the Kurdish liberation movement in the world was the public face which defended Kurdish human rights and its cultural identity. Our movement took a new position, determined that we needed to benefit the most and the greatest from it, especially at that moment more than ever in the past. Socialism and western capitalism both seemed to agree that the Kurdish issue in general in the Near and Middle East, particularly in Iraq, should move towards a peaceful and democratic solution, and that without it, in the common countries in which they lived, stability in the region would not be achieved and it would continue to have problems. These problems would arise, develop and end to the detriment of world peace and contrary to the legitimate interests and aspirations of the population of the region.

Our Party and the Iraqi Kurdistan council needed to be involved at the highest level in our movement. Together, they strived, day and night, alongside the new partisan struggle, giving special importance to the political, diplomatic, organizational, media and humanity struggles, so that our nation would be preserved and the homelessness and poverty in which they existed would be changed.

The war between Iraq and Iran, and the attitude of our party (PDK) and the opposition forces of Kurdistan and Iraqis.

With the fall of the regime of the Shah and the success of the Iranian revolution, a new situation emerged in the Middle East against the unjust plans and intentions of imperialism, Zionism, and old-fashioned-ism. A multi-faceted approach was opened in the interest of the freedom and development movement of the nations, including the oppressed and deprived Kurdish people, so our Party's attitude towards this revolution from the first day, even before its success, was a stance of support and friendship.

The decision of the ninth congress, held in 4/11/1979, says:

Our congress supports the successful revolution of the Iranian people under the leadership of Imam Khomeini; the revolution that destroyed the regime of the Shah, the pillars of colonialism and the old-fashionedness of the region, and their authority to strike the liberation movements. He also declares his readiness to strengthen friendship relations with the Islamic Republic to stabilize its pillars, by trying to unify all Islamic, democratic and progressive forces around its flag, to root out the plans made by American imperialism and Zionism and The old-fashioned Ba'athist regime is being opposed from Iraq.

The colonialist and conservative elements of the region suddenly began plotting to attack the Islamic Republic of Iran in the hope of destroying and returning Iran to being the appendix of colonialism and their own regimes in the region. Of course, the fascist regime of Baghdad was busy implementing this immoral plan. It was, internally, a suitable economic, military and political reality. Abroad, as we said, it received unlimited promises of financial support from the West, which in 1980 resulted in the war against the dictatorship of Iraq. Iran announced that the Iraqi army had invaded a large area of Iran from several areas in the south and middle and had previously announced the cancellation of the March 6 Algiers agreement with the Shah, which destroyed the great and national revolution of Aylul, which was Kissinger and the Shah's biggest plan against the movement.

The freedoms of the region in general, the Kurdish liberation movement and the Democratic and Progressive Path of Iraq in particular, were discussed. Kissinger and the Shah hoped that the Kurdish movement would not return for a long time, Iraq would be fully restored (as a western appendix) for a long time, protecting western and old-fashioned interests in the region, and would become a hundred and more strong obstacle.

The decision did not give real autonomy to Iraqi Kurdistan, because they did not believe in this scientific solution because according to him, his party and Arab conservatives, Iraqi Kurdistan is part of the Arab nation, belonging to the Arab people. In evaluating the September revolution in the course of our party Our ideological, political, military, organizational and administrative mistakes have shown to a reasonable extent as to how we lost the historic morning of March 11, 1970, so we did not consider it necessary to reaffirm them.

By hitting the Aylul revolution and the Kurdish liberation movement in Iraq, a progressive democratic Iraq was also lost and turned into a chauvinist dictatorship, unconditionally colonial and restricted by old-fashioned handcuffs. To a large extent, the Iraqi people in general and the Kurdish people in particular in Iraq, were suffering from oppression and the war of annihilation, and if it had not been for the success of the Iranian people's revolution, the breath of the liberal nations and their forces, democracy, progressive, national and Islamic, would be somewhat suppressed.

We hoped that we would all take a good stand and be able to get rid of the harms of this unstable situation, providing us with the necessary strength in the hope of surviving and achieving our goals yet we as Iraqi Kurds, PDK, and the Iraqi Kurdistan council in all The Iraqi people, the region, the democratic and progressive forces, the Arab and Islamic peoples have suffered more. As we have explained before, nearly two-thirds of Iraqi Kurdistan had been destroyed and the nation moved. More than half a million people were made homeless in foreign countries as refugees living in poverty, and to some extent disrespected.

About 8,000 Barzani brothers were taken to southern Iraq in the forced camp under the name of prisoners of war, all having been identified, just as the Faili brothers were expelled and all their money, property, identity and documents confiscated.

Here, we need to defend that the truth of the struggle and the way of the Kurdish movement and its success in establishing the beginnings of a policy of coexistence and alliance with other nations. These, and the success of democracy were the only guarantees of solving the Kurdish problem, especially In Iraqi Kurdistan. Only in this way could we pave the way to remove Arab conservatives, chauvinism in general, and Saddam and his officials in particular, who said that the land of Kurdistan was Arabic. From this viewpoint the Kurdish nation and the Kurdish struggle were subject to danger and potential destruction. As described in the report of their party's eleventh national congress in the fall of 1977 and published in the April 1979 Al-Thura newspaper, it was the chauvinist view that was the root and foundation of the Iraqi regime's racist policy towards the Kurdish people.

We had to disagree with that opinion, and to provide an opposing ideology, as well as to explain to all Arab liberal, democratic and understanding forces that the Ba'athist party's chauvinist and racist ideology was the root cause of the killings and destruction of Iraqi Kurdistan, meaning we must respond to this chauvinist view with a deep democratic and progressive stance.

We also knew that such opinions state that we, as Kurds, are a national mentality in the Arab nation, not a common Iraqi political entity that has consisted of two main nations since 1921; the Arab nation and the Kurdish nation, with other minorities, of course. Saddam, his party, his regime, and his national leadership did not just spout these chauvinist and unscientific opinions, but they even organized them, and they continued to support them with all their brutality to change the reality of the population of Kurdistan. They sought to completely Arabize Kurdistant, and we sought to oppose this from the ninth congress on.

We made a decision on emigration and racist resettlement, admitting that we were struggling to stop the actions of the fascist Tikriti regime suspected of forced emigration and Arabization in Kurdistan, which was carried out against our Kurdish people, trying to remove all traces of our history. We decided that it was necessary for the progressive, national, Islamic forces of Iraq, Arabs and the world to compete more against changing the national reality of Kurdistan than we did, because it harmed the brotherhood of Kurds and Arabs, their shared struggle and the past historical light in which our blood has been mixed in a barricade against colonialism and invaders since the heroic time of Islam, Salahaddin Ayubi.

The actions of the government had a great impact on the Kurdish nation psychologically and made it think about a lot of special ways to defend the rights and dignity that belonged to it, against the enemies trying to take both from them.

It meant that the progressive Iraqi, Arab and international forces, must bury their ideological and political mistakes, in order to solve the Kurdish problem in Iraq within the framework of a common homeland in a peaceful and democratic solution.

According to Saddam, he would replace the Shah's role in the Gulf and bring the oil fields of Ahwaz and Abadan back to Iraq. According to Ba'athist calculations, when they attacked Iran, there would be very little defence, which was certainly a huge mistake. On the contrary, they faced the fierce defence of the Iranian people who showed themselves to be determined during the eight years of war. If the officials of the Islamic Republic of Iran had properly considered the reality of Iraq and cooperated with the Iraqi opposition in general and the Kurdish opposition in particular on the right basis and common interests, we would have been able to ensure that Baghdad's fascist regime was destroyed.

As PDK, and along with all opposition forces in Kurdistan and Iraq, we realized that we should take advantage of this opportunity and conflict in the region in friendship with the Islamic Republic of Iran, provided we maintained our independence and made our own decisions. We sought to achieve our political goals, because Saddam and his regime were the instigators of the war, with the support of imperialism and the conservative countries of the region, without the opinion of the Iraqi people and its leaders.

The Iraqi people, with Kurds and Arabs, faced this devastating war, which ended with the greatest loss of life and property in Iraq and Iran, destroying both countries, particularly near the borders. Because of the continuation of the war, 300,000 were killed, and half a million wounded. The loss of property was estimated at 163 billion dollars.

Many in both Iraq and Iran believed that ending the war was based on a peaceful fairness that properly considered the rights of the Iraqi and Iranian peoples in terms of protecting the independence of Iraq and Iran and their right to sovereignty over all their countries. The instigators of the war would be found and punished.

Here, we needed to explain to all the nature of the war, our stance and the opposition forces of Kurdistan and Iraq, because there were many questions about it, and even many different realities emerged against it, there was no reality or a position on it.

Of course, the natural nature of the war was not as a national war for Iraq, but as self-defence for Iran, and it was a defensive war. It was directed towards colonialism and some of the region's conservative countries. The largest and worst activities were exploited by the West and conservatives, with regions Arabized and radicalized to change the balance of power in Iraq's interests and increase their political and military influence in the region. By doing more and not letting the breath of liberal nations breathe in the region, they sought to force Iran to return to the western appendix, or to destroy the republican regime.

Iran's Islamic forces were strong, though, but because of the mistakes we mentioned earlier, they were put in a place of global isolation. The direct intervention of the United States in the Gulf ended to the detriment of themselves and their friends, in the interests of Saddam, his regime and the West. When agreement 598 was adopted, they should have accepted it from the force's headquarters. At the same time, it would have been better to warn the Kurdish and Iraqi opposition forces before it was accepted, because of the fundamental shortcomings in resolution agreement 598. Iran should have shown in full that it had interfered in the start of the Second Iraqi War against the Iraqi people and the Kurdish nation in Iraqi Kurdistan in particular, meaning that the Security Council was precisely the main reason for the March 6 Algerian agreement and the conflict with Saddam's regime.

The main causes of Saddam and his regime's attacks on Iran, apart from the unclean intentions of Arabs and the region's conservatives, have not been properly studied. After Iran accepted resolution 598 and stopped the Iraq-Iran war, Saddam and his regime brutally attacked the opposition forces of Kurdistan and Iraqis in general, and particularly our PDK forces, in the areas of Sidakan and Mergasor.

On July 19, 1988, in the Khwakurk region and in the areas of a heroic branch in Duhok and Mosul provinces, in Khwakurk, our peshmerga brothers protected the most liberated areas and the nation over 52 days. We proudly say that the likes of the heroic war of our peshmerga has not been seen in the history of the revolutions in Kurdistan. They did not stop and focused a lot on the areas of branch one in Duhok and Mosul provinces from August 25, 1988 to August 29, 1988, the Iraqi and Jash forces, with tanks, planes, chemical weapons, and biological weapons, entered the area but were not allowed to show the world that the opposition forces of Kurdistan and Iraqis in general, and the PDK forces in particular, had ended and that the liberated area in Iraqi Kurdistan was no longer isolated.

Here we need to take a stand and be very careful and in detail. We have to take into account the current situation and the future, and there is good criticism in some of the assessments that have been put forward.

Self-criticism is sacred, because it is the engine force to strengthen relations between the Kurdish and Iraqi opposition forces, but what is true is that we, the PDK, have tried to take advantage of the situation, especially when independent. We protected ourselves, made our own decisions and strengthened ourselves, which was in the interest of the Iraqi Kurdish and democratic movement. This was true not only of us, but of most Iraqi parties and the Kurdish parties in particular, who even more than us, wanted to take advantage of the situation.

As a result of our resistance, enemy forces withdrew from a large area of Kurdistan to the central and southern councils, or were evacuated by force. Our liberated areas were increasing day by day, and the energy of the people and peshmerga increased dramatically. The areas that were moved from 1975 to 1978 were well rebuilt, and the lives of the people and peshmerga improved, flourishing from Zakho to Khanaqin.

By forming the Jud council and the Iraqi Kurdistan council, the hopes and aspirations of the Iraqi people in general and the

Kurdish people in particular were very high. We all believed in the final success, because the balance was very strong. Power was working in our interest.

Most of our criticism of ourselves, and the opposition forces of Kurdistan and Iraqis, is that we did not benefit from the situation as necessary, because the internal situation of the Kurdish liberation movement in Iraq and the National, Democratic and Islamic Movement in Iraq was not at a high level, and unfortunately it is not yet ideal. That is why the enemy was able to strike us with this great military package, which meant that we had stepped in the interests of the Iraqi people and the Kurdish nation.

We certainly reiterated that the national holy revolution, and the progress of the 26th of May of Kurdistan, which emerged in 1976, challenging a bitter and difficult reality, continuing after the 1975 setback of the Great Revolution of September. It continued its relentless struggle to achieve the political, economic, and social goals of Kurdistan and Iraqis, and after the halt of the Iraq-Iran war with an enemy military strike would neither change its slogan nor stop continuing its revolution, because the revolution had not been linked to the Iraq-Iran war. It was not right to take responsibility for stopping the Iraq-Iran war without stopping the war in Kurdistan, destroying Kurdistan and striking the Kurdistan revolution to some extent, but that mistake included all of us.

Here, the damage to the Kurdish nation in this war had to be put to rest, and the damage included all sides of the Kurdish freedom movement, especially as a result of the war destroying nearly two-thirds of Kurdistan, killing or displacing 1.4 million people. In 4,000 villages, sub-districts, and districts of Kurdistan, they were transferred to the forced camps of Aflaqi, while more than half a million Kurds who were homeless crossed into Iran, Turkey, Europe, America, Canada and Australia, living as refugees in those countries, far from their home country and their cities, villages, and families.

This homelessness caused a new psychological situation for the Kurdish people and had a bad impact on the brotherhood of Kurds and Arabs within the country and abroad, the common struggle and their shared entities and their past, when their blood had been mixed in one barricade. Of course, if the Iraqi Kurdistan council had been formed before the Iraq-Iran war, the brotherhood war would have ended, there would have been no more conflict, and the minor problems would have been put aside, and all of us would have stepped in the light of the movement's interests.

The liberation of Kurdistan and the Democratic Movement should have been acted entirely in knowledge of the Covenant and the internal procedures of the Kurdistan council, meaning that there would have been complete integrity between the parties of the Kurdistan council and, scientific and political steps would have been taken to solve the problems, conflicts, and main and minor contradictions. An extraordinary effort would have been made for a multi-party coalition of Iraq, considering our views on how to form it in the way we have shown in front of us, and a regular political leadership in the Iraqi Kurdistan council and the multi-council of Iraq in general were formed. These believed in the spirit of the council and the goals of the Iraqi people and Kurdish people, and we could have benefited greatly from the situation.

Sadly, as there were no political, military and frontal agreements, we suffered a lot of damage, and admit that Kurdistan was destroyed in the Iraq-Iran war. As we mentioned earlier, the enemy had begun Arabizing Kirkuk's oil fields in 1963, and after that, it did not hesitate - year after year - to harass and Arabize Kurdistan according to chauvinistic and fascist thoughts. However, during and after the Iraq-Iran the war, it saw the greatest opportunity to change the national reality of Kurdistan, for ultimate success would lead Kurdistan to Arabization, and of course, after the war in a way that was somewhat stopped, Saddam considered himself a survivor, so he poured out all the hatred towards the Kurds and Kurdistan in the second war.

As the leadership of the PDK Party and the leadership of the Holy Revolution on May 26, leaders of other parties in the Iraqi Kurdistan council prepared us on a regular programme to confront the enemy in all aspects, until the Iraq-Iran war ended.

This halt was the biggest mistake in terms of politics, military, organization and media, and we need to admit this mistake for our fighters and our people. These mistakes include all of us, not some parties to the Kurdish Liberation Democratic Movement and the Democratic, National, Arab and Islamic Movement of Iraq. Of course, by acknowledging the harm they had caused, they and everyone did not benefit.

One of the bitter consequences of the war was the displacement of many our citizens to Iran. Here we thought it good to thank the Islamic Republic of Iran for receiving them, and at the same time we asked them to look at our homeless citizens and Iraqi refugees with all respect in terms of humanity and friendship, paying attention to their needs for living and freedom to feel that they are a respectable revolutionary guest in the Islamic Republic. As many of the Kurdish and Iraqi refugees, especially the last refugees who were hit by chemical and biological weapons, were not left with anything, we begged that the officials of the Islamic Republic, ideologically, politically, financially, administratively and via the health services, look at them with utmost respect, in order to reconsider their struggle and to ensure they had more hope for their future.

In short, the roots of the Iraq-Iran war are old, but the Algerian agreement renewed the attitude of the Iraqi regime and the old conflict. The Iraqi regime began a war in 1980/9/22. The war was conservative and against the interests of the Iraqi and Iranian peoples, for the Kurdish people, and it was in the interest of American imperialism and its allies, an excuse for them to gain power over the region's oil and wealth and therefore to dominate the Gulf.

The war was to strike Iraq and Iran's capabilities, both economically and militarily. The result of the war was detrimental to the nations, particularly the Iraqi and Iranian peoples, and the Kurdish people were more harmed than anyone else. The result of that war was not only a lot of destruction and sacrifice but also the entire war was directly against the interests of the Arab nation and the Palestinian issue. Under the shadow of the war, southern Lebanon was invaded in 1982 by Israel, where the Palestinian revolution was fought. Of course, apart from all the reasons for the war mentioned, the Iraqi regime started the war according to its dictatorial nature and without the knowledge and questions of the Iraqi people, so they must take responsibility for historical and political results.

On the first morning, we condemned the war and declared it an unfair and conservative war, and kept this view until the end. In our opinion, solving the Iraq-Iran problem with a fair democratic agreement, respecting freedom and national independence and the will of the peoples of both countries would have been a better approach. It would have meant a respect for sovereignty and independence but not a dictatorial authority for Iraq, but this returned to the opinion of the Iraqi people and was a deep and historical problem.

Above all, there is the problem of the democracy of power and the legitimate rights of the Kurdish people. And here it is good to say that we are with a fair peace and reconstruction of Iraq and Iran solving Kurdish problems.

Evaluating the role of revolution and PDK

From the ninth congress until today

In order to evaluate the holy revolution of May 26, led by our Party and the presidency of our loyal president since 1976, with reality and principles, we needed to show the positive aspects of the revolution and our Party to a good extent. In order to assess the struggle over more than ten years, since 10/11/1979, when our Party leadership began its duties after the election by the ninth congress, we needed to be careful and give a final opinion on the central committee's assessment. It meant a general report for those engaged in the struggle, according to points 15 and 16 of article 18 of our party's internal rules. We hoped to investigate and evaluate it with reality and context, exploring political, organizing, military, media, and administration factors.

In addition, consider the financial and health services that we will explain to you below, so that it is possible to make a good comparison considering our Party's internal programmes and pro-cedures and the decisions of the ninth congress, reaching a degree of awareness and evaluation. In light of the interests of our Party, the Revolution, the Kurdish Liberation Movement and the Iraqi Democratic Movement, make the right and correct decisions for you, especially as our nation needs real and political opinion more than ever in the current special situation, in the hope of rescuing them from a difficult situation, even if this causes disappointment among them.

There have been many difficulties. If we do not give people full hope by making the right decision and clarifying all the positive and negative aspects of the revolution and the PDK, their reorganization, direction and self-gathering may not be necessary, and this will be detrimental to our nation and our Party. The revolution will end, and our enemies will benefit from it, so we consider you, the commanders of PDK and Barzani, and have considered that they will feel your historical responsibility at a high level and will not give the atmosphere any time. our congress and its investigation and evaluation, in the atmosphere of Friendship, brotherhood, Kurdishness and scientific revolution shall emerge:

1) Politically:

Of course, as we portray and look at the Party's political line, we see that it progressed to a very direct extent to stop the Iraq-Iran war. Of course, when we discuss and explain the political issues of our Party and the revolution in more than ten years, we must consider and forget the programme of our Party and the political decisions of the ninth Party congress in order to review our strategies and tactics carefully. We know to what extent they were obliged to do so, and we did not leave them, the agreements that were given to our party, and the great and national revolution of

September and its leadership after the 1975 failure. It was quickly held in disrepute, and it was revealed to all the world's freedom movements, socialist camps, democratic movements, and western workers that the Kurdish liberation movement in general with the Iraqi Kurdistan movement and revolution, were an integral part of the world's series of liberal and progressive movements. Sometimes the zigzagging journey led into a path of struggle and the revolution was not intentional, to a great extent it was forced on them making political mistakes, so we were respected by our strategic friends and wanted them to look at us with a more far-sighted eye than before.

Even in the Western world, human rights organizations and many political, scientific and human figures appreciate our movement and defend it with faith. As we have shown before, our political plan of revolution and PDK over the past ten years has been accepted by our nation, the Kurdish nation in general, and the Iraqi democratic movement, and it was the Arab progressive movement, so we feel positive about our resurrection, which we stand firm on, and we can answer every loyal question of our nation and our party. Our relations with the opposition forces of Kurdistan and Iraqis and the Kurdish forces and parties, and the national and democratic forces of the Arab Progressive Movement And, the Islamic forces of Iraq and the region have been very good.

We may be criticized, and some have complained about some of the instability in our relationship with some of the parties in Kurdistan. Unfortunately, this criticism includes most of the Kurdish forces and has had various reasons why it does not solve the instability and problems that exist. The important thing is to always ensure that it is cut off and not allow civil war with any Kurdistan party in any way so previous errors will not be repeated.

2) In terms of organization

When we talk about the face of organizing PDK for ten years before all the explanation and evaluation of this aspect, it is important to show the positive and negative aspects of organization, the path of the successful nations of the world, their experience, their benefits. Comparing them with our way of organizing, our shortcomings become very clear. It is visible, because for all the movements and revolutions on earth, it has emerged that the political goal of each movement, or a revolution that has been touched by principle and reality, depends on the success of organizing that movement, or the revolution within it.

The world's liberal and progressive movements have succeeded in following this political and organizational beginning and have achieved their far and near goals. We, the PDK, who were founded on August 16, 1946, know that the reason for the situation is a major reason, but what is true is that our internal shortcomings have been the main reason for our lack of access to our close goals. We, the PDK, should not take this great responsibility, even in the last 15 years, which means that, especially after the collapse of the great revolution of September 1975, all the opposition forces of Kurdistan and Iraqis are taking responsibility with us, each force and its part. According to our ability and influence, all of us, the Iraqi Democratic and Islamic Movement, will be with the Kurdish liberation movement in Iraq, and we need to properly evaluate both positive and negative aspects in terms of organization by following the beginnings of the organization, to solve our internal shortcomings as soon as possible, because as we said, the main reason for our failure was internal issues.

In evaluating the September National Revolution, which showed the role of the Party in the leadership of the revolution, it did not play a full role, so it was considered an important factor in the 1975 crisis, but what is true is that from the ninth congress until recently, our Party has had a great deal of opportunity to play its role in the leadership of the revolution. We respect our historical responsibility, as we should not have been able to play our role properly, even though we have all been able to. We have been faithfully to our duties for a long time, but in general, as it is necessary at all times, our local situation has not been at the level to produce a very significant time of our subjective situation. Unfortunately, we have lost some opportunities because, although we need to be committed them, we have not followed the internal rules of the Party.

Article 19- Point (1) states: "The Central Committee normally meets every four months" and, at point 2, says: "The Central Committee will hold a multi-party meeting at least a year, except for reserve members, members of its public institutions. The branches will be ready."

In Article 29, point 3 states, "Congress is held at least every four years, and there is an unusual request for the central committee to be held at the request of two-thirds of its members, in accordance with article nineteen of article 18." This means that these three deviations are very clear, and we need to reduce the effects of these deviations, of which there are many. There is no need to explain them. The truth is that these three changes were not intentional or were in the personal interests of some friends. Even because of the work of some of our friends and the distancing of their duties, we did not want to follow the meetings of the Central Committee, although in the meetings of the Head of the Bureau, the friends of the Central Committee who were close to the political bureau were invited and participated in receiving decisions. There are many delays in congress, and the difficult situation of the revolution combined with the brutality of the fascist regime, was not only the reason for not holding the congress, but also the neglect and deviation from local rules and the central committee.

Due to the decision of the central committee, we have come to the top with all our power and we hope that it will be successful with support, loyalty, good thinking and a desire to solve the problems and imagine a bright future for our oppressed people. Of course, we have established the organization of the Party on the foundations of the democratic centre, which is the newest beginning in the organization. The rules need to be better followed in the future, so that the ideological union, which is the basis for the union of actions, will be better established, and our party discipline will be fulfilled.

We will not hide from you that until a fully aware commitment to our Party's programme, the political decisions of the congress, the internal rules of our Party, the Law of the Revolutionary Army of Kurdistan, and the instructions and advice of the daily Head of the Bureau, are fully achieved, success will not be achieved. There will be even more disappointment, because if these early ones do not follow our daily behaviour with faith and do not move in their light, especially the new leadership of our Party, it will be hard to be better off. Regrettably, the power within the PDK and the revolution will be very weak and cannot play its leadership role.

Unfortunately, we and the opposition forces of Kurdistan and Iraqi suffered to some extent from this long-term disease, but we have not been able to survive it well. Because of this disease, the fascist regime of Baghdad has remained strong.

Our arrangements are very respectable, our party's organization in the cities has played a good role, their organizational relationship is good, and until recently they have played a role in beating enemies and humiliating them both abroad and internally within the country. The big uprisings of the people in the cities of Kurdistan in In 1982-1984-1987, in Sulaymaniyah, Kirkuk, Erbil, Duhok, Halabja, Qaladze, Rawanduz, and Shaqlawa, are the best evidence of the positive aspects of our party's organization which means branches 1-4, Barzan force and Mergasor district have been good at organizing cities and peshmerga forces to strike enemies in the country.

The mujahedeen branch was much more successful in hitting enemies and organizing the masses of their area, even with the plight of the PDK, and was the strength and influence of the Party and the ability of the branch, which encouraged NATO member Turkey to support the Iraqi regime in attacking liberated areas in the provinces of Duhok, Mosul and Erbil. In May 1983 and the years of 1984, 1986, and 1987, those attacks were repelled with the bravery of the unskilled peshmerga of this division, the political support of all the institutions of the leadership of the revolution, our party and the friends of the Kurdish nation. That is why in 1988, the regime launched the largest and most widespread attack on all areas of the region with chemical weapons.

Branch 3 and branch 4 were also effective in hitting the enemy in Qaradagh and Garmian and forcing them back them properly, but the enemy also used chemical weapons there. Their most prolific role was in the Khwakurk offensive with the forces and organizations of the political bureau who proved that they are indeed the loyal commanders of PDK and Barzani in protecting the liberated areas and hitting the enemy. Branch 2 has played a proper role and it was the first branch to be hit with chemical weapons in the Balisan Valley in 1987, and some of them participated in the Khwakurk battle and were honoured.

Peshmerga and local inhabitants were badly harmed by chemical weapons. Here we bow our heads to all the brave peshmerga of PDK who became victims of their nation and immortal martyrs of the road in honour and Kurdishness; thousands of greetings to their pure souls.

Branch 6, too, has played a very good diplomatic and media role, especially for further humiliating the enemy, introducing the Kurdish issue to European nations, and shaming the use of chemical weapons against Kurds and Kurdistan. Participation in conferences and seminars on the Kurdish people's issue is respectable.

Branch 7 has also played a good role in demeaning the enemy in using chemical weapons against Kurds and Kurdistan, and the strike of the 7th branch friends in the United Nations Hall is respected, as well as the role of our relations committees and the Lebanese office.

Branch 8 is also respected for organizing our refugee brothers in Iranian cities and establishing arrangements and adherence to local rules.

The Azadi Branch and the Khabat Organization were able to properly supervise our refugee and peshmerga brothers in Zewa, Naghada, Wrme, Khana and their surroundings, most of which are the families of our peshmerga brothers and are always in place. Respect and obedience to the orders and advice of our Party leadership, to a great extent, have protected brotherhood, peace and tranquillity in the areas and cities in which they live, and have not allowed chaos among our people, so the Azadi Branch and Khabat organization has played a great role.

This is a summary of the lack of activity and positive aspects of our PDK branches, otherwise the heroism, activity and self-sacrifice of the peshmerga, masses of our nation, our party members and officials, and the epics recorded in dozens of books would not be completed. All of these are proud, and hopeful, and there is a right to demand such a thing. How will it be lost?

Our Party and the Resonance of Dialogue (Negotiations)

The Kurdish liberation movement in Iraq, after the July 14 revolution, since 1961, the National and National Revolution of Kurdistan led by our Party and immortal Barzani, against the government of Abdulkarim Qasim stated that we Kurds have taken every peaceful democratic way to achieve the rights of the Kurdish nation, which, according to the frank text of Article 3 of the Interim Constitution, is as a partner in the administration of the country and in the text of the constitution.

With the consent of the Iraqi people in general and all the parties in the Patriotic Union of Kurdistan (PUK), which largely represented the political opinion of the Iraqi people. Therefore, the last compulsory access to weapons was in September 1961, which is why it has since been called the Great Revolution of Aylul, meaning that in 1963, in 1964 and in 1970 the cabinet contacted our Party and Barzani. He was immortalized in solving the Kurdish problem, and of course, immortal Barzani and the Central Committee of our

Party have warmly welcomed these relations, but unfortunately, they did not want to go towards a peaceful and democratic solution, even on March 11, 1970, and took a stand. It was good to solve the problem, but later, as we showed, the result seemed to be that, immediately after the March 6 agreement between The Shah and Saddam, there were difficulties.

Our Party's political bureau, with the consent of immortal Barzani, called on the Ba'athist Revolutionary Leadership Council to discuss and resolve the issue, and they responded shamelessly. In 1982-1983, after their defeat in Khurramshahr and in 1988, in all the relations between us and the Jud parties at the same time, we and the parties of the Kurdistan Council later showed that we had our own cause, case and independence. It is our decision, provided that they honestly move towards solving the issue of a democratic authority and solving the Kurdish problem in the common country of Iraq; that is, our historical slogan, which is democracy for Iraq and the real autonomy for Kurdistan, because together they will not be separated, even in our opinion and in the interests of the Iraqi people and the Iraqi Kurdish people.

Unfortunately, they have always withdrawn and have not gone towards a peaceful and democratic solution, because they are ideologically and politically far from thinking about it, so the solution to power and solving the Kurdish problem in Iraq is becoming more complicated day by day, and will continue to do so until the end of the regime. Therefore, you, our struggling nation, our brothers around us, and our revolutionaries, do not think that we are in love with war, chaos, and exile. A path and a peaceful and democratic solution will come forward, with all faith. We go forward and consider it necessary, even with historical responsibility, because our case is very fair, and our nation is too relentless, free and patient, and we will be safe and free. With our goals, we will prove better to the liberal world, the Iraqi people, and the Kurdish people, that we have not really forgotten the blood of our martyrs, and that it is impossible to forget them, and on their unchanging path that the PDK's path and Barzani will continue, and success is guaranteed.

Kurdistan Councils and Iraqi Wide Councils

Since the ninth congress, our Party has carried the slogan of these two sides. Since 1976, it struggled to form the Iraqi Kurdistan council, which would become the foundation stone for the formation of a wide Iraqi front, because the formation of both sides is important to the situation. The internal Kurdish Liberation Movement in Iraq, which imposes the National, Democratic and Islamic Movement of Iraq, the Iraqi people in general and the Kurds in particular, were waiting for the formation of these two historical councils, because the Kurdistan council of Iraq, which has been active since May 12, 1988, is of great hope to the Kurdish nation.

This especially the case at a time when the struggle needs more strength and activity than ever before, instead of playing a historical role. More than ever, we see that it is not at the highest level of our nation, and that we must step forward with all our efforts to save ourselves from this inertia, in the light of the charter. We must take steps towards its internal procedure, and if, as a result of daily behaviour the political leadership and the executive office feels the need to amend its charter, or internal procedure, it should be both realistic and objective. The Kurdish liberation movement in Iraq, has not been convened for more than a year by the political leadership, and needs more meetings than ever. This is particularly true as the Baghdad fascist regime's genocide war, for Kurds and Kurdistan, is more violent and brutal than ever before. On the Iraqi Kurdistan council, if it does not play its role in this difficult situation that our nation is going through, when it calls for the loyalty of all of us and the peshmerga of Kurdistan, what will be our answer?

Just as in the formation of the movement, which should have been formed in 1976 and at the time of the outbreak of the Holy Revolution of May 26, the brotherhood war caused the greatest damage to our movement and our revolution. It involved discarding all beliefs, because in the history of the movement, there was no progressive and liberating speech of nations to start a revolution against a fascist regime. Instead, there was the war of brotherhood and the prohibition of Kurdistan's regions from each other, each side having its own region with no access to any other without consent to act against the main enemy in the region.

We need to think carefully about resolving the main and minor conflicts within ourselves (within the nation) and to see how the world's liberal nations could work to resolve these two conflicts; that is, the main conflict between the enemy and a nation. The sub-conflict within the nation itself, has taken steps to avoid the opportunity for resolution. We, the PDK and the parties of the Kurdistan council, as we need to do, have not gone towards resolving these two conflicts since 1976 until the formation of the Iraqi Kurdistan council. We hope that we will all be aware of the level of our historical responsibility, and that we will bring new light into the office of the implementation of the Iraqi Kurdistan Front. Whatever the problem, we must solve it and give it a new life, and as soon as the political leadership gathers, it is even more necessary to step in the light of the charter and its local policy, and to perform all our activities. Thus, the name of the Iraqi Kurdistan council will certainly be respected more by our nation and our friends, and our enemies will reckon with us in detail.

As we have said before, we will try to form the Iraqi council and the Iraqi Kurdistan council will be the foundation stone for the public face of that. It is necessary to act with speed so that the general populace of Iraqi and the Kurdish people in particular, will not be waiting for more. We, the Iraqi Kurdistan council, with a united attitude and an opinion, will go towards the efforts and struggles of implementing these wide councils, which are in the interest of the Iraqi Democratic and Islamic Movement and the Kurdish Liberation Movement in Iraqi Kurdistan. This means that we should all own our own land, have our personal independence and make decisions, and dare to tell all our friends what our views are. If steps are taken properly, the result will be in the interest of all of us. We hope that all the opposition parties of Iraq and Kurdistan will feel their responsibility at a high level and to a great extent for the sake of narrow parties and interests.

We will not sacrifice the interests of the Iraqi people and the Kurdish people.

Here are some important points we want to briefly highlight:

One of the reasons for not connecting the Kurdistan council was the civil war. This was a reason for the non-binding of a multi-Iraqi council (alongside other reasons for not connecting the Iraqi council).

On the other hand, there are other reasons that a multi-party Iraqi council has not been formed, including:

1. Internal deficiencies of the opposition in general, such as unfeeling, or not considering the general situation, its needs, and weakness of democratic spirit among the Iraqi forces, which unfortunately is a common inheritance of Iraq.
2. The old political work in Iraq, such as monopoly, unilateralism, narrowness, and considering the narrow interests of the party.
3. External influence. Foreign pressure was not in the interest of unifying the opposition. Instead of helping to form the United Front, Mehwar was established.
4. The opposition has been unable to agree on a united stance on the issue, particularly from 1983 until the end of the war.
5. Differences in attitude towards the Kurdish issue and the future of power in Iraq.

The tenth and future congress of our party and Kurdish liberation movement in Iraq

Of course, the internal and objective situation of the Kurdish liberation movement in Iraq, the foundation of the Party on August 16, 1946, has been a historical and inevitable event, so that the Kurdish liberation movement can emerge from the blockade under the leadership of the Immortal Barzani Party and its presidency. It means that 43 years have been filled with the pride, hope, and aspirations of all The Kurdish people in Iraq, indeed the entire Kurdish nation has looked forward to our Party and considered it their support, and even the beloved nations of Iraq, as a leading party.

They have looked at the leadership of the Kurdish liberation movement and support for the Iraqi democratic movement and may have often seen a glimmer of hope.

Our Party has succeeded since its foundation, and its success in the national revolution and the greatness of Aylul was led by immortal Barzani, who won victory for our nation on the morning of March 11, 1970. After these great successes, we faced this difficult situation because of imperialism and inaccurate plans, as we mentioned earlier. Even a year after the 1975 setback, the mountains of Kurdistan and throughout Kurdistan, with peshmerga activities and their stand against the enemy, proved that they would not stop until the Kurdish nation achieved its goals, and now they consider it more necessary than ever to continue a tireless struggle to achieve our goals.

We don't mind many parties in Kurdistan and Iraq, who, at the time, were very critical of the great Aylul revolution, even sometimes with non-objective assessments, because of the reality and its problems. They were far away, and now we ask them a very realistic question and say:

Since the 1975 setback, has it been possible to fill the gap of Barzani, the immortal, who left?

We don't mind that they say it's very difficult and can't be done. It is right for the opposition forces of Kurdistan and Iraqis to reconsider their previous assessments, so that our future political plan can be more accurate.

We, the PDK, have bravely engaged in all aspects of the great September revolution, but in this regard, and the attitude of the subject, we have not seen any positive from the opposition forces of Kurdistan and Iraqis. That's why we're all in this bad situation. We must all feel our responsibility at a high level, always in the interest of the Kurdish liberation movement and the Iraqi Democratic Movement, through the dark times until we see the day when we reach our nation's goals.

The people of Kurdistan in general, and particularly our movement's friends, have looked forward to the tenth congress, which is waiting for its righteous decisions to give full hope to our nation and advanced cadres, to please our friends, and to be completely disappointed by our enemies. They also want to make sure that all decisions are committed and because of that they will be treated under supervision.

The role of the Central Committee of the ninth congress

Since the ninth congress was held, our Party has been under attack politically and in the media as well as being blockaded although we were given various opportunities for false accusations.

The leadership and the new ninth congress's task was difficult, but friends firmly came under the historical responsibility to complete the path that began in August 1946, so that the PDK could hold its own position in Kurdistan and Iraq. This is a summary of the important tasks they performed:

1. Since the 1980s and 1981s, the ninth congress has fulfilled several basic duties by following the decisions of congress and its approach, Including:
   A. By the end of 1980, all the blockades around the PDK were destroyed, contrary to the opinions that the PDK would not be able to fight for more than a few months.
   B. The leadership, foundation, and PDK peshmerga showed their strength and put great hopes and belief in the hearts of the Kurdish people.
   C. PDK proved to have a clear progressive approach, rejecting all the privileges given to other names and characteristics.

D. In a short time, it became a place of respect, appreciation, relations, and friendship with the parties, organizations, people, and natural national allies in Kurdistan, Iraq, the region, and at the Arab and global levels, and everyone came proudly to the PDK's call.

E. Thousands of Kurdistan's people, as they wished, joined the Kurdistan Army, which was properly established, and a law was enacted.

F. They contacted internal cities and organisations were strong.

G. Tens of thousands of people joined the Party as members or gathered around them as supporters and friends.

H. The media, especially the Iraqi Kurdistan Voice Station, which had been working properly, played a good part in raising awareness and conveying the voice of the people.

9. The most important step in the one or two years of post-congress efforts was the Party's efforts to form a national front, as a force was mainly involved in the formation of Jud, which was a major political success for the PDK, the Kurdish movement and the Iraqi people, both internally and around the world.

10. As a result of these successes, until the mid-1980s, the PDK went on with its activities, the most important of which are:

A. PDK went to the hearts of the Kurdish people and became a place of appreciation and respect for our nation's friends inside and outside Kurdistan.

B. The brave peshmerga of Kurdistan recorded a great epic in the history of the Kurdish people's struggle and strengthened the belief and trust of the Kurdish nation that their commander's unrelenting struggle and ability had not been lost and had the honourable role that they have played in defending with their lives and homes to the last breath. They sacrifice themselves on the way to salvation.

C. Therefore, the PDK became a major force in the Kurdistan and Iraq arenas and gained importance in a political position, and, with the help of other Kurdish forces and parties, succeeded in implementing public reconciliation in Kurdistan and forming the Iraqi Kurdistan council, which was a great historical political victory for the PDK and its parties.

D. Over the past ten years, several PDK leadership delegations, led by immortal Idris Barzani or Masoud Barzani, have visited middle eastern and European countries, which has always been a source of warm respect, support, and happiness for our movement's friends and allies. Of course, this goes back to the importance of PDK's role in the field of struggle.

E. The commanders of the central committee have according to their knowledge and ability. Through ten years of Rabaqi they have taken their struggle loyally and maintained their united ranks, although they have faced the most difficult political and military problems, despite any differences of opinion towards the complex and difficult problems of this decade, which is a positive thing and in such a difficult struggle, they were there.

Many members of the central committee and the political bureau have not been in the country for many years with the peshmerga and the masses of the people, but some have directly led the multi-party activities and great epics of the peshmerga, except for organizing affairs and other tasks.

    F. The PDK played a good role in managing and directing the internal uprisings of the country, which is due to the strengthening of urban arrangements and the Party's relationship with the public.

    G. Conveying the voice of Kurds and the issue to the worlds' public.

As we mentioned, the PDK delegations established successful relations with our nation's friends. Of course, the basic forces of these successes were due to the sacrifices of the peshmerga and the Kurdish people. In other words, the sacrifices of the people, peshmerga, members of the Party and other parties in Kurdistan and Iraq have not been wasted. Every drop of blood and suffering of any displaced family has become a cry, and it has been heard in the world's gatherings, calling for the Kurdish issue to be dealt with justly. As a result, the matter has come to the attention of many forums and groups of the world.

Today, if the PDK and other forces can better organize themselves, they can establish and deliver political achievements and, as a result, overcome the issue, which is the aspirations and goals of our martyrs and oppressed people. That's what heals our wounds, and it doesn't need any sacrifice to be given freely.

This was a summary of the central committee's agenda, which was achieved through the struggle, loyalty, sacrifice of foundation, peshmerga and PDK people.

Of course, if the PDK congress were to be held on time, it would have gained much higher respect and pride, because in the four or five years after the ninth congress was held, it succeeded in all aspects, but that was it. The conference continues to this day, and the situation in the countries has changed over the past ten years, including the balance of the region's forces changing, resulting in the use of chemical weapons, which directly caused the failure that faced PDK and the entire liberation movement.

In such a long period of time, ten years, seeing the most difficult circumstances of the war between the two countries, plus the sudden and major changes in the global situation, especially after the defeat of 1988, many shortcomings and agreements, the Central Committee emerged as revealed in the leadership of the party and other forces.

When the crisis in the region and the war turned violent, the nature of the Iraq-Iran war and the international stance changed, the leadership, or the Central Committee could not properly understand the new situation, and could not take advantage of these changes properly, and as a result, it was hard to get out of the moment.

What follows is a summary of the deficiencies and disadvantages of the Central Committee leadership:

Deficiencies:
It is clear, that the Kurdish liberation movement in Iraq suffered a military failure in 1988, which hurt the cause of the entire Kurdish liberation movement due first and foremost to:

- The shortcomings of deficiency, which was the natural result of the social relations that made up the leadership crisis throughout the movement, meaning that the movement was involved in a crisis situation of leadership, thought, and ability political research.

- Once again, ignoring the geopolitical circumstances in the region, which, although the situation remains the same, has been repeated by the movement's misguided tactics, as it has benefited from regional and international conflicts and clearly understands it. Taking advantage of the situation has not been done, and this has been reflected, when in 1974-1975 the Spirit of The State was not expelled, and in 1980-1988, the laws and rules of the war did not come to an end.

- The circumstances of the Kurdish movement in general, which has not been able to survive its negative line for more than a hundred years, were still falling into the same mistake that it repeated.

- An inherited lack of democracy in the Kurdish national struggle, which is historical and as a result, the opinions of the Kurdish forces' popular bases and the people's masses have been ignored.

- There were no platforms and public opinion institutions, such as holding congresses and conferences, or forming the Kurdistan National Assembly. Also, before the Kurdistan council, the simplest form of coordination, cooperation, and agreement between the Kurdish forces were not about the demands of the people.

- The disintegration of the Kurdish movement's parties in Iraq, which fought until the last two years before the Iraq-Iran war stopped, and had sometimes been competing over which one seemed to make more mistakes, or were competing for small gains from both political and military perspectives. This resulted in the movement being insufficiently strong and dynamic, and it was not united to stand up to the central authority with one voice and demand or stand against the central authority during the war, or to be united on the main issues, such as the war, the matter of friends, enemies and other problems. Also, the military movement, or the form of armed struggle, dominated the entire movement that imposed unrealistic demands and, as a result, it put it under unwanted retribution.

- The Kurdish movement in Iraq, years ago, but also even recently, was in a state of distancing itself from its sectarian status within the framework of the Iraqi national movement, and that this turned into a big mistake.
- The absence of a national Iraqi and Kurdistan council (the reasons for this are reported elsewhere).

Second, our Party, despite the consequences of the basic policies and reasons it faced with the other forces of the movement, itself had several reasons for its failure:

About organization and culture (which are two central tasks):

1. The remainder of the main leadership and institutions outside Iraqi Kurdistan were ignored by the decision of the ninth Party congress, as they should have entered the country, even though the liberated areas were very widespread

and the situation was better. The biggest part of our party's problems came from this return to these parts.

2. The tenth congress was not held in time, the party's grass-roots opinion was ignored, and the conferences were not held.

3. Political and ideological awareness had been ignored, and the PDK did not had a local cultural programme.

4. The phenomenon of dispersion and organized humiliation in the party's ranks, which was also reflected in al-Qaeda, was ignored by the leadership. The Foundation also felt some deviations from the early days of organization and justice at the leadership level, which negatively affected the morale of peshmerga, cadres and the public, and, as they became more concerned, social differences, other phenomena.

Political: Our Party has been involved in many political mistakes, the most important ones being:

1. The PDK leadership did not rely on the energy and power of our people, instead pinning its hopes to the Iraq-Iran war, in the view that the war would end the Iraqi regime.

2. As necessary, we have not benefited from the proverbs of the September Aylul National Revolution. Also, we have also not followed the Party's agenda and the decisions of the ninth congress as necessary.

3. Mis-assessment. In political assessment, in addition to exchanging situations and reversals, this, as we said, is due to internal shortcomings.

4. The PDK's programme and its slogans were clear, and the Party's practical policy was far from the programme under unusual and daily pressure.

About the disaster of branch one on August 25

The reasons for the situation that came before were negatively reflected in branch one and other branches of the Party. Also, because of the importance, pluralism, and boundary entity of branch one and its audience, there are also special reasons, which brought about the disaster, including:

1. After the End of the Iraq-Iran War, a negative psychological movement dominated the region's population, which resulted in the hope of the war.
2. Regime forces quickly invaded the main streets, divided the areas of branch one into parts, and cut them off from each other.
3. Regime forces were suddenly present in a large number, without the peshmerga leadership or leadership reorganizing the peshmerga forces under the new circumstances.
4. Increasing the number of peshmerga at the frontline war, which did not leave movement in the hands of branch one.
5. In the past years, the tests of the partisan war were initially ignored.
6. Most of the families were in the rescued areas, which were in a difficult situation and were affected by the disaster, especially as it was agreed that the transfer of families to the border would coincide with the commencement of the regime's attack..

7. At the time of the attack, members of the leadership, at the level of the political bureau or the central committee, were not within the boundaries of branch one.

8. In branch one, the military side dominated the affairs, on the account of the political, organizational and cultural aspects.

9. It was not prepared for the new military situation after the use of chemical weapons in the villages of Kurdistan (chemical weapons had been used since April 1987 in Sheikh Wasanan and Sargalu area). The peshmerga forces had to be reorganized in a new way (this was, in fact, the short-comings of all Kurdish forces), as there was no chemical weapons protection equipment .

Third, the main and direct cause of this failure was due to the use of chemical weapons by the Iraqi regime, which was directly reflected on the situation in branch one, because it was the main foundation of the PDK. That was after Iran agreed to the council's resolution 598.

International security announced that Iraqi regime forces were fully recaptured to attack PDK bases and other national forces in the border of branch one and used chemical weapons.

Of course, the use of chemical weapons, which was the first to be used in Iraqi Kurdistan, balanced the subordinate forces, after the regime failed to destroy the Kurdish movement, despite the use of all traditional weapons. it was the use of chemical weapons because of the military failure of the armed struggle of Iraqi Kurdistan.

Today, if it is not careful about its own situation the leadership of the Kurdish Liberation Movement (each party itself and the

Kurdistan council) will find that the military failure resulting from the use of chemical weapons will be a complete political failure of the Kurdish movement in particular, and the Iraqi national movement in general.

Our next programme

In our opinion, the general lines of politics and organization should be in the light of the following points:

1. We have suffered a major military failure, because in all aspects, we continue our struggle in the newest way to achieve our goals. We were hit with a big military damage, and the best evidence of the strength of the Kurdistan revolution.

   As we have shown, in previous chapters, if we prepare ourselves in light of the following needs, we will achieve the greatest success, especially as the regime has committed crimes against Kurds and Kurdistan and has become blackened in the eyes of the world. The Kurdish liberation movement is in a new position, requiring new preparations in all aspects. If we want to shoulder these responsibilities, we will invest and develop the growing part of our Party and Barzani.

2. Do not forget our strategy and our tactics, and we will continue to carry out our slogans, which are democracy for Iraq and true autonomy for Kurdistan.

3. Strengthening the leadership of our Party and centralization, strengthening the organization within our Party and the Revolutionary Army of Kurdistan, according to the internal rules of our Party and its beginnings (democratic centralism) and encouraging the proposal and inventive initiatives in PDK and revolution institutions.

4. Reorganizing the arrangements of the party and the army that are compatible with our new situation and to be done according to various needs.

5. Strengthening the Iraqi Kurdistan Front as soon as possible and fully adhering to its local policy.

6. We have shown the efforts to implement the Iraqi Front on all four main sides.

7. Going according to the programme in all our party and military institutions, especially in our leadership, and adhering to them.

8. Caring about our party's relationships, establishing relations with all the global, regional, Arab, and Kurdistan liberal movements, the Islamic Republic of Iran, the Republic of Syria, the Libyan Republic, and the countries. Our other friends, on a true and principled basis, consider the peaceful and progressive interests of the nations and against imperialism and conservativism, especially considering the interests of the Kurdish nation.

9. Raising the level of media struggle and caring about the announcement of PDK and revolution and finding options for continuing media affairs and development, both inside and outside, in all aspects (printing, station, technical and

cultural activities, whether in terms of content or using technology).

10. Establishing the spirit of brotherhood and alliance with the peoples of the region, especially those with which the Kurdish nation lives.

11. We will try to strengthen Arab, Turkish and Iranian relations and pay greater attention to the public opinion of these nations.

12. To try to strengthen Arab relations and pay great attention to the Arab public opinion on the following basis:

   a. Those who were our friends in the Arab movement, protect and strengthen their friendship.

   b. Those who are somewhat neutral to our issue (whether the popular forces, or the state) we should try to make our friends.

   c. Those who are not with us, or who are against us in some way, we should try to make neutral at least, and if they become friends, this is better.

   d. Give full importance to the Arab central issue in all aspects, and strengthen our relations with all Palestinian liberal organisations, and to show our support and alliance on all occasions.

13. Raising the slogan of national reconciliation and peaceful solution to the Kurdish issue and making it a weapon in the hands of the PDK and the Kurdish revolution to nullify the regime's manoeuvres, and violating the cooperation of all

parties that intend to implement this slogan, whether within the opposition forces, the regime's parties or institutions.

14. Considering the Kurdish national problem and affecting each other (i.e. the national dimension) in identifying and following the daily tactics and strategy of our Party.

15. Considering the new political situation in the world and new thinking on the basis of opening and showing flexibility to benefit from global relations within the framework of the interests of the Kurdish liberation movement. We assure you, if these necessary points are fully followed and are to be implemented properly, success is guaranteed. Therefore, our Party will play a better role in leading the 26th of May holy revolution led by Mr Masoud Barzani, and the Kurdish liberation movement in Iraq will achieve its goals as soon as possible. The least harm is success for the entire Kurdish nation. So we hope that we all feel the high level to be our historical responsibility.

Finally:

We send our endless and unforgettable greetings to the dear families of the martyrs of Kurdistan and Iraq.

Our warm greetings to all the Kurdistian and Iraqi fighters who have lost their lives and who are close to losing their lives in the regime's prisons under the cruelty of the Aflaqi Ba'athists.

Greetings to the refugees of the forced camps and the refugees abroad, the disappearances of Anfal, the areas of Barzan, Mosul, Duhok, and all the cities and towns of Kurdistan.

Greetings and respect to all humanitarian, global, Arab and Iraqi movements that have secretly condemned Baghdad's fascist dictatorship for using chemical and biological weapons against Kurds and Kurdistan.

Greetings and respect to the Kurdistan and Iraqi forces, and we hope that we will not hesitate to strengthen the Iraqi Kurdistan council and establish the Iraqi council.

Our greetings and regards to all the countries and humanitarian ceremonies that have taken our refugees with mercy and helped them. In particular, the Islamic Republic of Iran, which has hosted us, supporting us to a good extent in this occasion of our nation, even in the success of Iran's proud nations' revolution so far.

With our thanks, we hope that their help will continue to the extent of the needs of this difficult situation. We will re-establish our congress's success, and rely on God, our nation, and your struggling.

Central Committee
Kurdistan Democratic Party of Iraq
1989/11/20

The final declaration of the tenth congress of Kurdistan Democratic Party - Iraq

On December 2nd -12th, 1989, under the slogan "Strengthening the struggle for democracy for Iraq and real autonomy for Kurdistan", our tenth KDP congress was held. 332 representatives were present, along with a large number of guests from the Islamic Republic of

Iran, the Iraqi Kurdistan council, the Patriotic Union of Kurdistan, the Dawa Party, the Islamic Reaction Organization, the Kurdistan Socialist Party, Kurdistan People's Democratic Party, Kurdish Socialist Party, Assyrian Democratic Union, Kurdish Islamic Movement, Revolution Flag, Kurdistan Workers' Party and a large number of friendly and popular organizations.

The congress stood for a minute to mourn the souls of the founders of the Party, the immortal Mustafa Barzani, the late Idris Barzani, and the souls of the martyrs of the Kurdish liberation movement and the whole of Iraq.

The welcome speech was later delivered by Party leader Mr Massoud Barzani. Then the secretary of the Party, Haval Ali Abdullah, read the political report of the Central Committee for the congress, which highlighted the situation in Kurdistan, Iraq and the world, and highlighted the consequences of the war on extermination throughout Iraqi Kurdistan, in which the path of the Party's struggle over the past ten years, as well as the holding of the ninth-year congress were evaluated positively and negatively since 1979.

The report criticized the attempts and shortcomings that led to the military failure of the PDK and the Kurdish liberation movement, which was subjected to the use of chemical weapons by the dictatorship. It was a direct objective reason for the incident.

The report identified lessons from these years and made suggestions on how to continue the struggle for the next phase.

The report was discussed and investigated by a special committee convened by congress and decided after several manipulations.

The Central Committee then presented a new project for the PDK programme to congress, which was decided after a lengthy, edited discussion.

Guests read several speeches and greetings to the congress, as well as letters of assistance to the congress sent by more than one 130, organisations, social and intellectual figures.

During the congress meetings, many discussions were held on political, social and other issues, including the affairs of hundreds of thousands of refugees in Iran, Turkey, Pakistan and Kurdish refugees in particular in Europe, the United States of America, and further.

The congress issued a special resolution calling on the international community to take international law into account for our refugees and to be monitored by the UN Refugee Affairs Committee.

Some female representatives were present at the congress, with the problems and concerns of Kurdish women presented. They called for more attention to female social and democratic rights.

The congress made important organizational decisions to develop the future struggle in a way that would fit with the new situation in Iraqi Kurdistan. They also took organizational decisions to develop the activities of the party's highest sectors and to take decisions and strengthen the PDK.

The congress took some important political decisions on all levels and decided to prolong, strengthen and diversify the struggle appropriately, and in this way, the right to defend itself with arms and develop according to the circumstances. New to being against dictatorship and chauvinism, they emphasized creating some free platforms in which all Kurdish parties and personalities were represented in all the ways and sectors to express the public opinion of the people.

The congress also decided to strengthen the Iraqi Kurdistan council and expand joint national action to establish the Union of

The Kurdish Liberation Movement, and to try to unify the Iraqi opposition with all its fundamental parties, and to try to form a council in a wide-scale Iraqi national.

In a special decision, the congress called for the implementation of democracy for Iraq and real autonomy for Kurdistan based on public national reconciliation and the opening of a new page in the country's history by eradicating it. They called for an end to dictatorship, oppression, and cancelling all the actions of changing the national and historical image of Kurdistan and providing the rights of the national minorities in the opposition of Kurdistan and Iraq to strive for achieving a national reconciliation throughout Iraq.

For the first time in its history, the PDK congress had seen a free and wide horizon regarding various tasks, including evaluating the course of previous years, investigating important issues for Kurdistan, Iraq and the world.

The congress took a special decision about promoting democracy in the ranks of PDK and trying to promote it in the line of Kurdish movement in general and the importance of uniting Iraqi opposition, forming a wide Iraqi national council against dictatorship and oppression, and for the sake of democracy and social development.

The congress emphasized the strengthening of the Kurdish movement's union, particularly the Kurdistan council, and the Kurdish national right to determine its own destiny. At the same time, it pointed out that PDK supported any step through a peaceful and democratic solution to the Kurdish problem in each part of Kurdistan and any demands that the Kurdish people had there, adhering to their subjective circumstances and according to their own abilities.

The congress investigated the consequences of the Iraq-Iran war and its reflection on Kurdish society in particular and Iraqi society in general and concluded that neither war nor peace was a peaceful situation for the children of the people. It would endanger us, and only a democratic government based on public reconciliation in Iraq could solve this issue; it was not capable that a dictatorial regime could produce a fair solution.

Congress asked for an end to this unusual situation of shooting in order to reach a fair peace with Iran on the basis of respect, taking account of the national sovereignty of both sides, considering the will of the Iraqi people and their basic freedoms in general and the legitimate demands of the Kurdish people in particular.

The congress called on the international community to participate in a fair, democratic peace between Iraq and Iran and to set obstacles to the emergence of a new war in the Middle East. It also pointed to the fact that any other future war would be a chemical and/or biological, so congress took a special decision to remove the Middle East from the disaster of conflict and war, as well as to stabilize peace, justice and harmony in a way that would entirely include the nations of the region and the Kurdish people.

Congress expressed its appreciation for the support of our Party, the Kurdish Liberation Movement, and the Iraqi opposition to the Islamic Republic of Iran, which helped shelter thousands over the past ten years, Kurdish refugees in particular and Iraqis in general.

The congress congratulated the Arab Republic of Syria and the Libyan Republic on their cooperation with the Kurdish people's liberation issue and the Iraqi opposition.

On the Arab level, the congress expressed its greetings to the Palestinian people's uprising in order to defend their rights, to support the establishment of a Palestinian state and to hold an international conference including all parties in order to achieve the full national rights of the Palestinian people and the right to form its national state on its own land.

The congress congratulated the steps taken to achieve democracy in the countries of the region, as it expressed its cooperation with the friendly people of Lebanon and its national movement for the sake of stabilizing the legitimate government, establishing peace, unity of land, and freedom for the Lebanese people; and its support for the peaceful and just solution of the problems of Eritrean people and southern Sudan and the West Sahara people expressed.

Congress talked with great importance about the democratic changes that had taken place in socialist countries and talked about the spread of the wave of democratic changes in the world in general, and the disappearance and withdrawal of most of them. The dictatorial and racist regimes of the third world countries, deepening the general path of the countries towards widening the general freedoms and respecting human rights and increasing pressure on regimes that violate laws and certificates of rights and freedoms.

The congress emphasised the importance of opening the world, in the interest of human and nations' problems, especially those who have been oppressed throughout history, such as the People of Kurdistan.

Congress expressed its belief in the Universal Declaration of Human Rights They also congratulated the international efforts for strengthening the opening and elimination of atomic weapons, and eliminating the danger of global atomic war whilst strengthening cooperation between countries and nations for solidifying peace on earth and saving them from the danger of environmental destruction, hunger and delays.

Congress called on the international community to expand cooperation with the Kurdistan nation and its legitimate problems, and Kurdish right to take it into account, observers from the United Nations and other international institutions, except the legal status of refugees from Turkey and Iran and others, improving the situation and considering humanity in a way that is compatible with international law and justice.

The congress thanked the government, organizations, international parties, humanity, parties, cultural and social figures of the world who helped our people in their suffering, especially during the use of chemical weapons in Halabja and other parts of Iraqi Kurdistan.

Once again, they demanded that 16th March be announced every year as International Day in the name of Halabja, as a tribute to the martyrs and an expression of the global struggle to ban and destroy all weapons which have been stored.

The congress expressed its dissatisfaction with the attitude of the newspapers and the ignoring of some of the world's public opinion on the crimes of mass extermination committed by the Iraqi dictatorship against our people. The congress issued a special decision about the memory of immortal leader Mustafa Barzani and then all the representatives visited the holy grave to renew the loyalty agreement against the Kurdish nation's liberation problem and continue on the path of his struggle to success.

The congress elected Massoud Barzani, as the party's leader, with a unanimous vote. After deciding on the new internal procedure and cancelling the secretary Ali Abdullah's position, the Congress gave him the position of Vice President at the suggestion of the party's president and to respect the commander's struggle. Then the congress consists of a new Central Committee consisting of 21 members who were elected.

Congress honoured several former members of the central committee, who withdrew from the leadership because of their health; they had formed the core of the Party's leadership for decades and a younger group replaced them.

Holding a tenth congress of this size, and on such a democratic horizon, means the PDK's had great confidence in itself and the people. It was also a reaction to today's problematic situation that our people, its liberal movement and the Iraqi National Democratic Movement were going through. On the other hand, congress's arrival at this conclusion, in fact, the progressive line and democratic content of our party, from its establishment to this day. The congress came out with united respect, making the Kurdish movement stronger and stronger. The congress ended with a national anthem (Ay Raqib, the Kurdish speaking people are still alive).

Central Committee
Kurdistan Democratic Party/ Iraq 12/12/1989

December 2, 1989 - Hashmawa, tenth congress

December 2, 1989 - Hashmawa, tenth congress

December 2, 1989 - Hashmawa, tenth congress

December 2, 1989 - Hashmawa, tenth congress

Activities after the tenth congress

On the first day of the beginning of 1990, we met with the branch six of the Party. The meeting, attended by friends Hoshyar Zebari, Dr Muhammad Salih Jumaa and Dr Pirot Ahmed, discussed in detail the situation in Europe and how to organize the Party abroad and made a decision.

The meeting of the political bureau began on 5th January, 1990, in order to evaluate the general situation and take new and appropriate ways and procedures for managing affairs, formulating modern work strategies and programmes for the next stage. In the meeting, after discussing the topics and a detailed discussion, many decisions were made:

1. Seal stamp for all departments PDK Political Bureau.
2. Determining the duties and powers of the political bureau and setting a budget for them.
3. Select the section syllabus.
4. Appointing a new official to the political bureau administration.

At the 14th January 1990 meeting, attended by friends Fazil Mirani, Dr Jarjis Hassan, Dr Kamal Kirkuki, Said Salih and Abdulaziz Taib, the situation of refugees and residents of the Turkish camps was discussed and managed. During the meeting, the subject of setting up the committees was discussed in detail and considering the public interest, these friends were selected to run the camps:

For the Diyarbakir camp: Saado Kurki, Osman Qasim, Hussein Chalki, Salih Haji Hussein Guli, Said Nayef, Saeed Kestai,

Mohammed Shafiq, Dr Ghazi Abdullah Bamarni and Jamil Maghawir.

For the Mardin camp: Zuber Mai, Jamil Besfki, Amin Ahmed Uzmani, Badal (Zeravan) Kuvli, Izzat Muhammad Suleiman, Fariq Farooq, Karim Habib, Sadiq Galanski and Haji Abdulrahman Banavi.

For the Mush camp: Engineer Hassan Zawitai, Mohammed Abdullah, Sha'ban Maher, Tofiq Bahadin, Ali Tarwanshi, Muhammad Salim Shukri and Sadiq Salih.

Mullah Ahmed Dutazai was scheduled to be respected and consulted on the matter.

On 16th and 17th January, 1990, friends Mr Ali Abdullah, Abdul-Muhayman Barzani and Lieutenant Babakir presented the results of the Tehran meetings to their friends. A committee of friends, Fazil Mirani, Hoshyar Zebari and Abdul-Muhammed Barzani, was scheduled to form a committee to prepare an agreement on the basis of the discussion with Muhammed. On the twentieth day of the same month, we had a meeting with branch one to be aware of the situation with them and to solve their problems. The next day, in order to comfort them after the helplessness and distress that had arisen in Khwakurk, we met Rashid Beshuni and his friends fell, and Yassin Berukhi came with him.

At 10:30 pm on 25th January, 1990, in a letter, Dr Nasseh Ghafur presented the results of his visit to the Soviet Union. He appeared to have met with a representative of the Soviet Communist Party on the issue of the Soviet Kurds, and in another part of his message, the unstable situation of the Azerbaijani Kurds was discussed. Also, according to Shakaro, the situation of Armenian Kurds was talked about, with an emphasis on their Kurdish feeling and their pride in being Kurdish.

After Newroz 1990, a conference on organizing work for branches one, two, three and four was held on 25th – 27th March, 1990, to review their affairs, to adopt and set new working methods, and after presenting the topics and problems, a good and necessary set of decisions were made. The political bureau meeting was also held on 1st May, 1990, to review and reorganize aid and funds, and reorganize financial issues. The meeting detailed the financial issues and decided to revisit and review the financial issues and reorganize them appropriately according to the available income. In the frame of carrying out the affairs on 14th May after the conference of the four branches, friends Dr Kamal Kirkuk, Said Salih and Masoud Salihi returned to their duties.

According to the Mardin letter on 15th May, 1990, an Iraqi delegation, including Khalid Hamzani and Hajar Bamarni, visited the Mardin camp and Zeravani went to them. The people were expelled from their homes in the camp. After the incident, the police were called. Police and military vehicles entered the camp and the camp's residents were hurt.

On 17th May, 1990, we had a multi-party meeting with the righteous. The meeting discussed the situation in the region and the Kurdish people's struggle for their rights, as well as the legal dimensions of our people's rights. Three days later, on 20th May, we held a multi-party meeting with branches one, two, three and four to prepare for what was going on and move to the location of their tasks.

On 16th – 18th July, 1990, a multi-meeting of the political bureau, the central committee and members of the central committee's reserves was held to assess the general situation in the region, and a number of important decisions were made. On the 23rd and

24th of the same month, in order to strengthen the organization's structure and to alter the need for changes in the board of directors of the branch two, held a meeting. After showing the situation and discussing the problems, it was decided to make a change in the board of directors of branch two.

On 4th August, 1990, Azad Qaradaghi informed us of the 758 communications on the same date. Hama Sur Hussein and Haji Obed arrived at the branch headquarters at three o'clock and asked for a meeting, and we responded that this would happen if they could send them. The next day, on 5th August, 1990, we held a multi-party meeting to assess and discuss the new situation in the region after the invasion of Kuwait. The meeting was followed by a detailed study of the Iraqi army's attack on Kuwait and the new situation in the Middle East and Kurdistan. At the end of the meeting and considering the expected developments, we warned all branches to stop all kinds of peshmerga and military activities and monitor the situation.

On 14th August, 1990, we held a party conference attended by 180 political, military and social commanders and cadres to read and evaluate the situation in the region and new developments. After much discussion about new developments and attitudes, and after exchanging opinions, we were unanimously supported by the Party's policies and stances on the developments and changes. We also promised our commanders and our community to put the interests of the Kurdish people above all interests and to continue our national attitudes. A few days after that meeting, Mr Ali Abdullah returned from London and arrived at Razhan.

On 5th September, 1990, Teacher Akhir Sheikh Jamal returned inside the country and prepared a detailed report on the new situation in Iraq. It seemed that in terms of food, goods, and supplies, the people were living in a bad situation, and because of the invasion of Kuwait and the blockades, everything became a receipt and food was stamped on and this was divided between the people.

In order to discuss the issue of hostages on 10th November, I met Hussein Shingal. In the meeting, after discussing the topics, we agreed on the secret of the activity (Ghazal) and announced that the satellite phone had arrived in Tehran and was arriving in Qasimrash in the coming days.

Invading Kuwait

2nd August, 1990 was an important day and a historic turning point in the region. On that day, the Baghdad station reported that Iraq had attacked Kuwait and destroyed the authority of Al-Sabahi's family. Following the incident on 6th August, 1990, the International Security Council launched an economic embargo on Iraq, with only China and Cuba did not vote against the international decision.

At 13:00 am on 15th August, 1990, the Baghdad station announced that in a letter to Rafsanjani, Saddam agreed to the 1975 agreement and on 17th August, 1990, withdrew his forces and agreed with everything asked for.

On 5th September, 1990, Tariq Aziz visited Moscow and met Gorbachev[10], according to news sources, was not a successful visit.

On 9th September, 1990, Gorbachev and Bush[11] met in Helsinki on the Gulf situation; to some extent both agreed that Iraq should withdraw from Kuwait.

---

[10] Michael Gorbachev was the eighth and last president of the former Soviet Union from 1985 to 1991.

[11] George W. Bush was the 41st President of the U.S. President from 1989 to 1993 and later in 2018. During his time, the United States led an international coalition to liberate Kuwait from Saddam's regime.

On 9th September, 1990, Tariq Aziz, Isam Talabi, oil minister and Barzan Ibrahim Tikriti, visited Tehran and were warmly welcomed by the Iranians. Indeed, the world of politics is like that, after all the wars and killings of interests, they sat down together.

On 11th September, 1990, Moscow Radio (Voice of Peace and Progress) reported:

What right has Iraq to do this? We assume that Iraq has faced economic crisis and needs to solve its economic problems, to capture Bubrean Island[12]. Why hasn't permission been given to Turkey to invade Iraqi Kurdistan?

During Friday prayers on 21st September, 1990, Rafsanjani spoke highly of the Iran-Iraq war era, claiming their withdrawal was planned. In another part of his speech, he said that they had intended to attack Mosul in order to rescue their captives, even the necessary weapons had been delivered to the destination, but the matter was postponed because part of the road was in Turkey's hands. Abbas Shabak's lies seemed to be obvious, unfortunately, the president of a country is at a level to deceive someone like Abbas Shabak.

On the night of 21st September, 1990, Iranian television published the first part of Saddam's letters written to Rafsanjani.

Saddam had shown himself as very weak, but Rafsanjani was very strong in his response and wrote at the end of a letter: "Peace be upon you, those who follow guidance."

On 22nd September, 1990, Syrian President Hafiz Al-Assad was scheduled to visit Tehran and as published, Assad led a

---

[12] The Bubian Peninsula belongs to Kuwait and is in the northwest of the Gulf and northeast of Kuwait.

delegation consisting of Abdul Halim Khaddam, Faruq al-Shara, and Mohammed Harba, the minister and Interior and Trade Minister Mohammed Amadi, which visited Tehran.

On 4th October, 1990, Yevgeny Primakov visited Baghdad to meet with senior Iraqi officials and discuss the Gulf crisis.

On 18th October, 1990, the Arabic section of Ankara Radio published the following news:

The Hurriyet newspaper is an article entitled "Mosul and Kirkuk are going to Turkey". In a speech delivered in front of his parliament, Malik Hassan II announced that, as king of Morocco - Malik Hassan II, the major countries had agreed to change the map of the Middle East in which the Palestinian state in Jordan and the Kurdish state would be established in Iraq, whilst Mosul and Kirkuk would enter Turkish territory.

On 28th October, 1990, Tariq told us that relations between the Shammar and Juburi tribes had deteriorated and many of them had been arrested. They demonstrated in Mosul and raised the slogan "We want bread, not Kuwait". In a special section, he mentioned in detail about invading Kuwait.

In response to the Iraqi regime's actions, the United States led a major international coalition to drive Iraq out of Kuwait. From the invasion of Kuwait in August 1990 to the beginning of 1991, more than 700,000 allied forces were stationed in the Gulf region, where the United States sent only 500,000 troops to the region for the operation to liberate Kuwait. In the same frame, thousands of warplanes and armoured vehicles were brought to the area by the allies for the purpose of confronting the Iraqi army.

The Iraqi regime did not heed the advice of the international community and the security council's decisions, and finally on

17th January, 1991, operation Desert Storm under the command of General Norman Schwarzkopf[13] of the United States was conducted to expel Iraq from Kuwait and the destruction of the Iraqi army's fighting machine began.

After 43 days of intense allied air strikes and bombardments, Iraq was forcibly expelled from Kuwait. This was at a time when coalition ground attacks began on February 24, 1991, and quickly managed to reach hundreds of kilometres, thus entering southern Iraq.

Finally, on 28th February, 1991, Iraq accepted defeat and signed a ceasefire agreement in the Safwan area, giving all coalition conditions.

With the invasion of Kuwait and the change of the equation, the Kurdistan Democratic Party and the Kurdistan council were in a state of preparation for adapting to the new developments and with Iraq's failure against the allies, paving the way for the mass uprising and the Kurdistan council according to a plan as the peshmerga forces had decided to enter the cities. On 11th March, 1991, we arrived in Rania, the gate of the uprising.

---

[13] General Herbert Norman Schwarzkopf JR, an American general who commanded the Desert Storm Operation to liberate Kuwait . He was born in 1934 and died in 2012.

Conclusion

THE GULAN REVOLUTION was rightly the holder of all the meanings of a perfect revolution. It was a rebellion and a revolt to reject and change the oppressive realities imposed on our people as a result of the failure and the ominous Algerian agreement. Tens of thousands of people were not ready to stay under the imposed reality and accepted homelessness with their hearts and souls. Mr Barzani and the Kurdish way remained.

After the regional and international conflict against the Kurdish people, rejecting the real setback, giving hope and reorganizing ourselves was our first strategic goal. This was a difficult task in a climate full of threats, dangers and obstacles to Kurdish enemies, and looked like it was impossible. To achieve this goal, we needed the spirit of struggle where there was hope and despair.

What gave clarity to all the activists at that time was that our nation had a legitimate and independent cause and a clear goal and should not make any obstacles, interests, and pressures of the enemies make us lose hold of our principles and issues.

The Gulan revolution was the message of not surrendering the Kurdish nation and the rise of the liberation revolution against oppression, occupation and dictatorship, and the international conspiracy to destroy the Kurdish revolution. This revolution was a continuation of the previous revolutions and an important stage in history in the struggle of our nation.

The Gulan revolution carried the message and goals of the great Aylul revolution and was one of the most important stages of the struggle of the peshmerga and the Kurdish people. This revolution proved that if the struggle of the people of Kurdistan had stopped at some stage, the will of the struggle has never been broken and will continue with a new breath and thirst to reach freedom.

The masses, the peshmerga, the organization and a holy way, with clear and continuous goals, formed the main dimensions of the Gulan revolution. The Gulan revolution was therefore able to succeed in a short time and continue, because all these dimensions worked on it carefully, were done and complemented each other.

The Gulan revolution soon led to the resurrection of the hope of all Kurds and the transfer of the struggle to its real field, which is Kurdistan's territory. This point was of strategic importance to us. Because the main purpose of the enemy's plan was to end revolution and struggle in the land forever.

On the other hand, the fall of the Shah's regime, the start of the Iran-Iraq war and the change of equations paved the way for the Gulan revolution and the Kurdish liberation movement to continue its struggle with higher breath and hope.

In this hard and difficult way, the Gulan revolution was able to successfully start its goals and activities and not be under the influence of any regional trend but at the same time take advantage of the circumstances and events, growing day by day and becoming stronger – a place of sorority and hope for all sides.

As mentioned in previous sections of this book, the Gulan revolution coincided with the terrible events and the emergence of conflicts, among the Kurdish parties. Behind much of the deepening conflicts and clashes, the fingerprints of the efforts of Kurdistan's enemies and the region's intelligence agencies were visible. They tried their best to create conflict between the Kurdish parties and their constituent wings, to take advantage of it and disperse Kurds preventing the brotherhood and unity of Kurds.

Of course, the inexperience, confusion and selfishness of some leaders also led to the spread of mischief and the wounding of our nation's tired body.

In order to reveal the truth in this book, I have tried to point out some of these terrible events. I have tried to make it clear to everyone what happened, where the mistakes and shortcomings were and be an experience for the current and future generations of our people. There were many other detailed subjects that I didn't want to talk about because the enemies of the Kurdistan nation would benefit, take it from it and use it to further divide our people.

In parallel with all that, from fifteen years between 1975 and 1990, the degree of hatred and brutality of our people's enemies increased. The crimes committed against our people during this period have not been seen in history. Relocating, Arabizing, Ba'athist propaganda, destroying villages, and destroying economic infrastructure.

These, alongside the demography, social, and psychological destruction of our nation on the one hand, Anfal, genocide, and chemical bombardment on the other, go into the context of crimes against humanity that were committed by the previous regime during this period. They have been committed by Iraq against our people. All of these are important lessons for individual members of our nation and they should not be forgotten at all. Our nation has faced genocide, cleansing and dissolving policies in those years. With all the systematic crimes and cruelty of the regime, the rising spirit of oppression, continuity, and insistence on struggle, the response of our people towards our enemies became more important than ever.

The more brutal and conspiratorial the enemy was, the stronger the spirit of struggle among the Kurdish people became. In this way, the Gulan revolution has become a tool for the Kurdish people to prove themselves, defeat the enemy, and thwart their plans and threats. In this, the fighters of the Gulan revolution have performed their duty well.

Another goal of the Gulan revolution and the Kurdistan Democratic Party was to open up to the outside world, to establish relations with the free world, the liberation movement, and to find friends and supporters around the world.

In addition, the KDP was always an initiative at this stage for brotherhood, harmony and unity among the Kurdish parties and Iraq's liberal and revolutionary forces, because they believed that eliminating conflicts and unifying the capabilities of the parties would be a strong factor in better standing together against our common enemy, dictatorship and oppression.

In the direction of PDK's strong belief in unity, the Kurdistan council was born, which was one of the most important achievements and caused the military, political, media, and diplomatic energy of the parties to oppose the regime. The Ba'athist strain, which had a major impact on the success of the great spring uprising of 1991, and subsequent elections after the invasion of Kuwait by the former regime and the creation of suitable conditions, established Kurdistan as regional institutions.

The forces, values and goals of the Gulan revolution have been an extension of other Kurdish people's revolutions as new tools and methods, in different and complex circumstances. Thanks to God and the efforts of the Kurdish people, the Gulan revolution achieved its goals and did not allow the silence and disappointment of the Kurdish people take too long.

Here, I think it is necessary to thank and appreciate all the families of the martyrs, activists, and fighters of the Gulan revolution, the brave peshmerga, our arrangements, our cadres, the secret arrangements in the cities and villages, and the people of the liberated areas, and refugees. I will do this to all the patriots of all parts of Kurdistan, the activists of Iraq and the political parties who have had a part in this great pride, have been tired and sacrificed in the fight against oppression, dictatorship and chauvinism. We should always remember that the success and achievements of the Kurdish nation are because of the unity of their patriots it has created.

Thousands of greetings to the pure souls of
the martyrs of Gulan revolution and all the
martyrs of Kurdistan freedom way.

References of the second part

Kurdish

- Kurdistan news, the news of the media department of the political office of PDK Kurdistan Democratic PartyIraq, No. 112, late February 1984
- Wrya Jaff, Journalism History of the Kurdistan Democratic Party, 1946-1996, First Edition, 1996, page 80
- Kurdistan Students' Union, some aspects of struggle and history, Sasan Auni, in the publications of the Secretariat Office of the Kurdistan Students' Union 1998, page 71
- Khabat Newspaper, No. 549, January 1984, page 6.
- Khabat Newspaper, No. 558-559, January 1986, page 13
- In the publications of the media section of the Political Bureau of the Kurdistan Democratic PartyIraq, May 1984
- In the publications of the media section of the Political Bureau of the Kurdistan Democratic PartyIraq, Khabat Printing company

- History of PDK cadre courses, from mountain to city, 1968-2014, Center for Studies and Research and PDK Academy 2019, page 58
- The law of the Revolutionary Army of Kurdistan 1980, in the publications of the Kurdistan Democratic Party Khabat newspaper, no. 52 of September 20, 1976
- A recording of the secret struggle of the Kurdistan Democratic Party's arrangements, in the Pshdar border from 1975 to 1991, Gulan revolution, Omar Hamza Salih, 2018, page 165
- The History of the Gulan Revolution, 1976/5/26, Asaad Ado, Page 106
- Khabat Newspaper, No. 541, July and August 1980, Page 8
- Khabat Newspaper, No. 545, January 1981, Page 1
- Khabat Newspaper, No. 547, September 1981, Page 3
- Khabat Newspaper, No. 554 and 555, January and February 1985
- Khabat Newspaper, No. 549, January 1984, Page 3
- Khabat Newspaper, No. 556 and 557, March and April 1985, Page 3
- Khabat Newspaper, No. 558 and 559, January 1986, Page 3
- Khabat Newspaper, No. 522 and 523, November 1987, Page 3
- Brayati Newspaper, No. 638, September 16, 1992, Page 1
- Khabat Newspaper, No. 551, End of April 1984, Page 3
- Khabat Newspaper, No. 562 and 563, April and May 1986, Page 3
- Brayati Newspaper, No. 638, 16/9/1992, Page, 1
- Kurdish Liberation Movement, Idris Barzani, example, Sami Shorsh, translation into Kurdish language, Dr. Rizgar, page 22

- Muhammad Haji Mahmud, peshmerga Calendar, 1976-1996, Second Edition, 1986-1982, page 492
- Idris Barzani, History Man, Saeed Mamuzini, Erbil, 2008, page 10
- Idris Barzani is a great human being, but he will not die, Rashid Mahla Ali Kolaki, Erbil, 2016, page 77
- Faranso Hariri, Brayati Newspaper, Sunday 1993/05/23, No. 1652
- Interview with Mustafa Nerwai, Brayati Newspaper, Sunday, 1993/5/30, No. 450 1658
- The reasons for barzani's continuation, Farhanso Hariri, Matin magazine, no. 100, Gulan 2000, pages 22 and 23
- Kurdistan News, News of the Media Section of the Political Bureau of the Kurdistan Democratic Party of Iraq, No. 115, 1984/4/30, page 1
- Kurdistan Students' Union, some aspects of struggle and history, Sasan Auni, in the publications of the Secretariat Office of the Kurdistan Students' Union, 1998, page 96
- Congress and conferences of the Kurdistan Students' Union, writing and preparing, Irfan Aziz Aziz, Erbil, 2012, page 91
- Kurdistan Women's Union: From yesterday to today, written by Dr Vian Suleiman, page 7
- Jaafar Mustafa Maruf, A Selection of My Notes, 1985-1990, Second Edition, Page 16
- The mountain writes itself, writing the hard days of struggle, 1988, Jamal Mortka, page 18
- Kambiz Ibrahimzada, Genocide (Genocide) First Edition, 2012, page 15

- Dr Marf OmerGul, Kurdish Genocide the vision of the new international law, 2010, page 35
- Halabja, 1988 chemical attack, Hawraman Ali Tofiq, Erbil, 2000, page 19
- After such knowledge, what forgiveness? KURDISTAN, or THE CULTURE OF A NATION, Jonathan C . Randall, page 290
- Strategic Security of Iraq and the Ba'athist Tribe: Tarhil, Arabization, Tabis, Amin Qadir Mina, page 210
- Kurdish people's sociology, Agha, Sheikh and State, Kurdistan's political and social structures, writer, Martin Van Bruin Sen, in Persian, Ibrahim Younesi, in Kurdish, Shukur Mustafa, page 9
- Diligence, The Short History of the Immortal Barzani Party and Culture, Muhammad Mala Qadir, Third Edition, 2012, page 79
- Political decisions and the final declaration of the tenth congress of the Kurdistan Democratic Party of Iraq, 2-12 December 1989
- Mustafa Barzani peshmerga and President, written by Hamid Gawhari, Stockholm: 2017, page 667
- London Radio 9/8/1988
- Dr Muhammad Khidir Mawlud, Khwakurk, Resistance and Turning Point, Erbil Newspaper, No. 3156, 9/10/2019, page 6
- Panorama of using chemical weapons in Kurdistan, Dr Najih Gulpi, Kurdipedia website
- Genocide Crime, 1988, Information and Documents, Taha Suleiman, 2015 Genocide in Southern Kurdistan: Past, present, and future, effects and duties, Taha Suleiman,

University of Garmian, July 2017 50 years old, Kurdistan Islamic Scholars Union, a history of service and pride, Mullah Abdullah Sherkawi, 2020, page, 191

The memories of these friends have been crucial in this work;
Hashim Sitai, Babakir Faqe Ahmed, Hamid Sharif, Fahim Abdullah, Khurshid Shera, Abdullah Salih, Nasreddin Hawrami, Ehsan Amedi, Muhammad Muhsin, Barzan Mahla Khalid, Masoud Salihi, Shukri Nerwai.

References of the second part – Arabic

- (Rezgari) then (Khabat), mouthpiece of the Kurdistan Democratic Party, Nidal Musharraf For More Than Half a Century, Historical Presentation, 1946-1998, Rezgar Nouri Shawis, pp. 77-83
- Salah Al-Khorsan, Political Currents in Iraqi Kurdistan, A Reading in the Files of Kurdish Movements and Parties in Iraq, 1946-2001, p. 269
- Kurdistan Democratic Party-Iraq, Political Office
- Pamphlet printed by the Kurdistan Democratic Party-Iraq, Sixth Branch Europe, July 1988
- Kurdistan News Newspaper, published by the Media Department of the Political Office of the Kurdistan Democratic Party-Iraq, September 1980, issue, 7, p. 15
- Kurdistan News Newspaper, Issue (157), May 1987, p. 1
- Kurdistan News Newspaper, Issue (159), July 1987, p. 1
- Kurdistan News Newspaper, Issue (163), September 1987, p. 1
- Kurdistan News Newspaper, 90s

- Issue, 169, 15-20K1988/2, newsletter issued by the Media Department of the Political Office of the Kurdistan Democratic Party-Iraq
- Kurdistan News Newspaper, published by the Media Department of the Political Office of the Kurdistan Democratic Party-Iraq, September 1980, issue, 7, p. 15
- Kurdistan News Newspaper, Issue (157), May 1987, p. 1
- Kurdistan News Newspaper, Issue (159), July 1987, p. 1
- Kurdistan News Newspaper, Issue (163), September 1987, p. 1
- Kurdistan News Newspaper, 90s
- Issue, 169, 15-20 K1988/2, Newsletter issued by the Media Department of the Political Office Kurdistan Democratic Party-Iraq
- Human Rights in Iraq, Middle East Woj, translated by Dr Rezgar, p. 18
- Arabization Policy in the Kurdistan Region of Iraq, A Documentary Study, prepared by, Dr Khalil Ismail Mohammed, Sirwan Kakiye, Dr Muhammad Abdullah Omar, Mahmoud Haji, 2003, pp. 18-20-21
- The policy of Arabization in the Kurdistan Region of Iraq, a documentary study, prepared by, Dr Khalil Ismail Mohammed, Sirwan Kakiyi, Dr Muhammad Abdullah Omar, Mahmoud Haji, 2003, p. 22
- Al-Taz Al-Sadami, The Chemical War of the Iraqi Government, Against the Kurdish Revolution and the Kurds, Dr Hallo, 14/5/1988, 4-5
- Anfal Campaign in Iraqi Kurdistan, Destruction of the Village of Korimi, Oral Testimonies, and Evidence of International Doctors, translation, Dr Rezgar, p. 33

– The Kurds, in the documents of the British National Archives, 1969-1978, prepared and translated, Shirku Habib, review and introduction, Dr Abdul Fattah Ali Al-Bhutani, Erbil, 2017, p. 121

– Dr Kazem Habib, Glimpses of Nidal, The National Liberation Movement of the Kurdish People in Iraqi Kurdistan, p. 563

– Documents on the plight of the people of Kurdistan-Iraq, Media Department of the Political Office of the Kurdistan Democratic Party-Iraq, Khabat Press, October I, 1988, p. 7

– Ofrabengio, The Kurds of Iraq: Building a State within a State, translated by Abdul Razzaq Abdullah Bhutani, pp. 205-208

– Military communiqué on the Khwakurk epic, September 5, 1988, Political Office of the Kurdistan Democratic Party-Iraq – Kurdistan

– News Newspaper, Issue (178), 16-31 May 1988, p. 1 454

Documents

Dear reader,

This part of the book is all original documents. None of those documents has been edited in terms of grammar and composition. Still, spelling has been placed on the current spelling, which is now standard and recommended by the Kurdish Language Academy.

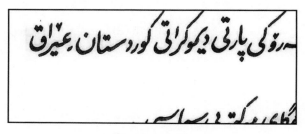

Document (1)

A Monsieur MASSOUD BARZANI

Monsieur,

Dans un esprit humanitaire, je vous demande de bien vouloir libérer dès que possible

Jean-Christophe LEFAS
Robert LAURENT
Yves MOY

et également

Hans KISTLER
Mario RIVA

qui sont actuellement entre vos mains.

Confiant dans votre compréhension, je vous exprime dès maintenant ma gratitude.

Toute oeuvre de miséricorde rend gloire au Dieu Tout-Puissant et nous permet de réaliser sa volonté.

Du Vatican, le 9 juin 1984

Joannes Paulus PP. II

Document (2)

parti
communiste
français
2 place
du colonel fabien
75940 paris
cedex 19
tel 238 66 55

Secrétaire général

paris, le   6 juin 1984

Monsieur MASSOUD BARZANI
Président du Parti
démocratique kurde
Irak

Monsieur le président,

     Dans un esprit humanitaire et dans la grande tradition de votre père MULLAH MUSTAPHA BARZANI, je vous demande de bien vouloir libérer dès que possible

Jean-Christophe LEFAS
Robert LAURENT
Yves MOY

actuellement entre vos mains.

Georges MARCHAIS

Document (3)

BRUNO KREISKY

Vienne, le 12 Juin 1984

Monsieur le President,

dans un esprit humanitaire et dans la grande
tradition de votre père, Mullah Mustafa Barzani,
je vous demande de bien vouloir libérer dès que
possible Messieurs Jean-Christophe Lefas,
Robert Laurent et Yves Moi, actuellement entre
vos mains.

Agreez, Monsieur le President, l'expression
de mes sentiments le plus distingués.

Bruno Kreisky

Monsieur
Massoud Barzani
President du Parti Democratique Kurde

I r a k

P.S. Je suis plein de sympathie
pour vôtre cause et vôtre peuple

Document (4)

١٩٧٨

حضرة الأخ العزيز م . ب

السلام عليكم ورحمة الله وبركاته . أن يحفظك و يوفقك لما فيه الخير دائماً

أ قبل بأشتياق حبينك والصافية

وأتمنى أن تكون بأحسن الصحة والعافية والجميع يقدموسركم

نحن هنا جميعاً الحمد سالمين والأهل والأولاد وكلهم سالمين ومتمتعين بفضل الله بالصحة والعافية

السلام والاحترام . أم مرور مع الأولاد سالمين وتحن هنا معدناالله جميعاً في محنتنا وتنألم

وليس هناك أية مشكلة ماعدى غيابكم عنهم مادعدنا الله جميعاً في محنتنا وتنألم

نتعالى أن يجمع شملنا جميعاً على الخير والسعادة ومرفوعي الرأس في أرض الوطن و

لوجود وسلامة الوالد . إذا سمحت لك الفرصة وتشرفت بخدمة الوالد

ارجو أن تقبل بدي نيابة عني أسأل الله تعالى أن يحفظ بعنايته و يو نقه لى

ما فيه خير وسعادة الدارين .

ما فيه خير متأكده مه دقت عودتك الى لندن ولذا لا أستطيع شرح المزيد مه

إنني غير متأكده مه دقت عودتك الى لندن ولذا لا أستطيع شرح لك

التفاصيل عه وضعنا وكلن ارجو أن تواجه الأخ محمد أمين إنه ليشرح لك

بعض الأمور وقد ارسلنا رسالة الى الأخ سامي خط الأخ على عبد الله ارجو

الاطلاع عليك أيضاً كما ما وصلت رسالة الى الأخ حسينه وأخرى الى الأخ

عبد الوهاب ارجو الاطلاع عليك أتى تصل على صورة أفضل عه

وضعنا .

جماعة الكلام يؤكدونه على شخصياً وبأ ستمرار وبأسم كبيرهم كى لا أقوم

بأي نشاط في صدورهم مع العلمه و أن لا يصل أفراد الى الطرف الآخر

ولا أتجاوب مع إرسال الطرف الآخر وحينها أن الحكومة

ولا أصل بهم ولا أتجاوب مع إرسال الطرف الآخر . ولكنني أعتقد

العراقية قد توفرت لديه معلومات وقامت بإحتجاج رسمي . ولكنني أعتقد

أن السبب يعود الى تأشيرنا الإيجابي على ترجيح حظ الوالد و تجاوب الناس

بصورة واسعة مع هذا الاتجاه . وكذلك تأثير العن هناك على رأي البعث

وما حلال مصول تغيير في رأي البعثين بتجاه إيجاد وسيلة للتقاهم معهم

وما حلال طرحت السفارة (الغيرد أعضاء الفارد) الطاقة أسئلة على جماعتنا

حظ الوالد و قد طرحت السفارة في آخر دعوة تحمي منها أنهم يقومون بتقديمه

المدعوين في بيت السفير في آخر دعوة تحمي منها أنهم يقومون بتقديمه

لتأكد فيما إذا كنا جادين للتقاهم معهم أستراتيجياً و تقديمه هذه الطريقه

هذه الأسئلة والدعوات تخويف بإراده بالتقاهم معنا وفعلاً فأن الموقف

الديلمي جباناً بالمرونة العجيبة مع العلمه حيث ما فرضوا النميرغلام رضا

الى بغداد وزيارة العتبات المقدسة تغزاه في أيام ثم تار الى البيتالله

يرللوي الى بغداد في زيارة رسمية للعلمه تغزاه في أيام ثم تار الى البيتالله

على كل حال هناك مصاعب كبيرة لا نستطيع تحريج

الحام في الصحة .

Document 5 (1-2), in this Document M.B IS (Fazel) Idris Barzani.

و يصعب في هذه الحالة ما عنه الرضا في الطرف الآخر ، يقول هؤلاء هنا أنهم
إنا ألقوا القبض على شخص ذاهب الى الطرف الآخر وقادم من هناك
سيسلمونه الى الحكومة العراقية . أعتقد أن هذه التسهيلات مقصورة
على شخصيا فقط ولا أصدره أن تكون هناك تغيير في أمور الجدد
ولكن ربما يرغبوا أن يرسلوا عناصرهم ويرسلوهم الى الطرف الآخر
ويتعاملوا هم مباشرة مع الناس هناك وفي نفس الوقت يتظاهروا
للعائد بأنهم لازالوا يتعاونون معهم ويظلون صداقتهم على أي نوع من
التواجد للأكراد . حل هذا في الحقيقة عندي مبني على أحسن صما دقة ولكن
يؤثر على وضعنا في هذه المرحلة الحاسة التي سنهيئ فيها العائد طيلة
كبيرة على بلادنا لانزال المقاومة . إ نني وأقم بعونه الله وقدرته
أنه إذا انفلتت جهود الأعداء لإنهاء المقاومة فأنهم سيضطرونه الى
الالتجاء الى السلم والتفاهم والتسليم الى الجود والمطهر السلم الذي يرمو
اليه يصعب مضطهد . ومما أجل إنهاء المقاومة لدي إفتراضين جيدا لو
أستطعتي الوصول للأعضاء في الوطن إ- ادلا السماح لجميع القرى الغير محتلة
ومن قبل قوت الجيش العلنية أن يتعاملوا مباشرة مع السلطات الحكومية و
يتظاهروا بنوع من اخلاصهم لسي كي يحافظوا على قراهم ومطانخ وثانيا
من الصعودي أن تستجنب قوات الأرضار هجمات الجيش العراقي ضامنة
إذا كانت القوت كبيرة ولاستعداداتي طافيه والعمل على إضافاء أنفسم
كي يوجهوا صذبا بني الصغيرة في الأعمال التي يستطيعون فيها القيام بها طم
والمهم في النهاية أن تبقى المقاومة المالكة وتحافظ قرى كردستان على
آلبم قدر ممكنه من السلامة ولذا ما كفقه هذين الهدفين تكون محاولة الأعداء
قد أحبطت .

ارسلناه مبلغ مع الأخ محمد أمين بك يرجى إعلامنا بوصوله
الأخ علي عبدالله نقدم له أحر السلام والاحترام . أقدم أحر التحيات الى الأخ
محمد و الدكتور نجم الدين ومحمد سعيد وجميع الأعضاء الآخرين في لندنه
دمتم جميعا في حفظ الله محروسين وبعونه موفقين
الصورة
فاضل   ٥/ح

Document 5 (2-2), in this Document M.B IS (Fazel) Idris Barzani.

Document 5
Document 6 (1-8)

Mr Idris's letter,

Dear Brother M.B
May the peace, blessings, and mercy of God be upon you

I Kiss and longing your eyes, and asking God to protect you and guide you to what is always good, and I hope that you are in the best health and wellness.

We are all here, praise be to God. Safe, the parents and children are all safe, and everyone offers you peace and respect. Masrour's Mom with the children safe and enjoying, thanks to God, health and wellness, and there is no problem except your absence from them. May God help us all in our ordeal, and we ask Him Almighty to reunite us all in goodness and happiness, and to raise our heads in the homeland with the presence and safety of the father. If you have the opportunity, and you honoured to serve the father, please kiss his hands on my behalf. I ask God Almighty to protect him with his care and guide him to what is good and the happiness of the two houses.

I am not sure when you will return to London, explain more details about our situation but I hope that you direct brother Mohammed Amin Beg to explain some affairs to you. We have sent a letter to brother Sami in the handwriting of brother Ali Abdullah, please ensure you definitely see it. I have also sent a letter to brother Shafik and another to brother Abdel Wahab. Please check these out to get a better picture of our situation.

The people of the Dukan constantly emphasize to me personally, and in the name of their elder, so that I do not carry out any
activity on their border with Iraq. They stress that I do not send
individuals to the other party or contact them or respond to the
call of the other party, and their argument is that the Iraqi government has information and has made an official protest. Personally,
I think that the reason is due to our positive impact on expanding
the Father's line and the people's response widely to this trend,
in that the impact of work there on the opinion of the Baath and
the possibility of a change in the opinion of the Baathists towards
finding a way to understand this, as well as the impact of work of
changing the opinions of the Baath and the possibility of altering
their perspective in understanding the line of the father.

The embassy (the Ambassador and members of the Iraqi
embassy) asked questions to our group who were invited into the
Ambassador's house in the last invitation. This was treated with the
presumption that they would be investigating to confirm whether
our intentions are serious about creating an understanding with
them strategically. This frankness may be one of these questions
and invitations, intimidating Iran with an understanding with
us. And to consider that the Iranian position is characterized by a
strange flexibility with Iraq, where Prince Gholam Reza recently
traveled to Baghdad to visit the holy shrines, and Princess Ashraf
Pahlavi travelled to Baghdad on an official visit to Iraq for five
days before travelling to the Sacred House of God in Saudi Arabia.

In any case, there are great difficulties that we cannot challenge,
and in this case it is difficult to help the Brotherhood on the other
side who say that if they arrest someone going to the other side or
coming from there, they will hand him over to the Iraqi government.

I think that these are personal stresses which affect only me personally, and I do not believe that there will be a change in border matters. However, perhaps they want to infiltrate their elements and send them to the other side, dealing directly with the people there and at the same time pretending to Iraq that they are still cooperating with them and prefer their friendship to any. A kind of presence for the Kurds.

All of this is not really based on honest foundations, but it affects our situation at this sensitive stage in which Iraq is preparing for a major campaign against our country to end the resistance.

I am confident with God's help and power that if the enemies' efforts to end the resistance fail, they will continue to resort to peace, understanding, and submission to the truth and common sense for which the oppressed people are calling. In order to sustain the resistance, I have two suggestions, if you could convey these to the Brotherhood at home:

First, to allow all villages not occupied by the Iraqi Baath forces to deal directly with the government authorities and to demonstrate a kind of devotion to them in order to preserve their villages and their inhabitants.

Second, it is necessary for the Ansar forces to avoid the attacks of the Iraqi army, especially if the forces are large and their preparations are sufficient, and work to hide themselves in order to direct their small strikes in places where they can carry out their activities of peace. If these two goals are achieved, the enemies' attempt will be thwarted. We sent a sum with brother Mohammed Amin Beg, please let us know of receiving if. Brother Ali Abdullah offers you the warmest peace and respect. I offer my warmest greetings to brother Mohsen, Dr Najm El-Din, Mohamed Saeed and all the other brothers in London and may all of you be in god's protection and with god's help.

Your brother Fazel
3/21/1978

In this Document M.B IS (Fazel) Idris Barzani.

الحزب الديمقراطي الكردستاني ــ العراق
المكتب السياسي

بلاغ عسكري حول ملحمة خواكورك

تتواصل المعركة البطولية لبيشمه ركة حزبنا في جبهة (خواكورك) التي تحولت الى ملحمة خالدة في تأريخ شعبنا ، سطرت ببطولـــة وتضحية مقاتلي كافة فروع حزبنا البطلة بوجه الحملة الشوفينيـة للنظام العراقي الذي يعمل منذ حوالي (٢٠) عاما على اخــــلاء كردستان من شعبها وتغيير واقعها القومي والتأريخي .

جاء التحضير للتصدي والمقاومة انطلاقا من قرار اللجنة المركزية لحزبنا في ٢٠/ تموز/ ١٩٨٨ وادراكا للطبيعة الشوفينية للنظـام التي دفعت وستدفع النظام الى شن حملات عسكرية واسعة على مقـرات وقواعد حزبنا وبغية القوى الوطنية الكردستانية والعراقية ، خاصة بعد اعلان الموافقة على وقف اطلاق النار في الحرب العراقيـــة ــ الايرانية .

شن النظام حملته العسكرية الضخمة على خواكورك في شمال محافظة اربيل ، في منطقة مساحتها لاتتجاوز (١٥٠) كيلو متر مربع .

وبدأت بذلك ملحمة تأريخية للمقاومة الكردية مستمرة حتـــى اصدار هذا البلاغ .

منذ ٧/١٩ وحتى ١٩٨٨/٩/٥ اي اكثر من شهر ونصف ، شنت قـــوات النظام عشرات الهجمات الواسعة ، مستعملة جميع انواع الاسلحــة المتوفرة لديها بدءا بالقصف الجوي والمدفعي المكثف والى الاسلحة الكيمياوية المحرمة حسب المواثيق والقوانين الدولية . وكسان سير العمليات ونشاطج هذه المعارك كالاتي :

Document 6 (1-8)

اولا : قواتنــا :

شاركت من طرفنا قوات مقر قيادة الثورة وقوات الفرع الرابع والثالث والثانى للحزب، ومفرزة من انصار الحزب الشيوعى العراقى الحليف .

ثانيا : قوات العدو المشتركة فى قتال خواكورك كانت تتكون من :

١- الفيلق الاول للجيش العراقى .

٢- الفيلق الخامس .

٣- اكثر من ٣٠ ثلاثين فوجا للمرتزقة، (من الافواج الخفيفة) .

٤- اكثر من (٥) خمسة كتائب مدفعية ميدان، واعداد كبيرة من مدافع الهاون .

هـ- ثلاثة كتائب دبابات .

٦- اسراب من الطائرات الحربية والمروحية .

٧- استعملت الاسلحة الكيمياوية فى قرية (زه روه) وغيرها شمـال جبهة خواكورك، وجرح (٦٢) بيشمه ركة من قواتنا .

ثالثا : خسائر العدو :

١- الوحدات العسكرية العراقية، التى تكبدت خسائر فادحـــة، وتحملت القسط الاكبر من الخسائر هى :

أ- الفرقة ٣٣ / الفيلق الخامس

ب - الفرقة ٤٥/ الفيلق الاول .

ج - الفرقة ٣٥ .

د - الفرقة ١٨ .

هـ - اللواء ٦٨ / قوات خاصة .

و - اللواء ٦٦/ قوات خاصة .

ز - الفوج الاول مستقل مغاوير من الفرقة ٣٣ .

ح - اللواء ٧٠٢ مشاة .

ط - اللواء ٤٠٢ مشاة .

– ٢ –

Document 6 (2-8)

ك‍ - اللواء ١٢٠ مغاوير .

ك‍ - اللواء الثانى مغاوير .

ل - وحدة كاملة من قوات الامن الداخلى .

٢- خسائر العدو فى الارواح :

ا - اصابة وجرح حوالى (٨٤٥٠) عسكريا ، ووقعت جثث اكثر مـــن
(١٠٠٠) منهم بيد قواتنا ، ومن ضمن القتلى عدد من الضباط الــذيـن
تم تشخيص هويات التالية اسماؤهم :

١- الرائد محمد صكر سلوم / آمر الفوج الثانى / لواء ٧٠٢ .

٢- الملازم الاول وليد اسماعيل آمر سرية فى نفس الفوج .

٣- ملازم عبدالكريم جابر محمد .

٤- ملازم محمد طعمة .

٥ - ملازم عزيز عطية عليوى .

٦- ملازم عبدالحليم مردان .

٧- الملازم الاول حسان عبداللطيف سلطان لواء ٦٨ قوات خاصة .

٨ - الملازم الاول محمد ياسين على آمر سرية ٢ / ف ٢ ل ٦٨ خاصة .

٩ - الملازم الاول احمد رشيد احمد

٣ - اسرى العدو : تم اسر اعداد من الجنود والضباط، وفيما يلـــى
اسماء الضباط :

١- الملازم الثانى حافظ جاسم حمادى آمر فصيل فى السرية الاولـى/
الفوج الاول ، مغاوير ، فرقة ٣٣ .

٢- الملازم الثانى ربح محمد فتحى / آمر فصيل لنفس السرية .

٣- الملازم الثانى سامر عبود وحيد آمر الفصيل من نفس الوحدة .

٤- الملازم الثانى محمد ناجى آمر الفصيل فى الفوج الثالث / لواء
المغاوير الثانى .

٥- الملازم الثانى عبدالخالق حمود من الفوج الثالث لواء ٦٨ قوات
خاصة .

٤- سقطت للعدو خلال المعركة حتى الان (٤) طائرات هليكوبتر، واصيبت

- ٣ -

Document 6 (3-8)

417

قواته بأضرار صادية جسيمة اخرى .

ه ـ الغنائم : وقعت بايدى فواتنا ، الغنائم التالية من العدو :

ـ اكثر من (٦٠٠) قطعة سلاح خفيف ومتوسط .

ـ ٣٥ قاذفة آر بى جى .

ـ ١٨ جهاز لاسلكى .

ـ كميات كبيرة من التجهيزات العسكرية ، بما فيها عدد من اقنعـة الغـاز .

رابعيا : خسائرنـا :

لقد كلفت المقاومة البطولية ، امام عشرات الهجمات العسكريـة الواسعة ، لمدة اكثر من شهر ونصف ، كلفت قواتنا تضحيات غاليـة يدفعها شعبنا ثمنا ، للدفاع عن وجوده وبقائه وكرامته وشرفه ومـن اجل الحرية والانعتاق .

لقد قدمت قواتنا حتى الان (٢٨) شهيدا خالدا ، و(١٠٤) جرحـى (٦٢) منهم اصيبوا بجروح نتيجة الاسلحة الكيمياوية .

وفيما يلى اسماء الشهداء الخالدين وهم :

١ـ الشهيد الرفيق حامد شيفى من هيز شاواره استشهد فى ١٩٨٨/٧/٢١

٢ـ الشهيد الرفيق احمد طه اسماعيل ورميلى من الفرع الاول استشهـد فى ١٩٨٨/٧/٢٧ .

٣ـ الشهيد الرفيق فتاح عثمان ارگوشى من منظمة موسكا استشهد فـى ٨٨/٧/٢٧

٤ـ الشهيد الرفيق ابراهيم ظاهر بيندروى من منظمة موسكا استشهـد فى ١٩٨٨/٧/٢٧ .

٥ـ الشهيد الرفيق مام على من الحزب الشيوعى العراقى استشهـد فى ٧/٢٧

٦ـ الشهيد الرفيق جمال محمد امين من منظمة كاروخ استشهد فى ٨/٧

٧ـ الشهيد الرفيق محمد چاوشين من منظمة كاروخ استشهد فى ٨/١٢

‏‏ـ ٤ ـ

Document 6 (4-8)

418

٨- الشهيد الرفيق قادر سعيد مصطفى من الفرع الشمالى استشهد فسو،
٨/١٩ .

٩- الشهيد الرفيق بابه رسول شيخ صالح من الفرع الرابع استشهد
فى ٨/١٩ .

١٠ - الشهيد الرفيق عبدالخالق احمد سعيد من اتحاد الطلبــــة
والشبيبة الديمقراطى الكردستانى استشهد فى ٨/١٩

١١- الشهيد الرفيق حسن خضر عقراوى من هيـز آوارة استشهد فى٨/٢٤

١٢- الشهيد الرفيق نذير محمد طاهر من هيز آوارة استشهد فى ٨/٢٧

١٣- الشهيد الرفيق ملا بحرى شكرى مجيد من اتحاد علماء الديـــن
الاسلامى الكردستانى استشهد فى ٨/٢٧

١٤- الشهيد الرفيق ولى حاجى عارف من الفرع الرابع استشهدفى٨/٢٨

١٥- الشهيد الرفيق رحمان مجيد من الفرع الرابع استشهد فى ٨/٢٨

١٦- الشهيد الرفيق حازم محمد شلى من منظمة چارچهلاستشهد فى ٨/٢٨

١٧- الشهيد الرفيق جوهر على شلى من منظمة چارچهل استشهد فى٨/٢٨

١٨- الشهيد الرفيق اسماعيل باسين حامد من منظمة چارچهل استشهد
فى ٨/٢٨

١٩- الشهيد الرفيق عبدالله حاجى ستونى من منظمة چارچهل استشهد
فى ٨/٢٨

٢٠- الشهيد الرفيق اسعد چهچو يحيى درى من منظمة چارچهل استشهد
فى ٨/٢٨

٢١- الشهيد الرفيق كيفى احمد برادوستى من الفرع الرابع استشهد
فى ٨/٣٠

٢٢- الشهيد الرفيق على سليم باجلورى مسؤول مدفعية الشـــورة
استشهد فى ٩/٤

٢٣- الشهيد الرفيق زوراب غازى ارگوشى مسؤول منظمة موسكا استشهد
فى ٩/٤

٢٤- الشهيد الرفيق حمه خان امين من الفرع الرابع استشهدفى ٩/٤
- • -

Document 6 (5-8)

٢٥- الشهيد الرفيق فريدون عبدالله من الفرع الرابع استشهـــــد
في ٩/٤

٢٦- الشهيد الرفيق احمد محمد احمد من مدفعية الثورة استشهـــد
في ٩/٤

٢٧- الشهيد الرفيق چاوشين خانو مسؤول منظمة بيران استشهدفي٩/٥

٢٨- الشهيد الرفيق جبار عثمان مردلن من الفرع الثالث استشهـــد
في ٩/٥ .

ايها المواطنون الاعزاء :

اثناء استمرار هذه المعارك الكبيرة ، شن النظام حملة عسكرية
واسعة جدا على مناطق محافظتي دهوك ونينوى ، بحوالي (١٠٠) الـف
جندي ، وبالدبابات والمدافع ، ومختلف صنوف الطائرات الحربيــــة
والسروحية ، مستعملا الاسلحة الكيمياوية على نطاق واسع،واقترفـــت
قوات النظام،الدكتاتوري ظلال هذه الحملة جرائم ابادة جماعية احرقت
ودمرت عشرات القرى ، وشردت حوالي (١٠٠) مئة الف كردي الى تركيـة
وايران،الا ان ذلك كله ، لم يقهر ارادة المقاومة في قلوب وافكار
الجماهير الشعبية الكردستانية الغفيرة ، سواء داخل العلن او فـي
مناطق العمليات العسكرية التي يحاول النظام تحويلها الى وطن بـلا
شعب . فقد تحدت فمائل البيشمه ركة لكردستان البطلة هذه الحملـــة
الهمجية التي تستهدف تصفية شعبنا وحركته التحريرية تصفية دموية،
فانتشرت في طول كردستان وعرضها المفارز الباسلة التي ستحـــــول
كردستان الى جحيم للقوات الشوفينيه المعتدية ، وسيواجه النظــام
في مستقبل ليس بعيدا مشاكل وازمات داخلية اشد حدة وستشور بوجه
الجماهير الشعبية العراقية المكتوية بنار الحروب والويـــــلات
والكوارث من جراء نهج النظام .

ايهـــا العسكريون العراقيون !

نحن لانحاربكم الا دفاعا عن النفس وعن حق الوجود القومي علــــى

- ٦ -

ارضنا وحفاظا على شعبنا من الابادة الشاملة التى ترون آثارهـــا
وآثامها بـأم اعينكم • وان النظام بعث بكم الى كردستان لابائكـم
بهذه الحرب الظالمة ، ولكى يفوّت الفرصة عليكم للتفكير فى ما جرت
من مآس ورويلات خلال ثمان سنوات، فيزج بكم فى حرب قذرة ضد الشعب
الكردى ، لكى يتقاتل الاخوة ، فيقتل العراقى بيد العراقى • وبدلا
من ازالة الاوضاع الاستثنائية الشاذة يواصل النظام حربه الظالمـة
ضدنا ، ليبرر استمرار هذه الاوضاع بل وتشديدها وتعميد الارهــاب
الشامل ضد كافة جماهير الشعب العراقى عربا وكردا واقليات ومطاردة
وابادة عشرات الالاف من رافضى الحرب ومنتسبى المعارضة ، وتشديد
الخناق على الشعب •

فندعوكم ايها العسكريون العراقيون جنودا وضباطا الى الانضمـام
الى كفاح الشعب العراقى ضدالحكم الدكتاتورى لاسقاطه ، ومن اجـــل
الحرية والديمقراطية والسلام للعراق والحكم الذاتى الحقيقـــــى
لكردستان العراق، واعادة اجواء التآخى والمحبة الى ربوع بلادنـا
بدلا من الحروب ورويلاتها وكوارثها التى ينذر استمرارها بحرب اهلية
مدمرة •

يـا ابنـاء الشعب العراقى ! ايهـا الاحرار والديمقراطيون فـــى
سائر الاقطار العربية !

ان النهج الشوفينى الدموى للنظام العراقى واصراره على ابـادة
شعب كردستان بممارسة جرائم بشعة وفظيعة ضده لهو نهج يضر بالغ
الضرر بالاخوة التاريخية بين الشعبين العربى والكردى، اللذيــن
لازالت مهمات تحررية ووطنية مشتركة كبيرة تواجهما فى الكفاح ضـد
الامبريالية والعنصرية والرجعية •

يا ابناء كردستان البواسل ! فى عشية الذكرى (٢٧) لثـــــورة
ايلول الوطنية عام ١٩٦١ بقيادة القائد التحررى الراحل البارزانى
الخالد فان معارك ملحمة (خواكورك) توءكد على عمق روح الكفـــاح

- ٧ -

Document 6 (7-8)

421

وارادة المقاومة فى اعماق جماهير شعبنا المستعدة لتقديم المزيد من التضحيات السخية حتى تحقيق النصر .

فندعو الى الامرار على المقاومة ومواصلة الكفاح بالاشكال الممكنة فمن الظروف الجديدة . فامامنا مهمات نبيلة عظيمة ينبغى تحقيقها . وكفاحنا هو كفاح عادل ومشروع ، ويتطلب المثابرة وطول النفس .

ان استمرار المقاومة بعزز ثقة الشعب الكردى بقضيته العادلة التى اتسعت دائرة الاهتمام العالمى بها سياسيا واعلاميا ، فينبغى استثمار كل ذلك من اجل قضيتنا العادلة.وكما جاء فى بيان اللجنة المركزية للحزب فى ٢٠/تموز الماضى فان العنف الاستبدادى لن يحل القضية الكردية بل يزيدها تعقيدا .

كما،وللمرة الاولى،تنضج داخل صفوف قوى المعارضة العراقية ظروف ملائمة لتوحيد جهودها فى تحالف كفاحى واسع ضد الدكتاتورية وحربها الظالمة فى كردستان ، فلنعزز هذا الاتجاه الوطنى الصحيح بتوطيد الجبهة الكردستانية العراقية على كافة الاصعدة .

- المجد والخلود لشهداء،ملحمة خواكورك والشفاء العاجل للجرحى .
- المجد والخلود لشهداء الحملة الفاشية على منطقة بهدينان .
- تحية الى اهلنا الاعزاء،، عشرات آلاف اللاجئين الذين دخلوا تركيا وايران خلال الاسبوع الماضى .
- الفشل والخزى والعار لحملة النظام الشوفينية العنصرية .
- عاش حزبنا برئاسة المناضل مسعود البارزانى .
- تحيا الجبهة الكردستانية العراقية .
- النصر الاكيد لكفاح الشعب العراقى من اجل الديمقراطية والحرية والسلام لعراق متحرر مزدهر يتحقق فيه الحكم الذاتى الحقيقى لكردستان والحقوق الثقافية والادارية للاقليات القومية والدينية .

المكتب السياسى   ٥ / ايلول / ١٩٨٨

للحزب الديمقراطى الكردستانى

- العراق

- ٨ -

Document 6 (8-8)

Document (6)

Kurdistan Democratic Party- Iraq
Political Bureau
Military declaration about the Khwakurk epic

The heroic battles of the peshmerga of our party continue in the front of Khwakurk, which turned into an eternal epic in the history of our people. This was both heroic and sacrificed the fighters within all branches of our valiant party in the face of the chauvinist campaign of the Iraqi regime, which has diligently worked for 20 years to evacuate Kurdistan of its people and change its reality both on a National and historical level.

The preparation for confrontation and resistance came from the decision of the Central Committee party on July 20, 1988 and in recognition of the chauvinistic nature of the regime, which prompted and pushed the regime to launch a wide military campaign on the headquarters and bases of our party, and the rest of the Kurdish and Iraqi national forces, especially after the announcement of the approval of the moratorium of shooting in the Iran-Iraq War.

The regime launched its massive military campaign on Khwakurk in the north of Erbil province in an area of only 150 square kilometers.

Thus, a historical epic of the Kurdish resistance began and will continue until the issue of this communication.

Since 19/7/1988, i.e. more than a month and a half, the regime forces launched dozens of large-scale attacks using all kinds of weapons available to them. This was to ward off intensive aerial and artillery bombardment and the use of chemical weapons prohibited according to international conventions and laws.

The conduct of operations and the results of this battle were as follows:

First: Our forces:

Participated from our side the forces of the Revolutionary Headquarters, the forces of the fourth, third and second branches of the party and detachments from the supporters of the allied Iraqi Communist Party.

Second: The enemy forces involved in fighting Khwakurk consisted of:

1. The First Corps of the Iraqi Army.
2. V Corps.
3. More than 30 mercenary regiments of light regiments.
4. More than five field artillery battalions and large numbers of mortars.
5. Three tank battalions.
6. Squadrons of warplanes and helicopters.
7. Chemical weapons were used in the village of Zerouh and others north of Jabtah Korek, and 63 peshmerga were wounded from Our forces.

Third: Enemy Losses

The Iraqi military units that suffered heavy losses and bore the bulk of the losses were:

1. 33rd Division/Special Corps
2. 45th Division/First Corps
3. 35th Division
4. 18th Division
5. 68th Brigade/Special Forces
6. 66th Brigade/Special Forces
7. First Independent Commando Regiment of the 33rd Division
8. 702nd Infantry Brigade
9. 402nd Infantry Brigade
10. 120th Commando Brigade
11. Second Commando Brigade
12. A complete unit of the Internal Security Forces

Enemy casualties: about 8450 soldiers were wounded and the bodies of more than 1000 of them fell into the hands of our forces and among the dead were a number of officers who have been identified as follows:

1. Major Muhammad Sakr Salloum/second Regiment Commander/Brigade 702
2. First Lieutenant Walid Ismail, Company Commander in the same regiment
3. Lieutenant Abdul Karim Jaber Mohammed
4. Lieutenant Muhammad Tohme
5. Lieutenant Aziz Attia Aliwi
6. Lieutenant Abdel Halim Mardan
7. First Lieutenant Hassan Abdul Latif Sultan, 68th Special Forces Brigade

8. First Lieutenant Muhammad Yassin Ali, Company Command 2/F Two for 68 Special
9. First Lieutenant Ahmed Rashid Ahmed.

Enemy prisoners were captured a number of soldiers and officers, and the following are the names of the officers:

1. Second Lieutenant Hafez Jassim Hamdi, commander of a platoon in the first company/first regiment, commandos/33rd division
2. Second Lieutenant Rameh Mohamed Fathi/commander of a platoon of the same company
3. Second Lieutenant Samer Abboud Wahid, commander of the platoon from the same unit
4. Second Lieutenant Mohammed Naji, commander of the faction in the third regiment/Second Commando Brigade
5. Second Lieutenant Abdul Khaleq Hammoud of the Third Regiment, 68th Special Forces Brigade

Four helicopters fell to the enemy during the battle and their forces suffered other serious material damage.

Spoils

The following booty fell into the hands of our forces from the enemy:

- More than 600 light and medium weapons
- 35 RPG bombers
- 18 wireless devices

- Large quantities of military equipment, including a number of gas masks.

Fourth: Our losses:

The heroic resistance in the face of dozens of large-scale military attacks for more than a month and a half, cost our forces precious sacrifices paid by our people to defend their existence, survival, dignity and honour, for freedom and emancipation.

So far, our forces have provided 28 immortal martyrs and 104 wounded, 63 of whom were injured as a result of chemical weapons.

The names of the immortal martyrs are:

1. The martyr comrade Hamid Shifi from Haze Awara was martyred on 21/7/1988
2. The martyr Rafiq Ahmed Taha Ismail Worm Li from the first branch was martyred on 27/7/1988
3. The martyr comrade Fattah Osman Arkoshi from the Mosca organization, his martyrdom in 20/07/88
4. The martyr comrade Ibrahim Zahir bin Ibrahim, the organization is a Mosca, martyred in 27/7/1988
5. Comrade Mam Ali of the Iraqi Communist Party, martyred on 27/07/88.
6. Comrade Jamal Muhammad Amin of the Karukh Organization, martyred on 7/8
7. The martyr Comrade Muhammad Jaushin, of the Karukh Organization, martyred on 12/8
8. The martyr comrade Qadir Saeed Mustafa from the third branch was martyred on 19/8

9. The martyr comrade Baba Rasul Sheikh Saleh from the fourth branch was martyred on 19/8

10. The martyr comrade Abdul Khaliq Ahmed Saeed from the Kurdistan Democratic Student and Youth Union was martyred on 19/8

11. The martyr Rafiq Hassan Khader Akrawi from Haze Awara was martyred on 24/8

12. The martyr comrade Nazir Muhammad Tahir from Haze Awara was martyred on 27/8

13. The martyr comrade Mulla Bahri Shukri Majeed of the Union of Islamic Religious Scholars of Kurdistan was martyred on 27/8

14. The martyr comrade Wali Haji Aref of the fourth branch was martyred on 28/8

15. The martyr comrade Rahman Majeed of the fourth branch was martyred on 28/8

16. The martyr comrade Hazem Muhammad Salim Jarajel organization was martyred on 28/8

17. The martyr comrade Jawhar Ali Shali from the Jarajel organization was martyred on 28/8

18. The martyr comrade Ismail Yassin Hamed from the Girga organization of guidance in 28 August

19. The martyr Rafiq Abdullah Hajez Stoni was martyred on 28/8

20. The martyr comrade Asaad Jiju Yahya Dari was martyred on 28/8

21. The martyr comrade Kifi Ahmed Bradosti of the fourth branch was martyred on 30/8

22. The martyr Rafiq Ali Salim Bagliuri, responsible for the artillery of the revolution, was martyred on 4/9

23. The martyr comrade Zurab Ghazi Arkoshi, the official of the Moska organization, was martyred on 4/9

24. The martyr Rafiq Hama Khan Amin of the fourth branch was martyred on 4/9

25. The martyr comrade Fereydoun Abdullah of the fourth branch was martyred on 4/9

26. The martyr comrade Ahmed Mohammed Ahmed of the Revolutionary Artillery, martyred on 4/9

27. Martyr Comrade Gaushen Khan The official of the Biran organization was martyred on 5/9

28. The martyr comrade Jabbar Othman Mardan of the third branch was martyred on 5/9

Dear compatriots

During the continuation of these large battles, the regime launched a very large-scale military campaign on the areas of Dohuk and Nineveh provinces with about 100,000 soldiers, tanks, cannons, and various types of warplanes and helicopters, using chemical weapons on a large scale, and the forces of the dictatorial regime committed, during this campaign, crimes of genocide that burned and destroyed dozens of villages and displaced about 100,000 Kurds to Turkey and Iran, but all this did not defeat the will of resistance in the hearts and thoughts of the masses of popular Kurdistan, whether inside cities or in areas of military operations that the regime was trying to turn into a homeland with no people.

The heroic peshmerga factions of Kurdistan defied these barbaric campaigns aimed at liquidating bloodily our people and their liberation movement, which spread throughout the length and breadth of Kurdistan. Valiant detachments that would turn Kurdistan into hell for the aggressive chauvinist forces, and the regime faced, in the not-too-distant future, more severe internal problems and crises and would revolt against it in the face of the Iraqi popular masses who were shrouded in the fire of wars and the woes and disasters caused by the regime's approach.

Iraqi military personnel.
We were fighting with you the interaction of the self and the right of national existence on our land and to protect our people from the total genocide, of which you have seen its effects and sins with your own eyes and the regime sent you to Kurdistan to distract you with this unjust war and to miss the opportunity for you to think about the tragedies and scourges that took place during the eight years. You were thrown into a dirty war against the Kurdish people so that the brothers fought and killed the Iraqi at the hands of the Iraqi.

Instead of removing the exceptional anomalous situations, the regime continued its unjust war against us to justify the continuation of these conditions, and even to intensify them, to escalate terrorism involving the masses, the Iraqi people, Arabs, Kurds and minorities, to hunt down and exterminate tens of thousands of opposition members who rejected the war, and to tighten the noose on the people.

We call on you, Iraqi soldiers and officers, to join the struggle of the Iraqi people against dictatorial rule, to overthrow it for freedom, democracy, peace for Iraq, and true autonomy for Iraqi Kurdistan, and to restore the atmosphere of brotherhood and love to our country instead of wars, scourges and disasters, the continuation of which would portend a devastating civil war.

To people of Iraq
Dear liberal democrats in all Arab countries,

The bloody chauvinist approach of the Iraqi regime and its insistence on exterminating the people of Kurdistan by committing heinous crimes was a method that would be deeply detrimental to the historical brotherhood between the Arab and Kurdish peoples, who are still major joint national liberation missions in the struggle against imperialism and racism.

To brave people of the Kurdistan

On the evening of the 27th anniversary of the September National Revolution in 1961 under the leadership of the immortal libertarian leader Barzani, the battles of the Khwakurk epic confirmed the depth of the spirit of struggle and the will to resist existed in the depths of the masses of our people who were ready to make more generous sacrifices until victory was achieved.

We call for persistence in resistance and to continue the struggle in the forms possible under the new circumstances.

We have great noble tasks ahead of us to accomplish and our struggle is just and legitimate and requires perseverance and longevity.

The continuation of the resistance enhances the confidence of the Kurdish people in their just cause, which is expanding the circle of global attention politically and in the media, so all of this should be invested for our righteous cause, and as stated in the statement of the Central Committee of the party on July 20, authoritarian violence will not solve the Kurdish issue, but rather increase its constraints.

Also, for the first time, suitable conditions have matured within the ranks of the Iraqi opposition forces to unite their efforts in a broad coalition of struggle against the dictatorship and its unjust war in Kurdistan, so let us strengthen this correct national trend in consolidating the Iraqi Kurdistan Front at all levels.

Glory and eternity to the martyrs of the Khuakurk epic and speedy recovery to the wounded.

Glory and immortality to the martyrs of the fascist campaign on the Badinan region.

Greetings to our dear people for the tens of thousands of refugees who entered Turkey and Iran last week.

The failure, shame, and disgrace of the chauvinist regime's racist campaign.

Long live our party headed by the militant Massoud Barzani.

Long live the Iraqi Kurdistan Front.

The definite victory of the struggle of the Iraqi people for democracy, freedom and peace for a liberated and prosperous Iraq in which the true autonomy of Kurdistan and the cultural and administrative rights of national and religious minorities are achieved.

1988/9/5
Political Bureau
Kurdistan Democratic Party - Iraq

Document 7 (1-2)

خۆ دەبێ تریکۆ کۆمیتە لەرەوبار، جولان جالیزدا ئەگۆبی بەرەشوە کاربکا.

١. وەکوه،بان جولایندا بو فردە جارەکات دەوۆاک لگ دەنسوبیری کاران لۆ دەنبکۆربسین.

ج. ھەمان بکرو دەکرە جبار بربابرداو، به هشتکی کاربکرن ومکاربو ئو بەرنامەبن لۆزدا
    بجولێن.

ئەگر نقش بکم لەماھۆدا جچاک لۆزانی جدوا جنزبکرن ئاکاۆلتا کئك مبندسس بلدان
دەبدتن بدیۆبارکابن، خۆلگیر نقطبردبم بیگ کۆازن لۆد جدت جۆلانی دەبوو
ئاکۆلاربیف وتملایتن،بربۆ کردگرگی نوژنی لدیفقاۆردا بکرو لابد ئەبوو ـ سعہ بلبگ.
بەجۆردوجالت بی ھانسکیان نی ئگگرین نقش جلادە بیسدا، جلم بیگ خدت کرۆشنبن
لە سەربربۆیف لردۆدربانن جۆن کاربکن.

متیق هاملردا لانم جدربانی دەقدم.

کۆئاۆبرو دەربسلاوم صر لۆضت جنابت دەقلاۆردۆا ـ بیۆمسب سلامدتم کردگۆتنی

١٩٨٨/٩/٨

Document Number (7)

Dear Mr Masoud
Warm greetings: I hope you are well and prosperous.

I warmly congratulate you and the brave peshmerga on the unique wars of Khwakurk, whose direct leadership at this delicate time and during the events played a major role in destroying the attacks of the invading enemy. Unfortunately, our forces were unable to participate in this great honor, because, as Your Excellency warned, many of our forces in the Martyrs' Valley in Qandil were ensuring traffic and withdrawing a part of Erbil's forces that they were able to successfully do. The enemy has been heavily attacking the area since 26th August, although it has attacked some places, but hundreds of carcasses have been damaged, and are still about to capture the entire area.

I would like you to be aware that we have completed the remembrance of the peshmerga organization in the following areas, as well as the small detachment of the cities and the preparation of secret arrangements in a way that is political. The organization will remain in all or in most places, and if their development and strengthening capabilities come forward in the next few months, they will be re-strengthened by forces drawn to the border and beyond. I did explain In the meetings of leadership of war frontier to all commanders. Of course, you have been informed of Tehran meetings and the results.

Mr Mam Jalal and our friends in Europe have warned me to inform you. So far, the PDK branch abroad, Haval Hoshyar Zebari, has not been informed of your instructions and the decisions of the political leadership of barricade about united work and the committee that was decided to be the representative of all political parties will be formed and will work as united, as the friend has told our commanders.

You know what a great importance working abroad in the political-diplomatic-media field is currently for our people's revolution. In the past few months, Mam Jalal and our friends have not hesitated and had good results, so Iraq has caught fire. We repeat our suggestion that overseas work in the name of war frontier would be of greater value and importance to any current abroad, so it is appropriate in this case to work in two ways:

1. As before, each side should work for itself and coordinate so that the actions are not against each other.
2. Everyone work together as a council decided, to work together and to act according to the programme set out.

If you consider the first point to be good at this time, we would like to inform us that friend in Europe work accordingly, and if you consider the second point to be good, it's important to notify and advise all friends in Europe to meet with the other parties' representatives should work together in the media and politics.

For both cases, we have no problem, although we prefer the second point, but we would like to be clear about the decisions to see how we work.

Now Mam Jalal is waiting for an answer in Sham. Finally, I have greetings again at the service of your excellencies and friends there. I hope for your safety and success.

08/09/1988
Nashirwan Mustafa

پارتی دیموکراتی کوردستان / عیراق

قوەتی بارزان

ژماره / فـ

رۆژی ۱۸/۱۲/۱۹۹۰

بۆ / م . س . بە نزربەشی ریکفتن

سلاوی شۆرشگیرانە

بۆ ئەوە ستی پتەوکردنی و ریکفتنەوەی تەنزیماتی سنوری ریکخراوی پیرات و هاتنە دانی
هێلانی سەربە ریکخراوی بۆ زیاتر خۆ ماندوکردنی و هەست بە مەسئولیە تەکردنی بە ماوبر
بە ئەوری سەدرشانی و ئەنجام دانی بە بارتی ریکفتن و هەروە هابۆ ئەوە ستی دیارکردنی
هێلانیئت بە لیرساوی ستم ریکخراوکە باش شەهیر بوونی کاتی چاوشتن فانو وە حیزری
سلیمان ستم ریکخراوە بە نئ لیرساوی مابوە ولەرۆزی ۱۸/۱۲/۱۹۹۰ کوبۆونەوە یەک
سەرکرا بە ماعادە بوونی لیرساوی قوەتە ولئژنە ی ریکخراوی زۆربە ی شانە
سەرکی و باردیدە دەرو شانە قاعدیە کانت . وە باش ئاموژگاریەکی زۆر لەلایە نی
لیرساوی قوەتەی سەباریە بە توندوتۆل کردنەوەی ریکفتن و تەنزیات وەبە نز
کردنەوەی روحیەی شۆرشگیریی و مەردومام بوونت لەسەر فبراتی و وەسلام و وەسلام دانەوە
لەبەینەهێلانی ، لیزنەده ستم ریکفراوەی بەشیوەی خوارە وەدانراوە وەهیوادارین
جیگاوی رزامەندی بەنزرتانبیت

۱- هەڤال خیدمیروفتاح کە کارگیرو بەشی مەسکەنەکەی ریکخراوی بوو کرابە لیرساوی ریکراو

۲- شیومر خانوشیومر کە لیرساوی شانی سەرکی بوو کرابە کارگیرو بەشی مەسکەن

۳- انوەر حسین وەفقن وەکوەخۆت بە کارگیرو بەشی ریکفتن دانراوە وە

کوبۆونەوە کەمانی بە روحیە تیلی پرلە هەستی شۆرشگیریی و براوی وبەرزاەفەنری
ئشت لەمە نیت کۆتایی ی هات . بۆ ئاگاداری بەنزرتان

ئیتر بۆ نیشیم وە - - -

ق . بارزان

د ۔ شەمیر احمد بارزانی

ئەو چەك و تەقەمەنیانەی قوومێ بارزانے کەلە دنوی دەولاتے حیال کراوے :

۱- تووی (۵۷) مام (۸) عەدەد
۲- تووی (۸۱) مام (۲) "
۳- تووی (۱۲۰) مام (۲) "
٤- تووی (۲۰) مام (۵) "
۵- تووی بی عەشرە (۱) "
۶- دوشکه (۷) "
۷- قەدیفەجاروح (۶) "
۸- کالس (۵۰) (۱) "
۹- رەشاش گرینوف (۲) "
۱۰- ثر-۳ (۷) "
۱۱- روسی (۲) "
۱۲- چەکی ئاریەجی (۳) "
۱۳- چەکی ژ-۳ (٤) "
۱٤- کرنو (٤) "
۱۵- کلاشنکوف (٤) "
۱۶- سمنوف (۳) "
۱۷- ام تك (۳) "
۱۸- لولەی دوشکا (۱) "
۱۹- دوربینے (۱۲) مام (۲) "
۲۰- موحی (۲) "
۲۱- فیشەگی گرینوف (٤۱) تاک
۲۲- برنو (۲۳) صندووقی
۲۳- دوشکا (۱۳) تاک
۲٤- ژ-۳ (۵) صندووقی

Document 8 (2-2)

438

Documents number (8)

Kurdistan Democratic Party/Iraq
Barzan Forces   **Number/f**   **Date: 18/12/1990**
to / Political bureau, Department of Organizing

A revolutionary greeting,

In order to strengthen and reorganize the organization within the borders of the Piran Organization and to encourage its friends. To further pursue and feel responsible for the duty of the organization, as well as to appoint a friend in charge of this organization who remained unresponsible after the martyrdom of Mr Chawshin Khano and Safari Suleiman. In 17/12/990, a meeting was held with the presence of the head of both the committee and the organized committee and most of the organization members, and the main political organs. After a lot of advice by the Barzan force official about strengthening the organization, raising the revolutionary spirit, continuing the struggle and responding to the friends, the committee of this organization was set as follows: We hope it will be acceptable to you.

1. Haval Hamed Miro Fatah, an administrator member of this organization's military department, was appointed as organization leader.
2. Haval Shekhomher Khano Shekhomar, who was member of the organisation, was appointed as administrator of military department.
3. Haval Anwar Hussein Mustafa's duty stayed as the administrator and organizing department.

Our meeting ended with a spirit full of revolutionary and brotherhood feelings and with the consent of all parties.

So forward. . ..
Barzan Force
Dr Saeed Ahmed Barzani

The weapons and explosives of barzan force buried on the side of the state:

1. 8 Pieces 57mm artillery
2. 2 Pieces 81mm artillery
3. 2 Pieces 120mm artillery
4. 5 Pieces 60mm artillery
5. 1 Pieces artillery
6. 7 pieces Dshk
7. 6 Pieces Bomb
8. 1 Piece 50 Calibre machine gun
9. 2 pieces Goryunov SG
10. 7 Pieces Goryunov zh3
11. 2 pieces Russian Goryunov
12. 3 Pieces RPG-7
13. 4 Pieces zh3 Weapon
14. 4 pieces Brno rifle
15. 4 Pieces Kalashnikov
16. 3 pieces Suomi KP/-31
17. 3 Pieces M1 Weapon
18. 2 pieces Dshk
19. 2 Pieces 120mm Telescope

20. 2 Pieces 120mm Mogi
21. 41 pieces of Groyunov Bullets
22. 23 Boxes of Brno rifle Bullets
23. 13 Pieces of Dshk Bullets
24. 5 boxes of Zh3 Bullets

بغداد ١٤/٤/١٩٨٨

اخي العزيز الشيخ مسعود البارزاني المحترم

تحية اخوية خالصة .. اخوان تكونوا بخير .

اخي .. كلما تتألم لهذا الوضع المليء بالمآسي الذي يمر به شعبنا وبلدنا ، وكي نجد طريقة الخلاصة
للخروج من هذا الأزمة ونتشبثه بكل شيء نحزرون . قبل مدة كتبت رسالة طويلة الى رئيس الجمهورية ، وبينت
فيها هذا الوضع الصعب ، و بينت له ان الحل يكمن بأن لا نخرج لمشاكلنا الداخلية الاسلوب طريق
المصالحة الوطنية الشاملة ، لأن الطرح المسلح يستنزف القدرات المادية والبشرية للبلد ، ومهما
كان المنتصر والخاسر ، فان خسارة الحاصل هو خسارة البلد ونفر الشعب . حيل العام جابهه سنة
على بلده وتكلمت معه بصراحة وبينت له ما جرى في كوردستان و بالتفصيل ما جرى للبارزانيين .
و بينت ان تعامل القادة مع الغير لم يكن من عنه ذاته ، بل الظروف جرت علينهم ذلك ، نحن شردوه
ارضه وجرت محاولات لإبادته ، فانه يتشبث بكل وسيلة يضمن بقاءه ، ومهم عتبونه الجزء الأول
وان تاريخهم يثبت اعتزازهم بوطنهم .

قال ، " ان الظروف ادت الى هذه التجزئة والفرقة ، وقدرها والاتصال بمختلف الجماعات
ولكن كي الذي توسطوا كانوا ينطلقون من مصالحهم الذاتية ، فان كانت مصلحتهم مع الفرقة والنضال؟
فانهم يؤيدون الفرقة؟ تحدثنا عن مختلف الجماعات الكوردية ، (هشج) ، (بدران) (جلال) (ادك)
.. الخ ، ، بينت له ان المحاولة للاتصال بهذه الاحزاب جعفراً يليه على النية في التفرقة بينهم و
انطوانهم ، ولكن اذا كان لهذا لهدف نية مبادرة لحل مشاكل البلد ، يجب الاتصال بهم جميعاً ولحرصهم
الى مائدة المفاوضات مجتمعين لبحث مشاكل البلد وايجاد السبيل السليم لها بتظافر جمهور
الجميع . كان بيني وبينه على رؤى ، فطلبت منه التوسط لحل المشاكل بينهم وبين الحكومة . قلة
اعتقد انني غير خاسبة لهذه المهمة ، ولكنه بين بأن انسب سواي شخص آخر ، مادمت لا
استهدف مصلحة خاصة ، بل مصلحه البلد ومستقبل الشعب .

اخي .. انا لا ازكي احد ولا اجعل البلد جنة عدن .. ولكن كما قال (ان السياسة
هي فن الممكنات) و انما نتعامل مع الواقع لا بما ينبغي . والانسان عندما يتعامل مع السوق
ايضاً يسأل نفسه : كم اربح وكم اخسر ، وبع مع اربح وبع مع اخسر . الايرانيون لهم مطامع
في العراق او على الاقل العراق اصبحت لديهم مطامع . نحن ليوا اصدقا ، الاكراد ولا الى هانيتهم حقوق
المشروعة ، ونفض المشكلة القائمة في العراق ، قائمة في ايران واشرشها . اذن الضرورة هي
البرجه هي اللذان يرفعانكم وغيركم الى الوقوف لهذا الموقف ، ولكن كم يدوم هذا الموقف وماذا
سيكون نتاجه ؟!

وهو ان المشكلة ستبقى على أمد اصبر الذين تلطّخي بدماء شعبهم وهم شعبنا الكردي بازرة؟
وما دمنا نتعرف الآن ظروفاً عليه جنّة مشاكل البلاد وإيجاد طرق لحلها، فالمانع من اختبار
هذه الرغبة من جانب الحكومة ومعرفة مدى جديتها في الأمر؟ ربما تقولون انها لا تؤمّن
وللتوحيد فمانات لاستمرار الوضع السلمي أو الحل السلمي .. أنا معكم، ولكنه في مثل هذه الأمور
لا يمكنه ان يكون هذا الشيء أو ذاك فما نا لحق وما لحقوق، بل عندما نأخذ الشيء لفقه
بيده، فإنه بصورته ويدفع عنه هيئة النهاية.

أخي .. للبارزانية مشكلة خاصة إلى جانب المشكلة الكردية العامة ولا
تتعارض مطالب البارزانية مع مطالب شعبهم الكردي في الفصى انها مكملة من نعظم بعضاً.
ولا يعقل ان تحل مشكلة البارزانيين خارج مشكلة شعبهم الكردي. وهنا أسأل المرء
نفسه: "بجيماكم سأحقق من اهداف هذه القوة المتيسرة لي؟"

أنني كتبت الرسائل إلى الإخوان الآخرين، فإذا أنذر أية جهة ارعب في التباهي
قد يضعف جانب الإخوة الآخرين. أنني أرى لا مانع من النظر على وجهة النظر
نظر الحكومة في عرض المصالحة. وقد حررتم أمام "حلفائكم" ولكن لا بأس ان يكون
الايصال بمعزل عنهم، أي بصورة غير مباشرة، في البلة إذا أتوّم نرك، فإذا تـحـمـتـم
جديّة الحكومة في التفاهم والنضال، يكلّفتكم الحلوسى إلى مائدة المفاوضات مباشرة بصورة
سرية ارعلنها هنا في الأمل أو في الخارج، حسب أو بدون، هذا يعود لكم، ولكن
أؤكد ان التشاور بيتكم أنه الإجراء المذكورة اعلاه (حشم) (جدك) (ادلس) (حسل)
سيكـيـفه القوة والاحترام، وان السير في الطريق سيبدأ بالخطوة الدولى ثم تتلو الخطوات الأخرى.
وكم أكون مرتاح البال والضمير عندما أركم معنيين وتجلسون إلى مائدة المفاوضات وتتوصلون
إلى تحقيق مكاسب لشعبكم وتعاريتها إلى شاطئ الطمأنينة والسلام ونيل الحقوق المشروعة.

أنني انتظر منكم الجواب الأولى، وعندما تصلني أجوبة الإخوان الآخرين
سأعرف حسب إجماعكم، وعندما قناعكم جميعاً بجدوى الحوار، سأترك الأمر لكم
مباشرة لأقول لكم "قول حافظ"

تقبلوا تحياتي وتمنياتي لأخذتكم وأقاربكم
أخوكم

د. مكرم الطالباني

Document number (9)

Baghdad 12/2/1988
My dear brother Sheikh Masoud Al-Barzani
A sincere brotherly greeting. I hope you're well.

My brother. We all suffer for this tragic situation that our people and our country are going through. And everyone think in its own way of how to get out of this predicament and cling to everything for salvation.

Some time ago, I wrote a long letter to the President of the Republic in which I explained this difficult situation. I explained to him that the world is convinced that there is no way out of internal problems except by taking the path of comprehensive national reconciliation, because armed conflict depletes the material and human capabilities of the country, and whoever wins or loses, the achievement of what is happening is the loss of the country and the damage of the people. A few days ago, I met him at his request and spoke frankly to him and explained to him what is happening in Kurdistan and in detail what happened to the Barzanis. I indicated that their cooperation now with others was not at a personal desire, but the circumstances imposed on them that, so whoever was displaced from his land and attempts were made to exterminate them, that they are Iraqis and their history proves their pride in their homeland.

He said, "The circumstances led to a rupture and division, and we tried to contact the various groups, but all those who mediated were based on their own interest, and if their interest was with division and fighting, they were fuelling the division." We talked about the different Kurdish groups (Hasha) (Hadak) (Hask) (OK). etc., and showed him that attempts to contact these parties alone indicates the intention to divide them and weaken them, but if there is a sincere intention to solve the problems of the country, you must contact them all and invite them to the negotiating table together to discuss the problems of the country and find the right way to solve them by the concerted efforts of all. He was basing his agreement on my opinion so he asked me to mediate to solve the problems between them and the government. I said I think I am not suitable for this task but he showed that I am more suitable than anyone else as long as I do not target a private interest as it should be in the interest of the country and the future of the people.

My brother. I do not recommend anyone and I do not make the country the Garden of Eden, but as it is said (politics is the art of possibilities) and that we deal with reality as it is and when man deals with the market he also asks himself: how much will I earn and how much, I lose and with whom, I win and with whom I lose. The Iranians have ambitions in Iraq, they are not friends of the Kurds or besides their legitimate rights, and the same problem in Iraq exists in Iran and yet is more severe. So necessity and embarrassment are what push you and others to stand in this situation, but how long does this situation last and what will be its results??

Will the problem be solved by hands stained with the blood of its people, including our Kurdish people in Iran? Since circumstances now confirm the possibility of examining the country's problems and finding ways to solve them, why not test this desire on the part of the Government and know how serious they are in this matter? You may say that they are not trusted and there are no guarantees for the continuation of the peaceful situation or a peaceful solution. I am with you, but in such matters this or that person cannot be a guarantee of a right, but when the people take their right into their own hands, they protect it and defend it until the end.

My brother. The Barzanis have a special problem besides the general Kurdish problem, and the demands of the Barzanis do not contradict with the demands of their Kurdish people, on the contrary, they complement each other, and it is not reasonable to solve the problem of the Barzanis outside the problem of their Kurdish people. And sometimes one asks himself how many goals I will achieve with this power available to me?

I wrote letters to the other Brotherhood, and if any party is alone in the discussion, the side of the other parties may be weakened. I think that there is no objection to getting to know the government's point of view in the offer of reconciliation and it may embarrass you in front of your allies, but I do not have to contact their isolation indirectly. In the beginning I will do this, if you feel the seriousness of the government in understanding and reconciliation, you can sit at the negotiating table directly in secret or public here at home or abroad, with or without me, this is up to you. But I assure you that consultation between you the above-mentioned parties (Hasha) (Hadak) (Hask) (OK) will gain you strength and respect, and that walking on this road begins with the first step and is then followed by the other steps, and how clear I am when I see you united and sitting at the negotiating table and reaching gains for your people and leading them to the shore of tranquility, peace and obtaining legitimate rights.

I am waiting for your first answer and when I receive the answers of the other Brotherhood I will act according to your consensus and when you are all convinced of the usefulness of dialogue I will leave it to you directly to tell you «Khoda Hafez».

Accept my greetings and greetings to your brothers and relatives.

Your brother
Dr Makram Al-Talbani

العدد ٧٧/
التاريخ ١٦/١٠/١٨٢

الجمهورية العراقية
وزارة الداخلية
مديرية الأمن العامة

السيد الرئيس القائد المحترم حفظه الله

تحيه وتقدير

سيدي

أحيطكم علماً على أصل رسالتنا المرفقه على اليمين

من خلال إلقاء القبض على البارزانيين ، تجمعت لدينا

المواد العينيه التاليه .

"٨٧٣,، تسعمائه وثلاثه وسبعون ساعه يدويه وساعه

جيب ، وساعه ذهب واحده وثلاث خواتم وقرط

نائي واحد ذهب .

راجين التفضل بالاطلاع وأحيطكم ... مع التقدير سيدي؟

مدير الأمن العام

Document Number (10)

448

Date: 6/10/1983

Republic of Iraq Ministry of Interior General Security Directorate

Director of Public Security

Mr President, the respected leader, may God save him

I inform you, on the origin of our message attached on the right, and by arresting the Barzani's, that we gathered the following materials.

Eight hundred and seventy-three wristwatches, a pocket watch, one gold watch, three rings and one gold women's earring.

Please Kindly review with my respect, Sir.

Director of Public Security

باسم الجمهورية
السكرتير

العدد : ١٠٦٧/٤٦٠١/لك
التاريخ : ١٩٨٧/٨/٢٤

سري للغاية وشخصي

٥٧٨٢

الرفيق علي حسن المجيد المحترم

م/العوائل البارزانية

نظراً لاستمرار تأكيد المجرم مسعود البارزاني على موضوع
العوائل البارزانية التي كانت تسكن محافظة اربيل - مجمع قوشتبة
وذلك من خلال الاتصالات غير المباشرة التي تحققت مع زمرته منذ
عام ١٩٨٢ وحتى الان ، حيث انه يعتبر ذلك كشرط أو مطمح
رئيسي للبدء بحوار جدي من قيادة الحزب والثوره --

أمر السيد الرئيس القائد بتوجيه المسؤولين والاجهزه الامنية المعنية
بالقضية الكردية - الذين من المحتمل الاتصال بهم من خلال طرف ثالث -
بان يكون الرد محدد وموحد بأن (لا أحد يعرف عنهم شيئ سوى
قيادة الدولة وأن المسألة الاساسية اكبر من قضية هذه العوائل)
وأن يعتمد هذا الجواب في الرد على أي استفسار منهم تدليل عن
مصير هذه العوائل .

نرجو اتخاذ ما يقتضي -- مع التقدير

سكرتير رئيس الجمهورية

(١-٤)

Document 11 (1-2)

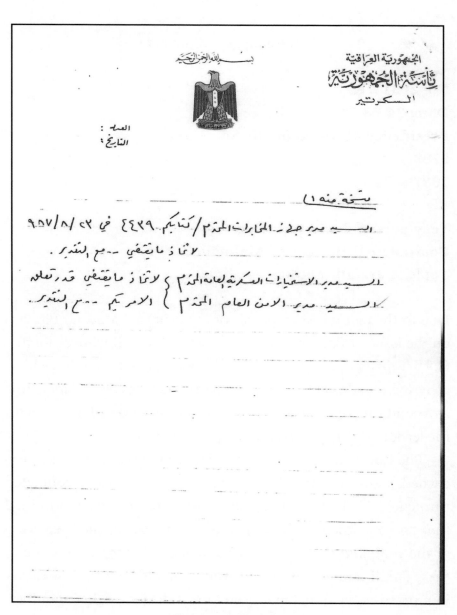

Document number (11)

No: 2651 / K
Date: 24.08.1987
Presidency of the Republic Secretary
5783
1987/8/24

Very personal and secretive
Comrade Ali Hassan Al-Malmajid
Topic/ Barzani families

Due to the continued emphasis of the criminal Masoud Barzani on the issue of Barzani families who lived in Erbil Governorate - Gosh Tappeh complex, through indirect contacts that have been achieved with his clique since 1983 until now, as he considers this as a condition or a major proposal to start a serious dialogue with the leadership of the Party and the Revolution.

The President ordered the officials and security agencies concerned with the Kurdish issue - who are likely to be contacted through a third party - that the response be specific and unified that "no one knows anything about them except the leadership of the state and that the main issue is greater than the issue of these families" and that this answer be adopted in response to any inquiry from them that may occur about the fate of these families. Please take what is necessary.

With my respect
Secretary to the President of the Republic.

A copy of it to the Director of the Intelligence Service / your book 4439 on 23/8/1987 to take the necessary action with appreciation. Mr Director of General Military Intelligence, Director of Public Security, to take what is necessary as far as the matter is concerned. With Regards,

رئاسة الجمهورية
السكرتير
مديرية الأمن العامة
العدد ٨٥
التاريخ ١٢/٧/ ١٩٨٩
٢٤/ شعبان/١٤٠٩ه

السيد سكرتير السيد الرئيس القائد المحترم

تحية وتقدير

الحاقاً برسالتنا المرقمه ٨٤ في ٢٢ شعبان ١٤٠٩ه
الموافق ٢٩/٢/١٩٨٩م

نرفق لكم مايلي :-

١. قائمه تتضمن أسماء « ٥٢٢٥ » من البارزانيين الذين نفذ بحقهم حكم الشعب بالأعدام ، وهم موضوعي بحث الفقره « ٢ » من رسالتنا أعلاه « قائمه رقم- ١ » ومن ضمنهم البارزانيين من سكنة حرير ، علماً بأنه لم يتم فرز الأسماء في حينه (عام ١٩٨٣) حسب المناطق والمجمعات .

٢. قائمه تتضمن أسماء « ٨ » أشخاص لهم علاقه بالحزبين وهم من سكنة حرير ، والذين نظمت بحقهم قضايا أصوليه ونفذ بحقهم حكم الشعب بالأعدام ، موضوعي بحث الفقره « ٦ » من رسالتنا أعلاه « قائمه رقم- ٣ » .

٣. قائمه بأسماء أفراد العائلتين المحجوزتين كونهما من ذوي الحزبين الذين قاموا بتنفيذ عمليات تخريبيه في الفقره الأخيره ، وهم موضوعي بحث الفقره « ٦ » من رسالتنا أعلاه « قائمه رقم- ٢ » .

راجين التفضل بالأطلاع .. مع التقدير .

Document (12)

Document number (12)

Presidency of the Republic Secretary
Directorate of Public Security
Issue: 85
Date: 3/3/1989
24 Shaaban / 1409 Hijri

Mr President's secretary
Greetings and appreciation following our letter numbered 84 on
22 Shaaban 1409 corresponding to 29/3/1989 AD.

We attach herewith the following:

1. A list that includes the names of (2225) of the Barzanis
   against whom the people were executed by death, and they
   are the subjects of paragraph (2) of our letter above (List
   No. – 1) including the Barzanis from the Harir population,
   knowing that the names were not sorted at the time (in
   1983) by regions and gatherings.

2. A list that includes the names of (8) people related to the
   saboteurs, who are residents of Harir, and who were organized against them fundamentalist cases and the people's
   death sentence was carried out against them, the two subjects of the research paragraph (6) of our letter comment
   (List No. - 2).

3. A list of the names of the members of the two families
   detained as they are relatives of saboteurs who carried out

sabotage operations in the recent period, and they are the subjects of paragraph (6) of our letter above (List No. - 3).

Please read with appreciation.

Public Security

Documents 13

بەشی یەکەم

بەندی یەکەم

لەشکری شۆرشگێری کوردستان :

لەشکری
پارتی دیموکراتی کوردستانسی
عیراقە ، لە و پیشمەرگە دلسۆزو
خۆیان بە خۆیانە وەیە (نیشتاوی
تەبەرانە پێکهاتووە کە) گیاشهیشتان
هاوپشتوتە سەر بەلی ئەستیان لە پێناو
بەندەشیپیشانی مافی گەلی کـــــوردو
دیموکراتیەت بۆ عیراق لە ژیر شەلای
بارش و جیمە چیکردنی پرۆگـــرام ر
نویبارە سیاسمیەکاشی کۆنگـــرەی
نویەمەرید ١.

٣

بەشی دووەم

بەندی دووەم

پیشمەرگە ر مەرجەکانی :

ا) پیشمەرگە ئەو خەباتکەرە قلیرە
کوردستانی بیان عیر القیەیە کـــــە
ئامانەیە بە شارەزووی خوی و بەرو
باوەرەوە لە ریزی لە شکری شۆرشگیری
کوردستان لە سەرانسەری کوردستاندا
لە (زاخو)وه نتا (خانەقیـــــــــن)
بچەتگی دزی رزیمی بەعس فاشسـتی
عیراقی و نوکەرەکانی لە کـــــوردو
مەرەبدا؟ ، واتە بەبی جاوازی لــــــــــە
نیوان ناوچەبەلا و ناوچەبەکی شـــردا
جونکە (پیشمەرگە پیشمەرگـــــــــسی
کوردستانە) ملگەچە بۆ فرماشسـیی
سەرگرد لە تیپی شۆرش و ئەبی بەپیـــسی

٤

باسای لەعگری شۆرشگیری کوردسـتان
رەفتار بکات .

ب) مەرجەکانی وەرگرشی پیشمەرگە :
١. هەشیکی باشی کورد لە شـــــو و
نیشتمانیە روەری عیرالی هەبیت و زور
باش بزانی بوجی چەکی هەلگرسـووە و
لە پیناوی جیەدا ؟
٢. دلسۆز و ئەستپاڵە و دامین پاللە
بیت .
٣. ئەبەز و دلیر و زیر و ئەخسری
بیت لە دوژمن .
٤. لە تی ساغ و بەشوانا بیت بـــسۆ
خەباتی پارتیزراشی و تەمەشی لە (١٦)
سال کەمتر تەبیت و پیر و بەلا کەوشە
تەبیی .
٥. گوی رایمەلی فەرماشــــــــسی
لیبررەواشی خۆی بیت بەشابیە شـــسی
لیبررەواشی راتشە وخۆی و؟ دریغـــسی
ئەکات لە جیمە چیکردنیان بە باشی .
٦. راشی لە لیبررەواشی خسوی و

٥

سەرگرد ئیە شتیی شۆرش ئە غاریشتـــــە وە
ئەگەر لە ناوبردنی خوشی عید ابیت .
٧. ئەبی لە لایەن ریکفر ئوەکاشـــی
پارشیمەوە بەسندی وەرگرشی کر ابیت .
٨. خسارە هاشووەکان (بلشحق) :

ا) ئەو هاووڵاتریمانەی کە لەسـمار
زەبرزوبگی دوژمن راشەکەن و تەگەشە
ریزی شۆرش .
١. ئەگەر شەشدام و پالیســـمور اوی
پارشی بن بە پیشمەرگە وەرشەگیرین .
٢. ئەگەر شەشدام و مەرجی پالیسوراوی
پارشی شەبن و مەرج پیشمەرگە بکایەشیان
شیدا اهەبی باش لیکولیشتە وەیەکی وورد
ئەگەلمیان وەکو (بلتحق)ابك ، بەلای
کەمەوە (٣) ماشگ لە ژیر جاودیسـری
ئەمیتن باشان بە پیشمەرگـــــــــە
وەرئەگیریـــن .

٦

Documents 13

بەشی شەشەم

سزا دانی پیشمەرگە
:

ئەی جورە سزا بۆ پیشمەرگە هەیە :
ئ) سەرزنج ر اکیشانی .
ب) گو استنەوەی .
ج) جەڵ کردنی .
د) بە شدکردنی .
ھ) دوورخستنەوەی لەریزی لەشگری
شورشگیری کوردستان بە پەکجاری .
ئ) چ کاتیک سەرزنج ر اله کیفریت
:

۱. ئەگەر بە پیچەواندی فەرمانشی
لیبەرس اوی خۆی رەفتاری کرد بسسو
جاری بەکەمی .
۲. ئەگەر غیر ازەی ئەشزیمی تیلە دا
راتە تخلی مرجی کرد.
۳. کردەوەی بچووکی شاغیریشسسی
وەهای لی رووبدات کە زیان بگەپەنی

۱۲

۶. لەکاشی پیویستیدا و بەپسسی
شیمگان سارمەشی بۆ خۆی و مسسال و
مندالی ەەرف بکریت .
۷. ەەول بدریت شاەشی ز اتیساریی
عەسکەری و سیاسی بەرزبکریتەوە بسە
کردنەوەی دەور اتی عەسکەری و سیاسی
بۆیسان .
۸. نیماشا جنبودان و لیدەاسسی
پیشمەرگە لەلایەن لیبەرس او اتیسسەوە
قدەقەیە ، چونکە بار استشی کەر امەتی
پیشمەرگە قەرمانیکی نیشتماشیسە .

۱۱

دووەم تیلە د ابیت .
۴. بۆ جاری دووەم کسسسردەوەی
شاغیریش بچووکی وەهای کردبیت ، کە
زیان بە سومعەی پیشمەرگە بگەپەنی
لە شاوچەکەیدا .
۵. بەی مواقەفەت بە گورپیسسی
چکی شورش ەەلساپی
د) لە چ کاتیک بە شدەکریت.

۱. ئەگەر جنبوی بە پیسسسرا
پیشمەرگەکی بان کەسیک لە خەلکی
ئەوچەکە د ابیت .
۲. ئەگەر غەری کردبیت لەگەل سرا
پیشمەرگەکی بان کەسیک لە خەلکی
شاوچەکە .
۳. ئەگەر (زیانیکی مسسادی)
ەەرچەندە بچووکیش بیت بە کەسیک لسە
خەلکی شاوچەکە گەپاندبیت بەپسی
شوەی عکایەتی لی کر ابیت .
۴. ئەگەر بە پیچەواندی عبادات و

۱۴

بە شاوپانگی پیشمەرگەی کوردستان لە
شاوچەکەیدا .
ب) لە چ کاتیک نەگوبزریتەوە

۱. نەگوبنجاشی لەگەل پەکی با چەند
سر ا پیشمەرگەپەاک ، کە ەسسسوی
نەگوبنجانەکەی ەەر خۆی بی .
۲. نەگوبنجاشی لەگەل خەلکی شاوچەکە
لە بەر ەەندی کردەوەی شاغیریش کسە
لیی رووبەدات و دەبنە ەۆی ناز ەز ایی
خەلک .
ج) لە چ کاتیک چەک ئەکریت
:

۱. ئەگەر بۆ جاری دووەم قەرمانشی
لیبەرس اوی پەکەمی جیبەجسسسی
ئەکردبیت .
۲. ستی و کەمتەرخەمی و ترسنوکی
نواندبیت لە جیبەجیکردنسسسسی
قەرمانە کانیدا دژی دوژمن .
۳. غیر ازەی ئەشزیمی بۆ جسساری

۱۳

Documents 13

460

Panel ١٥ (15):

ته‌قالیدی كۆمه‌لایه‌تی بجولینه‌وه‌ و
شه‌جیره‌اس ئه‌عاشیری دیش نه‌كریت .
٥٠ ئه‌گه‌ر به‌ندیه‌ك (زیندانسی)
له‌ ده‌مش راپكات .
ه) له‌ چ كاتیك دوور ئه‌خریته‌وه‌ له‌
ریزی (له‌شكر) بۆ ماوه‌یه‌ك . لـــــ
(مانگیك تا سالیك) :

١٠ دووباتی كرده‌وه‌كاش سه‌ره‌وه‌ی
كردبیت بۆ جاری جیم‌م .
٢٠ شیخشیفلالی مه‌ركز ولیبه‌رسراوی‌ش
خوی بكات له‌ناو غورده‌ئا بۆ سوودی
تایبه‌تی خوی .
٣٠ شیخجیر اس لیبه‌رسر اوی خــوی
ئه‌گریت به‌ شیازی سوك كردنی لـــه‌
ریزی بیشمه‌رگه‌دا۱ .
٤٠ نه‌مش له‌ چه‌ك و لیشكی خـــوی
دابیت به‌ شكشین یان به‌ فروشتن بـه‌
بی موافه‌قه‌تی كارگیری لی بـــــیان

Panel ١٦ (16):

سه‌ركرد لیه‌تی .
و) له‌ چ كاتیك له‌ ریزی له‌غسكری
غوركگیری كوردستان ده‌رئه‌كریت :
١٠ شپهنریه‌كاش غوری بگه‌ه‌نی بـه‌
دوژمن .
٢٠ دزی له‌ چه‌ك و لیشــــه‌ه‌او
مونشه‌له‌كاش غوری كردبیت .
٣٠ سه‌ریجی بكات له‌ جیمه‌ جی‌كردنی
فه‌رمانه‌كانی غوری .
٤٠ كرده‌وه‌یه‌كی بیه‌خلاقی بكات كه‌
زیان به‌ سومعه‌ی خوی و غوری و پارتی
بگه‌یه‌نی و جیگه‌ی شاره‌زایی و بیزاری
میلله‌ت بیت .
٥٠ دوژمن یا شاخه‌ر انی ئه‌خسی ی
خوی بكوژیت ، یان بیلان ریك بخــات
بۆ كوشتنیان ، به‌ هه‌ر شیازیك بیت ،
له‌بیت سه‌ركرد لیه‌تی شـــــوریو
لیبه‌رسر انی ، وه‌ بیویسته‌ بیـــساش
ده‌ركردنی له‌ ریزی له‌غكری غوركگیری

Panel ١٧ (17):

كوردستان بخریته‌ ئادگای غوری بـسر
سر‌قه‌انی به‌ی‌كی بیویست .
٦٠ چووش بۆشاو به‌كیه‌ك لـــــــه‌
حزبه‌كاش تر به‌بی شاگاد اری غوری .
٧٠ چووش بۆ شار ریزه‌كاش دوژمن .

Panel ١٨ (18):

به‌ندی هه‌فته‌م
گواستنه‌وه‌ی بیشمه‌رگه‌ :

١٠ بۆ لیبه‌رسر اوی غانه‌ی سه‌ره‌كسی
هه‌یه‌ بیشمه‌رگه‌یه‌ك له‌ غانه‌یه‌كه‌وه‌ بۆ
غانه‌یه‌كی تر بگویزیته‌وه‌ ئه‌غــــــر
بیویست بور ، له‌گه‌ل دیبارکردنی هـوی
گواستنه‌وه‌ بۆ ریكغر او .
٢٠ بۆ ریكغر او هه‌یه‌ بیشمه‌رگه‌یه‌ك
له‌ غانه‌یه‌كی سه‌ره‌كیه‌وه‌ بـــــــو
غانه‌یه‌كی سه‌ره‌كی تر بگویزیشــــه‌وه‌
ئه‌غه‌ر بیویست بور له‌گه‌ل دیبارکردنی
هوی گواستنه‌وه‌كه‌ بۆ كارگیری غاوچه‌ .
٣٠ بۆ لیژنه‌ی غاوچه‌ هه‌یـــــه‌
بیشمه‌رگه‌یه‌ك یان چه‌ند بیشمه‌رگه‌یه‌ك
كه‌ زماره‌یان له‌ زماره‌ی غانـــــــه‌ی
سه‌ره‌كی تیمبر بگویزیته‌وه‌ لـــه‌
ریكغر اویكه‌وه‌ بۆ ریكغر اویكی تر له‌
شووری غاوچه‌كه‌یدا۱ له‌گه‌ل دیبارکردنی

Documents 13

بۆ لقێکی تر به سەرباری سەرکردایەتیی
شۆرش دەبێت .

بەندی هەشتەم

بشووردن (اجازه) به پێشمەرگه
----

۱. بۆ هەر پێشمەرگەیەك لە یسه
سالی (۲) مانگ شیجازه وەربگریسیت
به جارێك یان به چەند جار ، به مەرجی
زروووفی ناوچەکەی شاسایی بێت .
۲. هەموو لیمەرسر اوانی پێشمەرگه
شەم مۆقیان هەیه به کاری بچن به
مەرجیك لەگەل سەرکردایەتیی سەرووی
خۆیانەوه رێك کەوتبن وه موافقه سیت
وەرگیر ایت لە سەری به مەرجسیه
زروووفی ناوچەکەیان به ساهیسی
هەلسه نگاندیت ، شاوەکو بشوورد اشی
خۆیان و پێشمەرگه کانیان دەبێت
هۆی ئارازی و سیخیزی لە ناوچه کانیاندا ؟

۲۰

خانەوه .
۰۲ خانەی سەرەکی لە لەشکریی ـ لسه
(۲ ـ ۰ ۵) خانه ، پاخسوود (۲۲ ـ ۲۷)
پێشمەرگه بێك دیت ، لەگسیسل
لیمەرسر اوی خانه سەرەکییه کسه و
پاریده ده رەکەی .
۰۳ رێكخراوی لەشكریی ـ له (۲) سی
خانه سەرەکی بێك دیت ، واته لسه
(۶۰ ـ ۱۱۲) پێشمەرگه لەگسیسل
لیمەرسر اوی و پاریده ده رەکەی کسه
کادری رێكخر او دەبی .
۰۴ لەشکری غورشگیری کوردستان لسه
سنوووری لیژنەی شاوجەدا ـ لیژنسەی
ناوجه ، که سنوووری جالاکی لەالیسەن
لقی پارتییەوه بۆ دەخبد دەکریت و
موافقه قەتی کومیتەی شاوەندی لە سسەر
وەردە گیری ، سەرکردایەتیی لەشتی
کۆمەلایەتی دەکات لەو قەواره ی کسه
بۆی دیاری کراوه و ، سوی هەیه بەی

۲۲

دزی دوزمن .

بەشی سێیەم

چەندی شووەم

هەیەکانی دەشریمی

أ) دانیان و لادانی لیمەرسر اوانسیی
رێكخراو و خانه سەرەکییەکان بسه
رەزامەندیی کارگیری لق دەبیت .
ب) دانیان و لادانی لیمەرسر اوانسیی
خانەکان لە دەسەلاتی لیژنەی ناوجسه
دەبیت .
ج) لەشکری غورشگیری کوردستان بسه
گویره ی هەیكالی دەشریمی ی خسوارەوه
رێكخراوه :
۰۱ خانەی لەشكریی ـ بریشیمه لسه
(۷) هوت پێشمەرگه به لیمەرسر اوی

۲۱

هۆی گواستنەوەکه بۆ کارگیری لق .
۰۵ بۆ کارگیری لق هەیه شالوگۆری لە
لیژنه ناوچەکانی سنوووری لقەکسە
خۆیان بکات به بیی بیوسیسسست و
دیبارکردنی هۆیه کانی شەو شالوگسسور
کردنه بۆ سەرکرد ایەتیی شۆرش .
۰۶ ئەگەر لقایه بیویستی به هێزیکی
زیاتر بوو لە هێزه کانی سسسنوووری
لقەکەی خۆی ، داوا لە سەرکرد ایەتیی
شۆرش ئه کات بویان ئه ثمین بکات بسه
رووی لەگەل دیبارکردنی هۆیه کانسی
بیویست بۆ دا واکەیان .
۰۷ هەموو شەو گواستنەوانه ، کسه
ئەکریته به چەکوه شەبیت ، واتسه
شاسی چەك لە و پێشمەرگانسسسه
وەربگیرێتەوه ، چونکه سەرای چیسسەك
وەربگیرێتەوه بی تەدراوه ، سەرەرایکشەوەئی
که چەك بەشیکه لەگیان و سەربسەرزی و
کەر ایەتی پێشمەرگەی کوردستان .
۰۸ گواستنەوەی ب ۰۰م له لقێكسە وه
رێكخراوه .

روویه‌كه‌وه‌ سه‌ر به‌ خوی ده‌بی ، سه‌ر
ده‌نجامدانی هه‌ر شیڤوگاری ـــــكی
شورشگیری ،

٦ ، كومیته‌ی شاوه‌ندی به‌ سه‌روكایه‌تی
ره‌ئیسی حزب كه‌ سه‌ركرده‌ی له‌ شكری
شورشگیری كوردستانه‌ سه‌ركرد ئیه‌تی
شورش ده‌كات له‌ هه‌موو روویه‌كه‌وه‌ ،

٧ ، مه‌كته‌بی سیاسی به‌ سه‌روكایه‌تی
ره‌ئیسی حزب به‌ گه‌وره‌ترین ده‌سلاته‌ له‌
سه‌ركرد ئیه‌تی شورشدا ، له‌ نهیوان دو
كوبوونه‌وه‌ی كومیته‌ی شاوه‌ندی ، بویه‌
هه‌موو ڤه‌رمان و شامووزگاریه‌كانـی
سیاسی و ڤه‌سكه‌ری و ئه‌نزیـــــــر و
ئیداری و مالی شه‌بی جیه‌جی بكریـن
به‌بی دوودلی (نردد) له‌لایه‌ن له‌شكری
شورشگیری كوردستان به‌ گشتی و له‌لایه‌ن
لیبه‌رسه‌ر انه‌وه‌ به‌ شایپه‌تی ،

٨ ، شه‌شجوومه‌ش شیشتمانی كوردستان
به‌شیك له‌ سه‌ركرد ئیه‌تی شـــــورش ،
به‌غدار له‌ سه‌ركردن له‌ ره‌شیدان له‌ هه‌موو

٢٤

خواشا و فراوانی شاوچه‌كه‌ی چه‌شـــــد
ریكخراوی له‌شكری له‌ گیری دروست بكات ،

د) لسق ،

ا) كه‌ شوروری جالاكی له‌لایـــــــه‌ن
كومیته‌ی شاوه‌ندی به‌پارتیه‌مانه‌وه‌ بسوی
نیباری كراوه‌ سه‌ركرد ئیه‌تی جه‌ ماوه‌ر له‌
له‌و ستوروره‌ی ده‌كات له‌ـــــه‌روری
سیاسی و ڤه‌سكه‌ری و ئیداری و مالی و
كومه‌لایه‌تی و له‌روری ڤه‌سكه‌ریه‌ه‌وه‌
بریاری نیمبایی به‌ده‌مشی لیبه‌رسه‌راوی
به‌كه‌می لقه‌وه‌ ده‌بیت كه‌ به‌ربه‌رچاره‌
به‌رامبه‌ر سه‌ركرد ئیه‌تی به‌پارتشـــسی و
شورش و شه‌مه‌شی له‌ سه‌ركرد ئیه‌تی بـــه‌
كومه‌ل نبای كه‌م بكاته‌وه‌ ،

ب) كارگیری لق بوی هه‌یه‌ له‌ {٣ـ١}
ریكخراو ، ئه‌مه‌زریبیت بو حیر اڤـه‌ت و
ئه‌شناد و بیویستیمه‌كانی تیـــــــری
باره‌گای خوی ،

ج) كارگیری لق بوی هه‌یه‌ هیزیكسی
ده‌ست وه‌ئین بیاخ بیمینیت كه‌ له‌ هه‌موو

٢٢

به‌ گشت روله‌ نه‌به‌زه‌كانی شورگیسری
كه‌ شامادمن له‌ بیشاوی ئامانجه‌كانیـدا ا
خویان به‌خت بكن ،

١٠ ، له‌كاتی بیویـــــــــتدا
سه‌ركرد ئیه‌تی شورش ده‌ند هیزیكـسی
ده‌ست وه‌ئین دروست ده‌كات كه‌ بـــه‌
راسته‌وخسو سه‌ر بسه‌ خویـــــه‌وه‌
ده‌بیت ،

―――

٢٦

كاریكی گرنگی غوری كه‌ چاره‌نووسـی
شورش و میلله‌تی بیوه‌ به‌حراوه‌ لـــه‌
روه‌ی سیاسی و ڤه‌سكه‌ری و مالــــی و
ئیداریه‌وه‌ ،

٩ ، شه‌گه‌ر بیشمه‌رگه‌یه‌ك لـــــــه‌
بیشمه‌رگه‌كانی له‌شكری شورگیسری
كوردستان حزبی شه‌سور و دلـــسوزی و
نیری و چاوشه‌رس و كه‌ڤناشـــــــن
له‌ بله‌یه‌كی به‌رز بسور كه‌ لیبهاتسروی
لیبه‌رسه‌راوی به‌كه‌م بیت له‌ سه‌ـــــره‌ك
غانه‌ی له‌شكریه‌وه‌ ئا لیبه‌رسه‌راوی
ریكخراوی له‌شكری ئه‌نشامه‌ت له‌ هیسزی
ده‌ست وه‌غینشندا ا سه‌ركرد ئیه‌تی بـــسی
شورش به‌ بیویشتی ده‌زانی بـــــــه‌
بریاریكی شایپه‌تی له‌روری ڤه‌سكه‌ریكو
ئیداری و مالیه‌وه‌ لیبه‌رسه‌راویشـسی
به‌كه‌می بی بیمیریت ، شه‌مه‌ش له‌بسه‌ر
شه‌وه‌به‌ كه‌ له‌شكری شورگیـــــری
كوردستان له‌ روله‌كانی كوردســـتان
بیگباتروه‌ و بو شه‌وه‌ی ماوه‌ بدریـت

٢٥

Documents 13

463

Documents 13

Document number (13)

The Kurdistan Revolutionary Forces

The rule:

At the second meeting of the Central Committee of the Kurdistan Democratic Party-Iraq, it was decided that at the fifth meeting of the Central Committee, necessary appointments were made, and it was decided that the revolutionary army of Kurdistan should be organized and led according to the provisions.

The source of legitimacy for this law is the Internal Program and Procedure of the Kurdistan Democratic Party, which was decided at the ninth congress, and the experience of the world's national liberation movement in the partisan war.

In particular, our Party's experience in the Aylul revolution, the Gulan revolution, and the partisan experience of immortal Barzani's Kurdish reputation.

Political bureau 1985

Part One:
Section One:
The Kurdistan Revolutionary Forces:
The force of the Kurdistan Democratic Party of Iraq, from these brave peshmerga, have put their lives on their hands to achieve the rights of the Kurdish people and democracy for Iraq under the flag of PDK and are part of implementing their political programmes and decisions ninth congress.

Part two

Section Two:

peshmerga and conditions:

A. peshmerga is a brave Kurdistani or Iraqi activist who is ready as they want and, with their beliefs in the revolutionary army of the Kurdistan throughout from Zakho to Khanaqin, fight against the Fascist Ba'athist regime of Iraq and its nomads in Kurds and Arabs, i.e., without distinction between one region and another, because the peshmerga is the peshmerga of Kurdistan, who is obedient to the order of the leadership of the revolution and must be under the law of the army and Kurdistan revolutionary behaviour.

B. Conditions for receiving peshmerga:

1. Have a good sense of Kurdishness and Iraqi patriotism and know very well why he is carrying a weapon and for what?
2. Be loyal, faithful, and honest.
3. Be patient, wise, and unafraid of the enemy.
4. Be competent in partisan struggle at least 16 years of age and not be very old.
5. Obey the orders of his officials, particularly the direct official, and do not hesitate to carry them out properly.
6. Do not hide the truth from its officials and the revolution's leadership, even if it will cost his life.
7. It must be approved by PDK organizations.
8. Newcomer:

Citizens who stand up because of enemy oppression and reach the ranks of the revolution.

If they are not members and candidates of the PDK and have peshmerga conditions, they will remain under surveillance for at least three months and then will be taken as peshmerga.

Part Three:
Section Three:
peshmerga orders (duties):

1. To be organized in the revolutionary army of Kurdistan.
2. Fight the enemy with all his might, according to the orders and plans he is responsible for.
3. Be against the spirit of being free and arrogant.
4. The relationship with the peshmerga brothers you live with is very good.
5. Always have a good relationship with the nation and always to be recognized as the protectors of the people's wealth, and dignity, so that they may believe.
6. Always try to increase the level of information in military and political terms.
7. Protect the secrets of revolution, goods, weapons, and explosives well.
8. He must be true and proud and not hide the truth from the revolution.
9. It should not pass the law of the Revolutionary Division of Kurdistan and protect the organization well, i.e. do not break the rules.

Part four:

Those who are not included in the The Kurdistan Revolutionary Forces:

1. enemy servants, or spies, or members of the sabotaging organization.
2. has bad history with nation.Be known as the opposition of Kurdish, democratic, and humanity beliefs.

Part five:

peshmerga rights:

1. It has the right to reach every position of responsibility according to its ability and competence.
2. Be awarded medals to those who harm the enemy more and are better active.
3. It should not be delayed in the weapons and explosives according to the ability and activeness, i.e. good weapons for the peshmerga.
4. In terms of protecting his health, home, and family according to the law, he should be looked after.
5. At the time of martyrdom, old age, or disabling, the life of the family, children and themselves must be ensured.
6. If his family and children need help when necessary and according to the law, it should be helped.
7. Try to raise the level of military and political information by opening military and political courses for them.

8. Insulting and beating peshmerga by officials is forbidden, because protecting the dignity of the peshmerga is a national order.

Part six:
The punishment of the peshmerga:

There are six types of punishment for the peshmerga:
  A. Drawn the attention.
  B. Transfer
  C. Disarm
  D. Imprisonment
  E. exclusion from the ranks of the Revolutionary Forces of Kurdistan
  F. expulsion from the revolutionary forces of Kurdistan for good.

A) What time will be drawn the attention:

1. If the behaves contrary to his official's order for the first time
2. If they are causing the problem for the organization's activities
3. A little attitude, arrogant, or disrespectfully that could harm the reputation of the peshmerga.

b) At what time is it transmitted:

1. Incompatibility with one or more peshmerga brothers, which causes incompatibility

2. Incompatibility with the people of the area because of some of the ugliness that occurs there and causes people to protest.

c) At what time will it be disarm.

1. If it does not carry out the first official's order for the second time.
2. He has shown inertia, negligence, and cowardice in implementing his orders against the enemy.
3. The second time causing the problem for the organization's activities
4. For the second time, it has made a small ugly openness to harm the reputation of the peshmerga in the area.
5. Without agreeing to change the weapon of the revolution.

D) At what time will he be imprisoned:

1. If he is swearing at a peshmerga brother or a person from the area.
2. If he fights with a peshmerga brother or a person from the area.
3. If it causes material damage, even if it is minor, it has been delivered to a person from the area, without complaint.
4. If it moves contrary to the traditions and traditions of society and does not hold the religious Sha'riah.
5. If a prisoner is escaped under their order

H) When will be removed from the Kurdistan revolutionary forces line (from one month to one year):